To *Love* Again

To Love Again

A Novel

Christina Hill

ISBN: 979-8-9857199-2-5

Edited by: imPRESS Millennial Books
Cover Design: Christina Hill
Cover Photo: Canva

To all of the social workers and foster families who have given their time, energy, and love in order to help the countless kids in the system. Your efforts are noticed and your impact lasts a lifetime.

And to all of the foster kids who thought their story didn't matter. It does. You matter.

PROLOGUE
June 16, 2011—Age 20

The cold night air wafted in through the open van door, causing a shiver to chase the length of my spine and the hair on my arms to stand on end. I looked down at my shaking hands and wondered for the hundredth time what the hell I was thinking.

I started rubbing my hands up and down my arms to keep them from giving way to my fear. My arms were covered by my favorite leather jacket that was supposed to shield me from the cool air that touched the rest of my bare skin, but I couldn't fend off the iciness. It was in my bones. I sat like a wounded animal hiding from her predator, hoping I wouldn't be discovered.

How I managed the courage to make it this far was beyond me. Maybe it was the look in Janet's eyes as she held my hand, or maybe it was the rose that the man with the warm brown skin and kind eyes handed me. Either way, it sparked something in me, like paddles connecting to my chest and jolting me out of my lifeless state. I was alive after believing I was the walking dead.

Gloria a Dios.

The familiar phrase leapt from the recesses of my mind as though Janet had said it aloud from her spot in the backseat. I angled my head in her direction slowly in case she had said something, but Janet was looking at her watch, unaware of the shock that had coursed through me. It couldn't have been Janet who said it anyway because that tone could only belong to one person: my mother.

It had been years, but I would remember the inflection of her voice anywhere. She always used to use that phrase—Glory to God. It had become her life motto the moment my Spanish-speaking father taught it to her. My mother was white, religious, and an addict. All reasons that my father should have run far away, but instead, he only ran closer.

I shoved the uninvited memories out of my mind as another woman was walking toward the waiting van.

"I'm Jordan," the blond man said with a small wave as he opened the van door. "This is Beau." He pointed to the driver's seat. "Mercedes," who sat behind Beau. "And Janet in the back."

I gave her a pinched smile and tilted my chin up in acknowledgement as the other woman climbed in hesitantly, checking the backseat to be sure there weren't any unwanted visitors joining us. A classic move when you're accustomed to watching your back on the streets. Things happen. Unplanned events that leave you exposed or scarred, usually both. Street life in L.A. was anything but predictable, and I had learned to roll with the punches—literally and figuratively.

"I—" she started to say, then stopped.

The regret for getting into this van was stamped all over her face, but Jordan just handed her a water bottle and blanket with a calm smile. He had offered me the same, but I didn't need those. I needed a gun, or a knife at least, knowing what we were about to do and the dangers we now faced.

I tucked a piece of long, dark hair behind my ear while the girl chugged her entire water bottle.

I cleared my throat to catch her attention and whispered, "I'm Kit."

I hated my street name. I carried it like a weight around my neck, paying penance for my choices. It disgusted me like the man who gave it to me did. I would rather be Kit, even if I didn't know who she really was.

I still wasn't sure if I could trust these people. I needed to know I had an ally. She looked more like me than they did with a short, black bodycon dress that hugged her many curves.

"Andrea," she said quietly.

She begged them to hurry up; we had to leave, and she was right. Bobby, my pimp, wouldn't like that I left. He didn't like when I was late or wore my hair up, either.

I looked forward when I heard Jordan climb into the passenger seat, watching as they started the van. I turned my head to peer out the window once more, expecting shadowy figures to appear and pull me from this seat and whisk me off to sudden death.

Death. That's exactly the kind of punishment I was facing for being in this van.

But I couldn't die. Not yet. I hadn't found Jacob yet, and I wasn't about to leave this world without finding out the real story of what happened to him after we entered foster care. I was doing this for my brother, I told myself, yanking my eyes away from the windows and forcing myself to breathe. Everything I did was for him. Whether it was working different blades to earn money, or looking for information that would lead me back to him, or getting in a van with strangers that promised to help me; I did it and I would do it.

The car started moving just as fast as my lips were, silently sending up the prayers I had heard my mother pray time and time again. I didn't know what value they had, since the prayers didn't work for her—maybe this time they would for me. I closed my eyes as we traveled down the cluttered L.A. streets until my fear forced them open to scan our surroundings. It wasn't until the words I dreaded most were spoken that panic overtook any ounce of calm I had left.

"Someone's tailin' us," Beau said, gripping the steering wheel tighter.

I stared at my lap as my heart started pounding faster. "Damn it."

"There's another SUV," Janet said from the backseat.

"Get down on the floor and don't sit up or look out the window," Jordan said. "Janet, you too."

Before I could second guess my next move, I dropped to the floor. "Oh shit. I knew I shouldn't have come. They always find you. No matter what, they track you down," I said out loud to the earlier version of myself who had made the decision to follow these strangers to a supposed freedom.

Beau wrenched the steering wheel, and the car careened around another bend in the road. The gas pedal had to be pressed close to the floor, but I couldn't open my eyes to look.

"Shh-shh-shhh," Janet said, reaching for my hand. "It's okay. We're in this with you."

Janet may have been a former prostitute on these streets, but did she know the kinds of pimps that were out there these days? They controlled everything on Figueroa Street, where the 110 and 10 freeways meet, and fear and survival mingled.

I had been fully catapulted into the darkest corners of my fear and dreaded every moment of what my brain told me would happen next. My terror was evident in my screams, and I channeled every bit of my sanity into the protection of my mother's prayers.

Save me! Someone. Anyone. Dios Mio.

My adrenaline was at its peak now, and I no longer had a grasp on reality. The words in my head were escaping out of my mouth, one after the other, tripping and stumbling on their way out. The van took another turn, and my body pressed into the side of the driver's seat, the speed of the vehicle itself threatening to kill me.

I'm going to die. I'm going to die. I don't want to die. Help. Please!

My pleas grew stronger, filling the small space of the van with a rush of frenzied emotion. My heart thumped wildly inside my chest, sweat gathered on my brow, and an instinctual will to survive had me pounding my clenched fists on the floor of the van, ready to fight whatever threat came. I had turned from a wounded animal awaiting a predator to an enraged one, ready to fight to the death if it came to that, and I knew it would.

Terror lived beneath the surface of every encounter I had on the streets. Some prostitutes were on drugs, which was easy to see by the glazed look in their eyes, but not me. I wanted a clear head and a sharp sense of my surroundings at all times. I had seen enough shit out there to know I needed my sanity in order to survive. Andrea had that glazed look in her wide, terror-filled eyes. Maybe that was why she was quiet, lying on the floor without so much as a squeak. My senses were alert, but that didn't mean they were helping. I was too afraid to face the demons that tied me up with invisible string. The demon that stole from me night after night, forcing himself on me when he pleased. I was nothing to my pimp. I lived every day of my life worried about what he could do to me. Today, I was doing the unforgivable.

You are nothing.

I own you, bitch.

You don't think I could kill you?

Threats. They were only threats, weren't they? At this moment, I was certain Bobby wasn't bluffing, and all of those threats were about to be proven true. The tears streamed down my face, and the thick layer of black mascara burned my eyes, mocking me for my choices. The voices around me were muffled. I couldn't tell who was speaking or what was happening. All I knew was that I'd die while wanting—needing—to live.

You have to survive.

You can't let him down, again.

Don't you dare give up.

The words in my mind told me to live, but I knew I wouldn't. It was impossible. Before I could lie to my thoughts that we'd make it out of this, the recognizable sound of battle hit the side of the van. Bullets. One...two...three bullets rang out, deafening the voices around me and causing Beau to punch the gas pedal further. I gripped the seat in front of my head and shrieked louder at the impending reality: our lives were a breath away from death. Time became nonexistent. My memorized prayers were silenced. The voices in my head came to a screeching halt as the battered metal box on wheels hit a bump and immediately stopped.

Death had found me.

Fear had devoured me.

It would all be over soon, I hoped.

Shaking uncontrollably, I covered my face and awaited my fate. Heavy breathing filled the silence that my cries hadn't stolen already, and I waited. And waited.

Nothing.

No, no. That's not right.

Where are the other bullets?

Where are the hands that owned me?

It felt like an eternity waiting to meet my Maker and solidify every mistake I'd ever made and those I didn't have the chance to.

Goodbye. I'm so sorry I failed you.

I'll miss you, Jacob.

"I love you," I whispered through cracked speech.

My world became small, and I realized how short my life really was. A wisp. A flash. I didn't want this life, not if I couldn't have my brother in it. I clenched my eyes tightly, and my whole world went dark.

CHAPTER ONE
Three-years-later
July 2014—Age 23

Thwack! Thud.

I startle awake at the sounds that fill the house. Opening my eyes, I try to locate any danger that could be hovering above me. Nothing. No one. I turn my head toward the clock, the time plastered in bright red, mere inches from my face: 7:10 a.m.

I groan as my dream state meshes with my wakeful consciousness. I must have slept through my alarm.

What in the world was that noise?

I fling the covers off of my legs and realize my heart is still pounding and heat courses through my veins, warming my skin and activating my sweat glands.

It's probably nothing.

Relax, Kit, I coach myself. *You aren't in danger.*

When I sit up on the edge of my bed, I finger-comb my short, dark hair as my bare feet graze the cool hardwood floors. I peer around the room until I spy the water bottle on my bedside table. Fumbling for it, I take a sip, trying to wake up while simultaneously calming my nerves.

Scrubbing a hand down my face, I push off the bed awkwardly and reach for a nearby sweater. I'm in a haze, drunk with sleep and alert from adrenaline. I blink rapidly, willing my eyes to start working. Needing to give them something to focus on, the framed picture sitting on my desk is the first thing they spy. Andrea, Dina, Olive, and I joined at the hip and smiling like we hadn't navigated years of hell without a map. Our smiles indicate we are four early-twenties women who are happy and living life to the fullest, and we are—*now*. That wasn't always the case, though. These women hold some of my darkest secrets, even the ones I'd rather not admit to myself.

It's weird not having Andrea around anymore. She married Jordan, started a new life, and moved out of the house. Our house. The one that turned the page to the next chapter of life. Andrea was my first confidant, first best friend, and first to assure me I wasn't completely jacked up. Once in a while, my brain likes to replay the scene where we first met, especially when I hear loud noises like I did this morning. It brings me right back to the fear of our escape like it had happened last night and not three years ago.

I clear my throat and take another swig of water. It's a memory I wish I could forget. A vivid flashback that leaves me shaking and feeling like bricks are stacked on my chest and preventing me from getting a deep breath. When the fear starts to creep up my neck and slither into my inner thoughts, I inhale deeply, utilizing the tools that my therapist has taught me.

Breathe. The memories are in the past.

No one is here that shouldn't be.

I exit my room cautiously, more from muscle memory than necessity. The commotion that woke me is now carefully piling books on the coffee table and wiping up a mess of what appears to be coffee. It's only Dina, my roommate. She glides her hand across the ground in search of her glasses. Finding them, she slides them on, and continues her stacking. People would never guess Dina had a drug addiction before coming to the Journey Center. Her sweet demeanor—the one that makes me want to pinch her cheeks and tell her how adorable she is—makes it difficult to tell she was once crazed and out of her mind.

"Morning," I say groggily, walking past her to snag a towel from the kitchen to help clean up the mess. Luckily, we still have some clean ones after the soup she spilled yesterday. She has a knack for dropping things, so we keep the towels nearby.

"Oh. Kit, I'm so sorry! Did I wake you?" Dina asks.

I yawn, making a few of my words less clear. "I needed to get up anyway. I must have slept through my alarm. Here, let me have that wet towel."

"I thought I could carry everything, but one of the books just started slipping and then…well, you can figure out the rest." She gestures to the mess.

"I can get the rest of this, Dina. You go change."

"Really?"

"Yeah, totally. I got this."

"Thanks, Kit. Er, so sorry…again, for the mess and waking you." Dina jumps up and moves hastily toward her room while I dab at the rug and couch that didn't quite make it out without something to show for it. I'm already awake and need to get dressed for an early morning meeting.

"Morning, Kit. Uh oh, what happened here?" Olive, our other roommate, emerges from her room as I'm carrying the second towel to the laundry room.

My morning voice sounds raspy. "Hey. Morning. Dina had a spill, but it's all good now."

Olive sweeps her straight, black hair into a messy bun then crosses her arms tighter across her body. "I thought I heard something hit the floor. It better not be the coffee pot because I was up all night and, to be honest, coffee is the only reason I am out of bed right now," she says, shuffling toward the kitchen.

I follow on her heels. "Were you helping out in the women's emergency shelter again?" Grabbing a thermos from the cabinet, I set it on the counter next to Olive's cup that I'm positive has a crude quote on it. Her humor is distinct.

"Yeah, Janet had some family things to deal with and asked if I could cover. It's been a while since I worked an all-nighter like that." Olive pulls the glass pot off of the burner and fills my thermos. "It doesn't seem real that we used to stay up all night on the regular," she says, shaking her head slowly.

My response is sarcastic. "The work you're doing now is a bit different." I nod in understanding. We both used to work the streets, and prostitution is a job better done at night. "Did you work with Andrea?" I ask, watching Olive fill her cup with the delicious dark roasted goodness.

"Nah. She'll work on the floor later today. A few of the girls are planning to apply for the program, so she's helping them with the paperwork." She places the pot back in its spot.

I tip my head, remembering the intake process well. "I can't believe you're still standing."

She nods toward her full cup. "Coffee. That's why I'm here, then a shower, maybe a nap later."

"Good. We wouldn't want a grumpy Olive to deal with," I say, with a smile.

"Hey, watch it. I'm not that bad."

I widen my eyes when Olive lifts her mug to tip its liquid gold contents into her mouth. I read the quote that is not-so-delicately worded on the side.

Punch Today in the Dick.

"Olive. Your mug," I say through my laughter. I'm glad I haven't taken a sip of coffee yet, or else I would have spit it out along with my laughter.

She glances at the side of her cup and gives a mischievous smile. "I love this one."

Olive is short and rail thin, a wisp of a thing really, which is why most people don't expect how forward she can be. I never have to guess what she's thinking, which is an attribute I didn't know I needed in a friend, but her honesty is refreshing, especially when it's written on the side of a coffee mug.

I catch a glimpse of the kitchen clock behind Olive's head. "Shoot. I have to get showered and dressed before I'm late. I'll see you later, okay?"

"I might be sleeping so don't drop anything else, alright?" Olive flips her hand in the air waving haphazardly as I leave the kitchen.

I yell over my shoulder, "It wasn't me!" and round the corner almost colliding with Dina and narrowly spilling my coffee on her new, fresh blouse.

Dina raises a hand to clutch her chest, releasing a nervous laugh while pushing her glasses farther up her nose. "Shoot. You scared me."

I give a small laugh, too, pacing the thump beneath my breastbone. "There's more in the pot if you want to get some."

Dina shakes her head. "I think I'll pass, at least until I get to the office. I can't risk ruining another good outfit."

Looking put together is important to Dina since she's the first person people see when they walk into the front office at the Journey Center. So, while her genuine smile and bubbly demeanor might distract from another coffee stain, I don't blame her for waiting.

I bring my other hand up to cradle my cup. "Alright then, have a good one."

We part ways when Dina walks out to her car, and I walk back into my room where I quickly pull out an outfit and head toward the shower. I turn the nozzle all the way to hot, allowing the water to warm before I turn it down. As I watch the billows of steam fill the small bathroom, the memories are tapping me on the shoulder, triggering a response I haven't felt in a long time.

You are dirty.

You are worth nothing.

I squeeze my eyelids shut so the pictures in my mind don't start playing. The face of the man speaking them flashes through my mind, but I breathe through it.

You are worthy. Period.

I inhale slowly and exhale even slower, letting the lies cool off like the temperature of the water. I have to continue telling myself everything I have overcome. I've practiced the techniques, uncovered the lies and processed through the loss of myself, and the celebration of finding her again, which is the only way I can still function. But the memories are still there.

They won't leave, even though I beg them to.

CHAPTER TWO
Three-years-earlier
June 16, 2011—Age 20

I saw darkness behind my eyelids.

My chest heaved with effort, but all I could do was wait for death. I had already said my silent goodbyes and whispered my regrets out loud. It was over. The tires quit screeching with every turn; there were no more gunshots clanking against the sides of the van. The engine was off, and all I heard was heavy breathing.

I didn't expect that part to feel like hours: the time when death had come and life had left, and I was somewhere in the middle. My mother talked about this middle-place—purgatory, I think she called it. I felt stuck there. Breathing but dead. Would I ever get out? Or, will I be forced to endure another life of searching and never finding?

I heard an exhale from the front driver's seat. "We did it. They're gone. We made it back safe."

My body didn't believe what my ears were hearing. I still didn't move; I couldn't. I was glued to my spot on the floor I named 'purgatory.' Someone pulled Andrea's hand from mine— the one I had grabbed at some point—and a gentle hand settled on my upper back. My eyes were still closed, shutting out the possibility of what was on the other side of them. If they stayed closed, I could stay in that place of unknowing a little longer. I wasn't ready to know.

Did I really die that fast?

"I didn't want to die," I said, clutching my head in my hands, still curled in the fetal position. "Not yet." I had seen too much, done too many things to believe I was worthy of living, but that didn't mean I was ready to die.

"You're safe, Kit. They're gone, I promise." The tender words had to belong to the same person that owned the gentle touch, but I still didn't lift my head. I shook off the hand and squeezed a fistful of my hair even tighter. The smooth voice and comforting hand continued their stroking, and I continued my shrugging to get it to stop. It wasn't real anyway.

How could someone survive that?

I know I couldn't, which is why I didn't.

I had lost the ability to cry. There are no tears in purgatory, I guess, but then why would I need them? Who needs to cry when they've already lost everything? My screams had left me, and my body was spent. Feeling the withdrawal from adrenaline, I started to shake and felt as cold as a corpse. I rubbed my damp hands over my face, feeling the skin that's wrapped around my bones and reminding me I'm still human. I'm still here—alive.

Is this how purgatory works? Dead but still human?

The soft hands that wouldn't leave lifted my shoulders, pulling them upward and convincing my body it could, in fact, move. I wasn't in my body though, I was watching it. I had to be. I sat up until my legs hung off the side of the van, leaving me to face the hands, the voice, and now, the dark face that looked at me with a mixture of protection and safety. He bent down in front of me with his brown, pleading eyes to assure me once again. Beau, I thought he called himself. But my ears sounded like they were full of water.

His voice was dull, until it became sharp.

"The men drove off. Your pimp isn't going to get you." His gaze shifted, and I followed it, seeing the reason my pimp had fled. A large group of burly men loomed behind the van, which had somehow survived the onslaught of bullets and breakneck speeds. All I saw was another threat. These men must be after me, too. I wasn't safe. They weren't safe. I gasped and scooted back into the van, trying to disappear. Death should've been the only thing that could separate me from that life. But they must have followed me to the other side. These men would make me pay, like my pimp. For fleeing, for lying, or just because they could.

Beau held out a hand and his warm smile encouraged me to take it. "It's alright. These guys are here to help, and I am, too."

I stared at his hand, wondering what it was offering me. Could I trust him? My gut reaction told me I could, but I wasn't sure if it could be trusted either. Guts lie sometimes.

"He's gone?" I had to ask. I needed to confirm. If he followed me there, he'd make sure I wasn't breathing.

Beau nodded his head. One of his hands extended toward me and the other braced himself on the sliding van door. I sat on the floor, gripping the seats on either side of me, half-believing it was safe to emerge and the other half convincing me that if I did, I'd never be able to get back in it. If I left that van, would I leave death, too?

I reached for the offered hand, choosing to view it as an ally rather than an enemy. He collected my other one as I inched forward. My feet touched the pavement, but my movements were hesitant, assessing the group of tattooed men who looked more like gang members than rescuers. In the dim lights, their harsh expressions could've killed me twice. No one held a weapon. Then again, no one needs guns or knives in purgatory.

They didn't move, so neither did I.

It couldn't be purgatory, though. It wasn't death. I knew that, because Beau's hand felt too real, the van too solid, the air too warm. Returning from the brink of death, I shivered and Beau swung his jacket around my shoulders. I hugged it tighter around me, inhaling my new favorite scent: safety. I was coming down from the high of escape and realizing how risky it was for me to leave the way I did. Bobby left, but he'll come back. He always did. The tears returned, running down my face one after the other while I tried to catch them with the sleeve of Beau's hoodie.

I was really alive, not only because I had breath in my lungs but because I was free.

CHAPTER THREE
Three-years-later
July 2014—Age 23

I brush my teeth and run a comb through my hair. It must be the added stress I'm under at work that's fueling so many of my anxious thoughts. The Foster Youth Program at the Journey Center constantly forces me to be one step ahead with so many young kids coming in and out of our doors. In many ways, I still feel like one of them, even though I'm a twenty-three-year-old woman. I was the girl who spent her adolescence in foster care only to age out of the system with no money, no guidance, and zero family to speak of. Until I met my pimp, *Bobby*. I shiver, because it's a name that still sends a chill through me like an ice cube on bare skin.

After getting dressed, I slide my feet into my sneakers, grab my side bag, and walk out the front door. My office is only a block away, but this morning it might as well be five miles uphill at the rate I'm going. I'm still sluggish, and both my body and brain are dragging.

When I finally push through the doors of my building, I feel my phone buzz inside my purse. Pulling it out, I smile at the name on the screen.

Andrea: Hey, don't forget game night tonight. Jordan said that Beau was planning to come too and will bring Catan.

I laugh out loud. I've won Catan every month since we first started playing a year ago. Minus the time that Beau won after placing a settlement where I was clearly planning to go. I am always ready to throw down at game night and send Andrea a snarky reply to remind her of this.

Switching my phone to silent mode, I tuck it back into my purse before taking the stairs up to the third floor. In this old, renovated hospital, there are plenty of elevators to use, but I choose the stairs as often as I can to get my steps in and work off the stress of the job and my life.

"Mornin'," a friendly voice says as I crest the last stair.

My head snaps up and my foot catches the edge of the last stair, almost causing me to pull a Dina. "Hey, Beau." I try to regain my composure while smoothing hands over my hips attempting to shake off the embarrassment. My gaze lingers on his deep, brown eyes, appearing lighter against his dark skin, before I snap back to attention. I could get lost there if I let myself. But that's just it, I've never let myself. I glance at the cup in his hand. "Are you holding what I think you are?"

"Coffee—for you. Black, no sugar, no cream, and no fun," he says, extending his peace offering.

Basically, how I like my men.

I flash him a teasing smirk. "You know I don't like any of that frilly stuff like you do."

"Since when is a little cream considered frilly?" he asks with a playful grin. How dare he try to arrest me with that smile before eight in the morning. It isn't fair. But neither are feelings.

I don't answer him, but I do pretend to snatch the thermos from his hands, indicating how greedy I am for my coffee. Although, after the morning I've had, it's not all for show.

A smile lights up his face and the rich, warm color of his skin practically glows. The depth of his dark hue makes me want to rub my hand along his skin to see if it's as smooth as it appears. I know it will be. There's no way it isn't. I'm convinced of this and would bet money on it.

Shaking my head, I force my brown irises to keep moving when I hear him start to speak.

"I see how it is. Wait a minute, is that…" Beau looks down at the thermos in my hand. "Is that another cup of coffee?"

"What? This?" I raise my still-warm thermos from home. "Psh. No. It's…tea." I know the second this three-letter word falls out of my mouth that Beau won't believe me. I could have said anything else: a latte, eggnog, goat's milk, *anything* else and he would have believed me, but he knows I gag at the thought of swallowing tea.

"Mhm, right. So, you're tellin' me you made yourself tea at seven in the mornin' *before* you had coffee?" There goes my front. Gone. Like the dream I have of possibly beating this quick-witted man at his own game for once, until I decided to pull out the word *tea*.

I shift my weight to the other foot. "Okay. Fine. It's coffee, but I will have you know there was nearly a coffee shortage at my house this morning and I could have been very close to making tea so…you're basically saving me and yourself, by proxy, in giving me this second cup of joe." I take a small sip from each of my cups to prove a point.

His laugh breaks the competitive air between us, and his bright, toothy smile finally gets me laughing, too. It's the way things are between us. Light, carefree, and uncomplicated. There's no way I'd complicate everything with feelings that can't be trusted.

We both start walking toward my desk. He doesn't have to, considering his desk is a few cubicles away from mine in another direction, but somehow Beau always finds a reason to do it.

"I'll see you, and your coffee cups, at the meeting in fifteen," Beau says, jutting out his chin as I stop to set my things down. "Oh, and Kit?"

With my shoulders back, I watch him push off the flimsy cubicle wall. "Yeah?"

He swipes a thumb over his bottom lip and my heart stops. "I want my cup back, ya hear?"

I swallow then remember to roll my eyes and pretend to consider his request. "Sure, sure," I say, flippantly waving my hand. Beau's the best guy friend I've ever had and that's saying something since I haven't had many. Our history runs deep rather than long, but I'll forever be in his debt since he saved me. And since he brings me coffee every weekday.

After he walks away, I shuffle over to steal a look around the corner of my walled office, noticing Beau already looking over his shoulder at me. Pulling my head back like a turtle escaping beneath its shell, I tell myself it's all in good fun. It has to be. But there's no way I wouldn't be able to notice a man like him. He's tall, as in, borderline gigantic, compared to my small frame that barely hits his shoulder; his dark skin is both warm and inviting, and his smooth, melodic voice is like a gentle caress that makes me want to draw closer to him. But I can't. We can't. We're friends. That's it.

As a prostitute, I learned not to have a type. The drastic variations of men I served incited a severe dislike of about every size, shape, and color of man out there—shout out to therapy for helping me work through that one. However, if I did have a type, Beau would fit the bill perfectly. Unfortunately, I need Beau's friendship more than I need a boyfriend.

Uncomplicated, that's what I'm going for.

Rolling my chair out, I sit down with a sigh and power on my computer. Needing something to do while I wait, I start organizing the random items in the top drawer and remember why I tend to avoid it. Among other things, it holds pens, lipstick, receipts, and whatever else I find at the bottom of my purse and throw in here. I should probably clean this thing out more often than I do. But it's kind of a catch-and-release place.

Shifting things around, I see the edge of an old business card. Tugging at it, a jolt of remembrance flashes through my body as the recognizable font becomes visible. The corners are bent and worn, and the once-white color is now a dingy yellow.

I thought I had lost this. I was sure of it. I shake my head at how I could have missed this. I haven't seen it for months, even years. Was it in my purse at one point? Possibly shoved between Target receipts and unopened mail.

The card held more than the first and last name printed at the top, and I'm not even sure the email or phone number still works, but to me, I'm holding a lifeline. One that has dropped into my lap, or my desk. Time is precious and I'm running out of it as the clock keeps ticking while the question mark of my brother's whereabouts hangs in the balance. He'll be turning eighteen in a little over a month and aging out of the system is in his near future. That is, if he's even in the system. This card means something.

Monica Castillo.

I silently read her name over and over. Would she even remember me? It's been years since I heard from, or saw, my old social worker. She was a part of my life before…well, before the streets.

The old business card rests between my thumb and pointer finger. The *what ifs* claim my attention. Life would have been so much easier if Jacob and I could have stayed in the same foster home, but there wasn't a family able to take both of us. It would have been different if my father was a more capable parent too. Not perfect, just caring enough to keep us around. Or if my mother didn't die at her own hands, we might have been a good family.

But Monica was different. She wasn't a parent, sibling or even a friend. But somehow she was everything to me when I needed her.

Monica was more than a name on a card.

CHAPTER FOUR
2006—Age 15

"You're all set, Kit," Monica said.

"Yeah. Right." I rolled my eyes and plopped down on the bed where I'm sure plenty of other foster kids had slept once, too. The room smelled like it had been freshly cleaned with notes of lemon and orange hanging in the air and clinging to the furniture.

Monica moved to sit down beside me, not too close but close enough that her elbow grazed mine. "The Thompsons are a seasoned foster family. They won't be like the last parents you were with."

The Thompsons would be like everyone else. Maybe they'd try harder, be a little nicer, but the truth would remain: they wouldn't be my family. I crossed my arms tightly so I was further away from her. "Is that supposed to make me feel better?"

"No, it's not, but it is to assure you that you'll be taken care of this time."

Like that was my only worry.

I didn't reply. Instead, I turned my face away from her and scanned the small, sparsely-decorated room. There was a desk and chair, an empty closet and a three-drawer dresser. It was better than the last place, but one thing was still glaringly obvious: that wasn't my room. It was for someone on their way to yet another home, another destination. It wasn't *my* room at all, only a rest stop and those aren't permanent. No, I wouldn't be there long either.

"Look, I know I haven't been your social worker for long, and I get it, you don't trust me yet. But I want you to know something," Monica angled herself in my direction, "I'll be here for you, Kit."

I scoffed. "Oh, like how Elise was there for me? Or Julia who came before her? Maybe Cynthia?" Their names ran together like they did when they were assigned to me. In two years, I had four social workers. Enough to know they were all the same.

I glanced at her briefly to notice the folded hands in her lap but turned my attention to the wall behind her head. A hole above the headboard was where my gaze landed. There was likely a picture that hung there before, maybe a family picture that one of the foster kids brought with them. I didn't have one of those. A family or a picture.

She allowed the silence to hold my cynicism for a breath. "I can't promise I'll always be your social worker. I'm not gonna lie to you."

"Then don't," I spat. Excuse me for not accepting those empty words but it was laughable, really. How would she be any different from all the others? The ones who promised they'd help me get in contact with Jacob after losing touch and were unable to do a thing about it.

The caged emotion in my chest came barreling out in the form of words. "You want to help me? Then let me talk to Jacob. Find my brother's foster family, and then maybe I'll believe you."

She stared at me but didn't speak.

"But you can't find him, can you? No one can. Everyone told me we'd be able to stay in contact. That I'd have his number and he'd have mine. You're all liars if you ask me." My words were harsh but I didn't apologize for them. Not when everything went down the way it did. They took him from me, leaving Jacob lost. Or maybe I was. Either way, we haven't spoken in two years. Long enough to know something was wrong.

"You're right," she said.

My countenance fell. *What?* Where was the defensiveness, the over-explanation of how the foster care system worked, or the promise to fix everything? Where was the rehearsed script that would roll off of everyone's tongues that I'd gotten used to hearing?

"You're right. We haven't been able to find him. He was moved to another home and likely another. The trail has gone cold and I hate that it happened." She leaned in and pinned me with her unblinking stare. "It should never have happened, Kit."

I wanted to nod in agreement, because it's true, we should have stayed together. But no one could take two kids at once back then. Maybe it was because I was a teen. Jacob was young enough that he wouldn't be seen as much of a problem. But me? I was thirteen when I entered foster care. A hell-bent teenager who'd talk back and cause more trouble than I was worth. And they were right.

I didn't respond with a nod or even a flinch. I could feel my body becoming numb with the pressure of this conversation, so I clenched my jaw, forming a hard line between my lips.

"But I can give you something else." Monica dug in the pocket of her purse and pulled out a white card. "I can give you my word that I'll be here for you now, tomorrow, the next day, and every day after, whether I'm your social worker or not. I want to find Jacob, too."

The card was suspended between us, and I debated leaving it exactly where it was. She wasn't the first social worker I had who offered to help find my brother, but for some reason, she was the first one I wanted to believe.

I studied the ferocity in her unwavering position beside me and not the blank wall. Her gaze was strong and insistent. I gripped the corner of the card and, without looking at it, tucked it into my jacket. I could always rip it up later.

CHAPTER FIVE
July 2014—Age 23

Tears hang on the rims of my eyes begging to be released. When I close them, they overflow and wash my cheeks, bringing memories of Monica with them. I snatch a tissue from the box on my desk; it's calling me like an old friend, ready to support me like that's its job.

Like I predicted, Monica wasn't my social worker for long; it was an inevitable circumstance. A new one came along but I never believed or trusted any of them more than I did Monica. But even still, we never found him. She made calls, got names, and drove distances I likely never knew about.

I open my desk drawer again and pull out the only picture I have of Jacob. His dark, curly hair touches his bottomless light eyes as it cascades over his forehead. In the picture, Jacob is wearing his favorite Angel's jersey—the one and only gift our dad ever bought him. Damn, if life didn't love to throw foul balls. Jacob turns eighteen in more than a month, and who knows if his name would show up in the system again. I hope that, unlike me, who jumped from home to home like it was a sport, he was adopted, which might explain why it was so hard to find him.

I have to call Monica. Today.

I stare at the card, aware that not only did I find it for a reason, but right now, it's my only option. She probably won't remember me, but I have to call. Looking down at Jacob's picture and Monica's business card, I renew that promise like I had done so often over the past ten years.

My voice is hushed when I say, "I promise I'll find you. I swear."

When I catch a glimpse of the time, I realize our department meeting is starting in two minutes. I reverently tuck both the picture and business card underneath a stack of sticky notes and push the drawer closed, wishing I could lock them away in a safe so they wouldn't walk off with all of the newfound hope I've got going on. I carefully pop the top off my thermos and pour the contents of Beau's peace offering into it, vowing to wash Beau's precious mug out later. He can wait.

Striding down the narrow hallway, I arrive at the conference room and notice everyone milling about to find a seat. I hear my name from the back corner of the confined room and notice Beau waving at me.

He is sitting in the adjacent chair, patting the back of the one meant for me. "Thanks for saving me a spot," I say, easing into it.

His smile grows bigger, but he doesn't say a word. He only reaches toward the coffee thermos in my hand, turning it so he can read the saying that's accompanied by a half-dozen birds. I look down and read it, too.

Nice Tits.

My mouth drops open. "Olive," I grind out and shake my head. "I'm guessing *tits* are a specific kind of bird not..." I feel the heat rise to my cheeks while Beau smiles and curls his lips inward, trying to hold back his laughter. It's clearly not working for him like it is for me. I'm trying to hide the words behind my palm. Laughing is the furthest thing from my mind, but I manage a breathy one before the meeting is called to order.

"Good morning, everyone," says our supervisor, Candace, and I catch Beau's wink before focusing on the front of the room. "I know you are all busy, so I don't want to take much of your time, but I'm excited to talk about our upcoming job fair. This is a chance for us to help the twenty percent of foster youth who age out of the system and end up homeless to find a different path."

I lean back and cringe at the statistic. When I first started working in this program, I had no idea people like Candace existed. She is every bit as committed to the kids she's met and those she hasn't.

Candace tucks her cropped hair behind her ears. "The job fair will be for foster kids who are preparing to age out of the system and need some resources for their next steps."

It sounds like a brilliant plan for a lot of our current kids who are still deciding what kind of jobs they want and how to train for them. It's no surprise that there are more kids aging out and looking for work than there are tools to get there. The foster care agencies in L.A. are slammed. Social workers with more cases than they should have and an ever-growing number of kids entering the system every day isn't a good mix. There are gaps and kids fall through them—like Jacob and I did.

"We will need a few folks to work our booth as well as help organize the other businesses, schools, training programs, and foster agencies that we want to invite." Candace scans the room for willing volunteers.

This could be another opportunity to find Jacob. If he's still in the local area, maybe he'll hear about the event and come to find potential job opportunities. If he's been adopted, that wouldn't be likely. But if he isn't, I have a shot, and discounting any one of them isn't an option right now.

In a rush of movement, my hand is in the air. "I'll help." My pulse races, knowing what this could mean for me, for Jacob. My search for him has been a perpetual dead end, and who knows what will come of Monica's business card. I need a real win.

Candace nods her head. "Thank you, Kit."

"Count me in, too," Beau says.

Seeing Beau's half-open hand reaching up to indicate he's in this thing now, too, makes my stomach flip. We'll be working closely together, and I can't tell if that's a good thing yet, since every nerve in my body stands on end when he's around.

It's only attraction. Nothing else. You aren't capable of anything more.

"Perfect. Beau, Kit, why don't you both plan to work the booth the day of the event. I will also want your help making calls to different foster agencies in our region. I am hoping this event will draw kids from all different counties." I internally high five myself as Candace moves on, acknowledging other volunteers and assigning different jobs.

Beau leans in and whispers, "Looks like we have a lot of work ahead of us." He's close enough that I can smell the cinnamon flavor on his breath from the gum he likes to chew as it fans my cheek, rendering me silent.

My breath halts in my throat, and I nod but don't turn toward him, knowing we'll collide if I do. "Yeah," I start to say, swallowing hard. "This could be big."

He pulls back, resting his elbows on his bent knees and starts tracking whatever Candace is saying, because I'm not. My thoughts would reveal more than they try to hide if Beau could read my mind, and not only what those thoughts would say about him but what they'd say about me. The parts of me that can relate to these foster kids we're helping. Events like this could have changed my life's trajectory, and I wish I had known, so I could've saved myself a lot of heartache.

Beau knows the basic scaffolding of my story, having grown up in foster care, but not all of the intimate pieces that make up the whole picture. There are times I feel guilty keeping such a large piece of myself from Beau, someone I consider to be a close friend, but that part of me is sacred. Private. Tender. He's seen me at one of my lowest points and that was vulnerable enough. No need to drag him into the other shadowy places.

When my attention lands back on what Candace is saying, she is already wrapping up the meeting. "Alright, everyone, now that you have your jobs, let's get to it. I'm here if you need me."

My coworkers prepare to leave and Beau joins in, standing slowly, offering me his hand so I can do the same. I tighten my hold on the thermos and accept his friendly gesture. I'm not expecting his hand to feel exactly how I've imagined it. Warm. Strong. Safe. I stare at our joined hands for the seconds they are together. The brief connection sends a spark up my arm and straight to my heart.

I clear the mounting desire from my throat. "We've never done an event like this before, but I know Candace wants to find new and creative ways to get the word out about how we can serve the community."

His body faces me head on, and maybe it's the way he's studying me, or the impact of the work we do, but it causes a swell of emotion to rise up. "I wish I had known about this place when I was in the system. It would have been…life changing." A program like this would have meant everything to eighteen-year-old me.

His eyes stay on my face. "You're right," he shrugs. "And it has been life changing, but not in the way you thought."

I nod and look down at my shifting feet. He's right. My life is nothing like how I envisioned it going.

He nudges my arm with his elbow and beckons me to follow him out the door, and I do, because I'm helpless to do anything else. I'd follow him almost anywhere. Anywhere other than the parts of my past that are off limits. The Jacob parts.

He peers over his shoulder and smiles. Heat travels down my spine and then back up, causing my hands to turn clammy.

This is only attraction.

My mouth tips into a smile, too. "Thanks, Beau." I swallow, breath shallow, and consider asking my body what just happened as I trail him out of the room and down the hall.

Beau's smile turns sly. "You gonna be at game night tonight? I've been waitin' to beat you since last month."

I laugh and strut up beside him, swatting his arm in jest. "Oh, I'll be there, but I'm not leaving without being the first to reach ten victory points."

"I'm comin' prepared this time. I've been studyin'," Beau says.

A short laugh slips out. "What are you studying, exactly?"

"Techniques. I have to beat you somehow."

"Hmm. I'd like to see what kind of techniques you're talking about." I squeeze my eyes shut, my words coming out differently than how I meant them. Gesturing with my hands, I try over-explaining so we're clear. "Game techniques, I mean. You know, like building roads and cities, maybe getting more development cards, that sort of thing."

He laughs and bumps my shoulder. "I can't give away all my secrets now." His reply calms my flustered thoughts while also leaving me wondering what he's holding back.

"If you're feeling that confident, why don't we place a friendly wager on tonight's game?" I offer, immediately regretting it. A wager? What the hell am I thinking? This is definitely a bad idea.

We pause at the crossroads of where our paths split to each of our cubicles, and Beau turns to face me. I can't help noticing the pull and flex of his muscles as he tucks his hands into his front pockets. Why do they have to be so loud and in your face? My gaze lingers for longer than it should.

He clears his throat and I snap my head up. "Hmm. What did you have in mind?" he asks.

This could be fun, right? Two friends engaging in a friendly wager over a game we are playing with other friends? Harmless. No big deal. Easy.

I purse my lips, thinking. "Loser has to…"

There is barely a pause before Beau says, "Buy the other one dinner."

I consider him for a moment, taking in his eager words and expectant expression. "Deal." I stick out my hand, leaving little room for either of us to change our minds.

His lips part into a full smile. The kind that exposes pearly white teeth and makes my insides burn. The kind that makes my heart stop its beating. And the kind that makes me break out in a sweat. *That* kind of smile.

"Deal," he agrees, reaching for my hand and pumping it a few times.

I drape a stray hair behind my ear. "So, I'll see you later then…loser."

"Not if I have anything to say about it," Beau counters, giving me a smug look as he walks backward. "You better watch out, Kit. I'm coming for you."

His finger is aimed directly at me, but I'm the only one who knows it's pointing at my heart.

CHAPTER SIX
July 2014—Age 23

I sit back at my desk feeling like I've already fit a full day of work into one hour. Rotating my chair side to side while cradling my thermos, I wonder if I should call Monica now or later. If I wait, I may lose my courage, and I don't have time for that. But if I call and she doesn't remember me, it could be a dead end anyway. Why does asking for help have to be such an event?

I pull open my desk drawer and unearth Monica's business card. Flicking the edge of it, I consider what I'd say to her. The last time I saw Monica was when I was fifteen. I had moved into a new foster home—the fourth home in two years—and I wasn't exactly nice to her when she dropped me off.

She kept me updated via phone calls on her search for my brother, and though there was not much to show for it, at least she'd tried. But it all ended when my case was transferred. Monica encouraged me to tell my new social worker about Jacob but I hit a wall. I was frustrated that nothing was working. There was too much change to keep up with.

Leaning my elbows on the desk, I hold each side of the worn card between my hands. If anything, I didn't have a reason *not* to call her; she said I could at any time. Though, does that still apply eight years later? She helped as much as she could then, but would she be able to help now?

Picking up the phone, I cradle it between my cheek and shoulder as I punch in each number. Then, I exhale a long breath.

"You got this, Kit."

"Got what?"

Startled, I drop the phone. Then scramble to pick it up and place it back on the cradle. "Candace, you scared me," I say, clearing my throat.

"Sorry. I heard you right as I turned the corner. I didn't realize you were on the phone. Do you need to call them back?" she asks, completely unaware of the nervous energy buzzing through my body.

"No, no. Not at all. I'll call them back later." I wave my hand. "Did you have something you wanted to chat about?"

Candace leans her shoulder against my cubicle, standing directly across from my seated position. I'm still trying to wade through the surprise of her sudden presence when she tilts her head and pauses, the silence filling with my questions.

"I'm really glad you raised your hand to help out today. We have a lot of work ahead of us, and while I know you are totally capable, I want you to know you can tell me if there's too much on your plate. You have a lot of kids in the program you're helping right now and I just want you to know you can tell me if it's too much."

I release a short exhale, thankful this is all she wants to talk about. "Of course. I think with Beau's help, we'll get it done, but I'll be sure to let you know if anything feels like too much."

No you won't, my brain reminds me, but I push the thought aside.

"Alright, great. I'm excited for what this could mean for the foster kids in our county," she pauses, holding up a hand. "Scratch that—our whole region."

I smile. "You have a big heart, Candace."

"When you've worked with foster kids for decades, they have a way of breaking your heart and then growing it ten times bigger." Her enthusiasm and sincerity make me think of Monica.

How many foster kids had Monica come in contact with over the years? How many cards had she passed out? There is only one way to know if the woman who handed me this business card is still the same person I remember.

I have to call her.

Candace stands to her full height. "As soon as I get to my desk, I'll email you the spreadsheet I've started with the names and contact information of local agencies and social workers. It's a long list, and we'll likely need to add to it."

Swallowing, I try using some words. "No problem, I can handle it. Send the doc my way and I'll get started." I use my most confident I-will-get-this-done-no-matter-what voice, because that's what I need right now. I need the go-getter version of Kit.

"Great," she says, waving goodbye.

I exhale sharply, leaning back into the support of my chair. I know I'll get this done despite the enormous project Candace has indicated, but I wish I could spend my days looking for Jacob. She isn't paying me to spend all of my time and energy focused on my search.

Picking up my cell phone, I read through the group text with my friends roasting one another before the cards are even dealt. I'm not in the mood to compete anymore. Not because I don't want to but because it reminds me of Jacob. That was what we did together when living with a drunk mother and an absent father became too obvious.

It was our escape.

. . .

2003—Age 12

I fanned the playing cards in my hand, pretending like I didn't know exactly which ones I already had. Jacob didn't need to know that. "Do you have any aces?"

He grunted before handing me an ace from his cards. "You always get all the matches."

I shrugged. "I remember all of the cards you ask me for."

He rested his chin in his palm, uninterested in our game. It made me want to let up a little and give him a shot at winning but I didn't. I was competitive, and it didn't matter that the game was Go Fish against a seven-year-old or a cutthroat poker game with money on the line. I was going to win.

It was my turn, so I looked down at my options. "Got any nines?"

Jacob huffed and handed me the nine I knew he had asked me for on one of his last turns. He flicked the card instead of passing it. "Here."

I thought about saying 'thank you,' just to make sure I played the annoying big sister role perfectly but we were interrupted.

The voice was high-pitched and slurred. "Why the hell is it so loud out here?"

I stood quickly and walked toward our mother who was stumbling down the hallway. "Sorry. We'll be quiet. Let's get you back to bed."

I hadn't even reached her before her body crumpled and fell to the floor. I peered over at Jacob; his lips parted as he sat turned in his chair, watching every movement our drunken mother made.

"No," she said brusquely. "I can do it myself."

Ignoring her, I adjusted her shirt so it wouldn't fall off of her shoulder and reveal more than it already was and grabbed under her arm to lift her up. "I'll help you into bed and bring you some water."

Yanking her arm away from me, her hazy eyes bored into mine. "You don't get to tell me what to do. I'm your mother." She tripped over every word like she stumbled out of her room.

The very idea that she would even give herself the label of *mother* was laughable. She had no clue how to mother considering it was more of an action rather than a title.

Her eyes were bloodshot, mouth hanging, open because apparently it took too much energy to keep it closed, and her hair was disheveled like she'd been in bed all day. She was in bed all day.

I sighed. "Let me help you up."

"I'll do it myself."

It was awkward and clunky but she finally stood to her feet. She rubbed her forehead and leaned a shoulder to the wall, then her head followed. Unmoving, I wondered if she had dozed off standing up, but as I moved closer, I noticed her blank stare in the mirror at the end of the hall. Her eyes were unblinking—lifeless—but she kept staring at me as I stared at her, neither of us moving.

When it started to creep me out, I reached out a hand and said, "Here, lean on me, and we'll walk back to your room."

She swatted my hand away, standing as straight as she was able, which wasn't much. "I said I'd do it myself." Tripping down the hallway, she used the wall for support until it refused to help her, and she fell again. Her arms shot in the air, and she waved her hand, calling me over without any words to indicate she needed help. I hesitantly padded toward her, avoiding the hall mirror and her dead eyes. I helped her up, and we took the last few steps to the room where she could sleep off whatever she dumped into her system.

Her loud groan followed me out of the room and down the hallway as I fetched a glass of water. Returning, I set it on her nightstand but my mother's snores were already filling the dank room; she was passed out and breathing heavily. Apart from her chest rising and falling, her body looked as hollow as her eyes.

I came back into the dining room to find Jacob facing the table, cards in hand, like the episode didn't happen. I wish it hadn't. At least then I wouldn't have had to explain it away. He was getting older now and started to question why our mother was always so "tired." Drunk tired was more like it, but Jacob didn't need to know that. He didn't need to know a lot of things if I could protect him from all of them.

He avoided looking at me, though I had picked up my cards and was ready to resume. All of the fun had been sucked out of the room by our mother's presence. She was a ruiner. A ruiner of lives, families, moments, and especially card games. She had taken enough from us; she didn't get to take this, too. Playing games gave us something to do when it was the two of us. There wasn't room for three at our table.

Staring at Jacob's sad expression, I cleared my throat. "Do you have a two?"

He shook his head and said nothing.

Searching for anything to pull him out of his shell, I asked, "Want to know something cool?"

He looked up at me briefly and answered with a shrug.

I took that as a yes. "The oldest deck of cards is at a museum in New York City."

Jacob still didn't respond and continued to stare down at the worn table.

But I kept trying. "Some say that a deck of cards symbolizes a calendar." He looked up and kept his eyes on me for more than two seconds. That got him. "Fifty-two cards is like fifty-two weeks in a year, four suits represent the four seasons, and…" I didn't finish my thought, because Jacob was gazing down again, uninterested in my random card facts.

I stared across the table at my one and only friend, the pain etched into the concerned creases of his face. It was hard to have friends when I had to be home to take care of Jacob. I didn't have anyone else, and neither did he. He was my everything.

His leg swung back and forth, bumping the table and causing it to shake.

Looking at my cards, I made a decision. One that I knew would put a smile on his face. "Do you have any fives?"

Jacob's head snapped up. Puffing out his chest as the air around him filled with confidence. We were both swimming in it. "Go fish."

I smiled and reached for the deck. He didn't need to know that I guessed wrong just like he didn't need to know that our mother was drunk and not tired.

The lightness in his eyes was worth it every time.

CHAPTER SEVEN
July 2014—Age 23

A new email notification flashes on my screen and, seeing it's from Candace, I click on the spreadsheet attachment and start scrolling…and scrolling…and scrolling, wondering when it'll stop. I finally hit the bottom and sigh in realization of the work I have ahead of me. Even if Beau and I split this list, we're still going to be on the phone all day, every day.

Groaning, I fold my arms on the desk and drop my forehead on top of them. This job will take up so much time that I needed to start last week in order to get it done.

I'll call Monica later, I tell myself, hoping I'll be able to knock out a good chunk of this list today. I need to figure out what I'm going to say to her anyway. Words are hard when they've been missing for years.

LATER THAT AFTERNOON, when the usual buzz of the office had quieted, I notice an ache twitching in my neck. I barely left my cubicle today. My mouth is dry from non-stop action, and my stomach growls at me like a hungry animal. I had no time for lunch as I'd called, emailed, and game-planned how

I'd be able to tackle this project. I'm beginning to understand why Candace warned me.

I was so busy that I never had a chance to call Monica, either. But it was probably for the best, because it gave me more time to come up with what I would say when she did pick up. Tomorrow I'll have the words and will call her.

I grab my things and rush home to change for game night having severely overstayed my welcome at work. The janitors had already come through to empty trash cans and vacuum the thin carpet squares. Wanting to get ahead on the list, I stayed even when Beau offered to drive me home.

Finally pulling up to the curb outside of Jordan and Andrea's apartment in Burbank, I throw the gear into park and pull the keys from the ignition. Their apartment is north of the city but still has innumerable stoplights, buildings stacked high and close together, and enough activity to make me scan the area outside the car before exiting. I'm late, but Andrea knows clocks aren't my friend.

Olive let me borrow her car again, and even though I had to say a prayer before, during and after driving it, I'm grateful she's kind enough to lend it out. Catching myself in the rearview mirror, I lean in to get a better look at my fresh makeup. My dark brown eyes sit beneath thick, well-shaped brows and long lashes while my face is glowing, but that might be sweat since the AC doesn't work. Feeling like something's missing, I sift through my purse and snag the deep magenta lipstick, then swipe it liberally over my lips, pressing them together to smooth out any unwanted lines.

Pleased, I exit the cramped Honda, leather jacket in tow, and shut the door firmly. Among other issues, the driver's side door can stick a little, so I repeat the motion three more times before it decides to properly shut. I smooth out any wrinkles in my black, fitted t-shirt and dark denim skinny jeans. Both of which are hugging every one of my curves like Olive's Honda hugged the white line on the side of the road.

As I walk toward the apartment complex, I reach up and tousle my short hair that's parted down the middle tonight. It's one of the first major changes I made when moving into my new digs and becoming better acquainted with myself. I've always worn my hair long, and it flowed nearly to my hips when I arrived at the Journey Center. I loved my long hair, but when I got off the streets, the hair had to go. I was ready, and I needed it gone as much as I needed to build the woman underneath.

"They had to live on the top floor," I mutter, trudging up the three flights of stairs, my complaints falling from my mouth and down the distance I just climbed.

Staring at their paint-chipped door, I lift my hand to knock as it flings open, filling my senses with strong notes of vanilla and revealing Andrea's cheerful face. Her smile is so wide I fear it might break or get stuck that way.

She wraps me in a tight hug. "It's been forever. So good to see you."

"I saw you a few days ago," I say, laughing into her dark, wavy hair through the heavy breaths I'm still trying to catch from the climb up.

"Sure but a few days feels like forever when I'm used to seeing you every day." Andrea steps back, cataloging every square inch of my face like she'd forgotten what I looked like.

I raise a hand to my racing heart. "I missed you, too."

We cross the threshold and Jordan, who has been waiting patiently, shuts the door behind us. "You know you'll always have a room here. Andrea keeps the spare bed made up just for you." He winks at his wife and pulls me in for a hug.

"Thanks, Jordan. It's good to see you," I say.

"You know you're the one who made the bed in there last, not me." Andrea nudges her husband's side as he tucks her under his arm.

Jordan shrugs. "Well, sure, but that's because we did it–"

Andrea cuts him off, "Okay, I think that's enough of that." She winks at me and raps on his broad chest.

Andrea sizes me up in obvious approval. "You're looking great tonight."

I look down at my outfit like I don't already know what I'm wearing. "Oh, yeah, thanks," I reply with a nervous laugh. I wasn't expecting such a public perusal, but then again, I never am. I don't like being the center of attention. Well, not anymore.

I look up from my all-black worn Converse sneakers, seeing Beau behind Andrea and Jordan. It's only been a few hours since we last saw each other, but that doesn't stop my breath from hitching or my stomach from dropping.

Now would be a good time to look away, I think to myself, hoping my expression doesn't give me away.

Beau studies me intently, and the awareness stirs up the desire rising throughout my body before I force myself to look somewhere else. One look. It used to take three, four, the occasional two, but now it's one.

I'm still shaken when Jordan's voice breaks the lingering silence. He looks back and forth between us. "Let's get Catan set up."

Andrea rubs her hands together. "I'm gonna get the snacks." She turns and disappears into the kitchen.

Jordan heads to the dining room table where I can see bits and pieces of the game board taking shape. I love this game and don't feel nervous about the competition; it's always friendly, but I am nervous about the shift I sense happening in Beau's eyes. Or, is that only happening in mine?

We remain standing in the entryway, feeling every part of the uncomfortable tension. This is new. Where is this coming from? When did it start? I want to dissect all of these questions right now, but I don't, because that would be downright reckless of me. More than friends doesn't exist for Beau and me. Hell, it doesn't exist for me and anyone, period.

He clears his throat and rubs the back of his neck. "Want me to take your coat…or something?"

I peer down at the leather jacket still in my hand and shake my head. "I'm good. I got it." Hanging it on the hook beside the door, I take a controlled breath before swiveling back around. "But I am ready to see the moves you told me about earlier."

Before Beau can answer, Jordan is calling to us. "The game's ready, let's play."

Beau waves a hand, inviting me to move past him and into the dining room. "After you," he says with a sly grin, and I bite the inside of my cheek to suppress a smile.

I pass Beau, and without even thinking—something I really need to do more of— I bump him with my shoulder, teasing but also adding more fuel to the fire we are building. The one I keep telling myself I need to dump water on. I don't listen.

"I DON'T GET it. How are you so good at this game, Kit?" Andrea asks with a mix of disbelief and awe. The evening passes in comfortable ease as the four of us joke and jeer over too many snacks and plenty of smack talk.

I laugh at Andrea's reaction while Jordan counts the ten victory points that won me the game, again. "She's got ten points." Jordan tosses his remaining cards on the table.

Andrea shakes her head in astonishment. "Seriously? I don't know how you manage to pull this off every time."

I set down my two remaining cards and reach for a carrot. Dunking it in the dip, I say, "It's all in the strategy. Beau can tell you a thing or two about that." I give him a side-eye while chewing and notice he is staring in my direction, still baffled by my second win of the night.

With his mouth hanging open, Beau says, "Let's play another."

"Come on, you already owe me for the two games I've won. You really want to make it three?" I lean back confidently in my chair and cross my arms.

"I studied all the techniques online, all of them told me expanding my settlements to cities is where it's at. I don't get it." Beau tips his head back to look at the ceiling and I stare.

Look away.

I can't help it sometimes. He makes small movements like this that set my body on fire. Who knew necks with scruff could be so attractive. Adam's apple, squared jaw, sultry eyes. Yes, apparently eyes *can* be sultry.

Look away.

I don't look away. "I guess that just shows you can't believe everything you read on the internet," I tease. "I can see how building cities would be good in theory, but if you focus on obtaining the Longest Road and Largest Army cards, then you're already halfway to the total amount of points you need to win." I may regret lending this information to Beau when he wields my own strategy against me, but for now, I get to stare at him longer.

Beau holds up two fingers. "I owe you two dinners. A deal's a deal."

My smug smile may tell Beau I'm proud to be winning a couple of free dinners, but all I can think about is the guy taking me. "I get to choose, right?"

His lips press together, and he nods his head slowly.

"Anywhere I want?"

"Anywhere," Beau confirms.

I rub my palms together, making him wonder what types of restaurants I have running through my head. Of course, I'm not going to tell him. Where would be the fun in that?

Andrea stands and it steals my attention away from Beau. "I'm going to get more dip. Kit, can you help me in the kitchen? Maybe the guys can get cards out to play Nertz?" She points between the table and the guys as she grabs my hand and pulls me into the cramped, outdated kitchen.

"Okay, what was all that?" Andrea asks.

"What do you mean?"

"Spill it."

I try not to smile; I really do but it's useless. Knowing exactly what she's talking about makes me smile broader and laugh harder. I have no intention of saying it out loud, though. The feelings swirling around my body are mostly new and one-hundred percent foreign. Seeing Beau again tonight and living in the realm we've created somewhere between his eyes and mine only confirmed this. I don't talk about these feelings with other people and definitely not myself, because they aren't real feelings. It's just attraction.

The tile floor is fascinating and steals my attention. "Spill what? I don't know what you're talking about."

"The flirting, the inside jokes…the eye thing you both keep doing. Don't even get me started on the lipstick you're wearing."

I jerk my head up. "What do you mean? I like wearing lipstick," I say defensively. I knew Andrea would notice; she knows me too well. I should have worn ChapStick.

Leaning against the counter, I grab a chip and scoop out a hefty amount of dip. I'm trying to choose my words carefully but they come out facetious. "Alright, you guessed it. I'm totally into Beau and want to marry him."

The shock on Andrea's face says it all. "You're serious?"

"No! Can you hear how ridiculous that sounds? Really, Andrea, nothing is going on. We're friends and always have been."

"Yeah, but it isn't so crazy to think that something could, well, you know…develop between the two of you."

I start to explain things away. "Actually, it is crazy. Don't you think something would have happened already? Nothing has changed in the last few years to make our relationship different than it always has been." I'm trying to convince Andrea of this as much as I'm trying to convince myself, but the fact is I'm not ready to give it a name, let alone describe it. If I do, I can kiss our friendship goodbye, and I don't think I can handle that since this is *just attraction*.

Arms crossed, Andrea leans against the opposite counter. "Relationships grow when they're ready. It wouldn't be all that crazy, if you think about it. You have history together."

"Andrea, I promise, it's nothing. Sure, we tease each other but that's it, really." I'm hoping these words will set my feelings straight; they have to, since I've got a brother to find and a limited amount of time to do it. Relationships take effort and men are needy, both of which I don't have space in my life for.

Besides, none of this even matters, because it's *just attraction*.

Andrea uncrosses her arms and picks up the extra bowl of dip. "Okay. I'll drop it but promise me something."

It's my turn to cross my arms and look at her sideways, telling her with my body language that I don't know if I can promise anything. I'm no good at those.

"If your feelings change, don't hold yourself back from feeling them. We've seen some shit in our lives, but that doesn't mean we aren't worthy of finding love, too."

Andrea sees straight through me to the pieces of myself that are the most broken, and it causes a lump of emotion to form in my throat. I have to avert my gaze if I want to hold it together.

It's different finding love for someone like me after living so long in a world where it didn't exist.

The only response I can muster is a nod, so she knows I've heard her. Plus, I can't handle any more of her wise words anyway.

Andrea moves closer to squeeze my shoulder and then exits the kitchen, leaving me to sift through the emotions surrounding this kind of promise. I turn to face the counter, gripping the edges until my fingers yell in protest. My heart is feeling things without asking for approval, but I don't know how to stop it now.

CHAPTER EIGHT
2004—Age 13

"Go Fish," Jacob said, void of his usual enthusiasm when I had to draw a card. He had a downcast expression, and I wished I could take it away, but that'd be impossible. Even for me. Not on a day like the one we had.

I reached for the deck and grabbed a card.

"Have any kings?" he asked.

I looked down at the cards in my hand and sighed with relief when I saw a king of clubs. "I do. You got me." Handing him the card, I tried to catch his eyes with mine, but he kept his head low.

Jacob nodded but didn't say anything else. I couldn't blame him. He'd been quiet ever since we got picked up by that social worker two days ago. Saying enough words to get by, but I knew better. This wasn't Jacob.

This was a kid that lost almost everything.

I didn't know how to fix it. Not this time. It wasn't as easy as closing my mother's door and playing cards in the dining room while she slept off her bender.

She was dead.

Gone.

And our Papa? He forgot to come home.

We were in a room that looked like it used to be an office but now held rows of pop-up cots, cribs and couches that were all filled with kids. Infants were being fed and rocked by workers, teens were curled up under blankets, and then there was Jacob and me. Sitting cross-legged on the cold, linoleum floor in the corner of the room, playing cards and trying to pretend like this nightmare wasn't real.

The room was dark, apart from a small lamp, and I'm sure the staff was hoping we'd sleep, though I don't see how we could. The wails coming from children torn from their families were too loud. I couldn't unhear those sounds, even in my dreams.

I cleared my throat and prodded his knee to get his attention. "You get to go again, remember? You guessed that I had a king, so you get to ask me again."

Jacob had always been easy-going but not today. Not yesterday, and probably not tomorrow, either. He threw his cards down between us with such force that it sent them flying in different directions. Dropping his head into his open hands, I could only stare in shock at his hunched body.

His voice was muffled by his sobs, and I didn't hear what he asked, but I did, because this question was coming from my own mind as well. "What do we do now?"

I swallowed every emotion and did what I'd always done. I protected him. "We'll figure it out. These people are here to help us, and I'm sure they're working things out." When I said those words, I knew he wouldn't believe them, because I barely believed them. Over the last couple of days, I'd watched kids enter and exit the doors of this room at an alarming rate. Some were siblings, others were strangers, but it was clear why we were all there. We were waiting. There was so much waiting. Two days of it for us while others were here for two weeks. We were waiting for parents to get their acts together; waiting for social workers to get assigned, waiting for homes to become available. So. Much. Waiting.

I set my cards down and started to gather the ones that Jacob threw. "We're going to get through this, okay? I promise. Come on. Let's keep playing cards."

Promises were all I had, and I hoped I'd be able to cash in on them one day, preferably soon. We're hanging onto whatever we can grasp in the middle of an ocean of uncertainty. We just needed to keep floating, keep waiting.

He dropped his hands away from his face and peered up at me through his long lashes. They were wet from crying, and I could see the fear even without much light. A shrill cry resounded somewhere else in the room, and it felt colder, a shiver caused goosebumps to rise on my arms. I'll never unhear those sounds. They'll be tattooed in my memory every time I think of that place.

Closing my eyes against the reality we were living, I handed him his cards. "I didn't look at them."

His smile was small but still there. "Liar."

"I swear. I'm not a cheat. I like beating you fair and square."

He shook his head, and the hunch in his shoulders started to straighten. "Fine. Do you have any jacks?"

Looking down at my cards, I had my answer to his question. My eyes met his, and I tipped my mouth into a teasing smile.

"Go Fish."

CHAPTER NINE
2014—Age 23

I tap my fingers on my desk and feel how sore they are after all the emails I sent yesterday. But, I don't stop my nonsensical fidgeting while I listen to every ring coming through the phone; my heart beats faster with every one of them.

Answer. Answer. Answer.

I lost sleep last night over what I would say. Waking up multiple times, thinking about Jacob and the crying children who don't have names but still take up space in my thoughts, didn't help any. But when I woke up this morning, I knew what I'd say to Monica when she answered. I'd remind her of the promise she made to me, like the promise I made to Jacob.

I don't expect her voice to sound so similar. It's been years, but the familiar inflections bring a rush of memory with every word.

"Hi, you've reached Monica Castillo, and I'm unavailable to take your call, but if you leave your name and callback number, I would be happy to contact you when I am able."

It's not until Monica's voice starts speaking those last few words that I realize I'll need to say something when the phone beeps. Should I leave a message for her to call me back? Do I hang up now and call back later?

In a rush of panic, I slam the phone down on the receiver like it's a hot potato about to burn my hand if I don't release it this second.

"What's going on?"

I scream at the unexpected question. "Beau!" I hold a hand to my pounding chest. "You can't sneak up on me like that."

"Why? I do it all the time," he says, moving into my cubicle and perching on the corner of my desk.

He's so close, I can smell his favorite brand of cinnamon gum as he chews. Who even likes that kind? I hate the flavor, but I like smelling it.

"Yeah, well, today I guess I'm just a little more…" I search for the best word to describe my reaction. "Jumpy."

"I can tell. What's up?"

I sniffle, trying to clear the smell of cinnamon from my nostrils. "Nothing. I was…making more calls. Have you made progress on the spreadsheet?"

"Yeah, I have, but it doesn't feel like it. That list is long," he says, crossing his arms over his broad chest and slowly shaking his head.

I scoot my chair back further, requiring the distance before I decide I like the taste of cinnamon gum. "It really is. I had no idea there were that many foster agencies and facilities to invite."

He blows out air. "We'll work our way through it. Don't worry. I got your back."

I smile briefly, feeling my nerves settle and my longing soar.

Beau surveys my meager decorations clearly lacking on the fuzzy cubicle walls. No pictures, notes, knitted something or others from the grandma I don't have. The walls are bare, unlike other coworkers who don't have any free space left. Even Beau has pictures of every member of his family, likely even first cousins.

His considerations make me squirm, and I attempt to recapture his attention. "So, Friday…"

"Friday," he repeats. "You gonna tell me where we're goin'?"

"I already told you I'm not saying anything, so stop asking." I point at him with a mock seriousness.

"Oh, come on, not even a hint as to where I'm takin' you?" he asks.

"No, because knowing you, you'll have some surprise waiting for me at the restaurant that I may or may not like. Need I remind you of the balloons?"

"We were celebrating a birthday. Balloons made sense."

"Not when it wasn't my birthday," I say through a short laugh.

"You have to admit the staff did a killer job of singin' to you, though."

I cross my arms. "But, it was also awkward and embarrassing."

He tips his head to the side. "I remember you gettin' a free dessert out of it."

A smile begins to form, and I bite down on my lips so as to not give into his arresting smile. I look down briefly and swallow my feelings. "Still. I'm not telling you until we start driving."

He lets out an exaggerated huff. "Alright. I'll trust you," he concedes, holding up his hands in surrender.

"Good."

A short silence fills the space between us before another head peeks around the corner of my walled space.

"Kit. Beau. How's it going?"

"Doing good, Candace. Beau and I were talking about the spreadsheet." I shoot a look at Beau.

"It's comin' together," he confirms.

"Great. Hey, uh, Kit. I found this in the break room, and Cami told me it was yours." Candace extends an arm, and I pray it's not what I think it is. "I figured you'd want to take that home," she says with a small grin before releasing it into my hands and backing out of the space to continue on her way. I don't miss the giggles she tries to hide as she leaves.

I focus on the coffee mug for half a second before palming my forehead, a flush of embarrassment climbing my neck.

"Olive's mug?" Beau stands to his full height again and beckons for the mug.

I nod and hand it over, too shocked to even watch Beau's reaction, but I hear it.

His laugh is hearty and deep, forcing me to look. "That's good," he manages to say.

I snatch the mug from him and look at the saying written above a small picture of the Excel spreadsheet logo.

Freak in the Sheets.

I raise a shoulder. "I mean, it's true. I am good at spreadsheets."

His smile grows bigger, if that's possible, and he backs out into the narrow hallway. "I believe you," he says, his laughter still ringing in my ears. I don't want it to stop.

Face burning, I whip around to face the desk. Planting my elbows firmly on its solid surface, I push my fingers through my hair. "What just happened?"

I let out an I-can't-win-today breath and then check the time. There is only one hour left before I can call it quits and head home. It leaves me enough time to call Monica back.

When I get her answering machine again, I think about hanging up but can't release the phone. It's glued to my hand, and I know I won't be able to hang up without leaving her a message.

I have to know if she'll be the ally that I desperately need.

CHAPTER TEN
July 2014—Age 23

"Kit," Dina calls from the living room. "Beau is here."

My stomach drops hearing his name, but I feign ignorance at my own reaction. *Friends. We are going out as friends.*

I run a hand over my short, wavy locks, grab my purse and tell my heart to chill out.

I see him first as I exit my room and round the corner into the living room. Beau is wearing a black button-up shirt with an olive green sports coat, dark jeans, and black leather sneakers. *Wow.* If I wasn't confused before, I am now. Beau knows how to dress, that's clear as day, and I try my best not to ogle him but my slack jaw isn't doing me any favors. His hair is buzzed shorter than it was when I saw him at work, and I'm having a hard time pretending like those clean, sharp edges aren't making my pulse thump faster.

"Hey," Beau says. "You ready to tell me where I'm taking you?" His smirk tells me he noticed my reaction as much as I felt it.

Just attraction.

As I continue to absorb the man in front of me, I realize there was a question mark at the end of his comment. I shake myself out of my musings and try out his line for size. "I can't give away all my secrets."

I'm stepping closer to him when I notice Dina and Olive spying on us from the kitchen. I give them a look that says to bug off but they don't turn away.

Smiling with a playful glint, he says, "I'm not asking for all of them…just one."

I laugh nervously, knowing full well that my roommates are within earshot. "I have a spot picked out, don't worry," I tell him, patting his arm in a very friendly way.

I know where I'm taking him, but if I am going to pull this off, I have to keep him in the dark for as long as possible. I'm the one who told him to dress up, which is more to satisfy my own curious mind than for the place I picked out. In order to make it believable, though, I dressed in a blush-colored blouse, dark skinny jeans, and neutral-colored wedges I traded for my usual sneakers. This better work.

"I told you I'd let you in on things when we got in the car. Remember?" I say.

He points to his head. "Short-term memory."

I lean further on one leg, pushing my hip out. "Like I believe that."

Beau sweeps out his arm, indicating that I should walk in front of him, and when I do, I inhale his delicious spiced cologne and I make a pleased face, one that makes Dina giggle, which leaves me feeling too exposed.

I grit my teeth. "Goodbye you two."

We walk toward the front door, where I snag my trusty leather jacket from the hook. I never leave anywhere without it. It doesn't matter that it's the middle of summer in California. This jacket has been through things with me. It survived them, too, like I did.

He follows me to the sidewalk, but before I make it to Olive's car, Beau reaches out and grabs my elbow.

"I'll drive," he says.

I glance over my shoulder at him. "I told you I could drive. Olive's letting me borrow her car."

Beau stays silent, and I lower my eyelids to get a read on him.

He looks past me. "I'd like to make it there in one piece."

I place my hand on my chest and let my mouth hang open in pretend shock. "What do you mean? Beau, are you trying to tell me you don't like Olive's car?"

I know exactly what he thinks of her car. He had to rescue me from the side of the road a time or two when it decided to die on me.

He pushes his hands into his front pockets and shifts his weight to his heels. "It's not Olive's car I have a problem with."

My mouth shuts and I frown, glaring at him through my painted lashes. "You aren't trying to tell me that you don't like my driving, are you?"

He shakes his head quickly. "Nah, I'm trying to tell you I don't like your driving in L.A. I can't speak for how you drive when there are no other cars on the road."

He's not wrong.

I straighten, crossing my arms. "You have a point. Alright, you can drive, but next time, you'll have to suck it up alright, Big Guy?" Beau nods once and moves to walk around me, but not before bumping my shoulder and knocking me off balance.

I catch myself before I tip too far on the edge of my heel. "Hey!" I stomp after him toward his car. I won't admit this out loud but it's enjoyable to be around someone who can dish out a jab as well as they can take one.

He opens the door and I climb in. When he rounds the car and settles in, I give his shoulder a light shove in retaliation, but of course his giant body barely moves.

"Where are we going, Squirt?"

"Squirt?" I say with an air of disbelief. "Since when do you call me *Squirt*?"

"Since you started calling me *Big Guy*," Beau says with a straight face.

"So, as of twenty seconds ago?"

"Exactly." He nods, and without waiting for directions, turns the key and pulls out onto the street.

"You might want to rethink the nickname if you want to know where you're taking me." I'm acting as if the nickname bothers me, but there's no need to let him know I secretly enjoy it.

"How about this," he states. "I will drive to where I know you're going to take us, and if I'm wrong, I'll stop calling you Squirt. Deal?"

A small laugh passes through my lips. "There are like, thousands of restaurants in L.A. What makes you think you know where I plan to go?"

"Oh, I know," he says, looking over at me with lifted brows and a smug grin that makes me believe he really does. "So, do we have a deal?" He rests his elbow on the center console and holds out his palm for me to shake.

I study the side of his face, which indicates an unwavering confidence that's both drawing me in and wanting to prove him wrong. "Okay, Big Guy. Deal," I say, taking his hand and shaking once. I can't resist a friendly wager and Beau knows it. I ignore the heat radiating from our touch, realizing how much it's affecting my pulse. If I'm not careful, he'll be able to hear it soon in this small space.

He continues driving, taking all of the necessary turns, and with each successive mile, I second guess our new wager. Eventually, he pulls into a small parking lot and navigates into a tight space before he kills the engine. Then, he looks at me. My arms are crossed and I'm sulking, because there's no way, *no way*, that he figured it out.

"I'll take your reaction as my answer."

His certainty radiates around the car's small cabin. I glare at him from the corner of my eye until my resolve breaks. "Fine. You got it right."

I jump as his hands meet in a loud, resounding clap, and the confidence turns into something akin to gloating. He's enjoying this. I'm enjoying this less.

I hop out of the car and meet Beau around the vehicle before we start walking toward the doors. "I thought I had you with the dress code," I say, revealing the plan I thought was bulletproof, or at least Beau-proof.

"That's how I knew where we were going," he says, stunning me with a wide smile. He opens the door wide and bows. "After you, Squirt."

I try hanging onto my irritation, but it's hard when Beau's gentle hand is on my lower back, guiding me toward the register.

The young kid with the sailor hat looks up as we approach. "What can I get you two tonight?"

Beau's smooth voice answers for me. "Two double-double burgers, animal style, both with fries and chocolate milkshakes." He takes our receipt, and we walk outside in search of an available place to sit. White, circular tables with red bench seats and matching red umbrellas dot the patio, and we choose one in the back. So far, I've managed to keep my mouth shut and am proud of myself for keeping my questions in for this long, but as we slide into opposite benches and Beau's knees nudge mine, I can't hold it in any longer. "Alright, you win. I know it wasn't the fancy clothes that gave me away, so what was it?"

"Because, it's your favorite place, and I know you wouldn't go for a fancy restaurant. That isn't your style." He rests his forearms on the small table. "You don't think I know what you like by now?"

I fiddle with one of my hoop earrings. I didn't think I was that predictable. There are things I like, preferences I have, but I didn't think anyone else had noticed. Andrea knows some of my likes and dislikes but I never expected Beau to.

I wave a hand in front of my outfit. "I needed to make it believable, though we can see how well that worked out." I toss him a playful smirk, which he responds to with a beaming smile and puffed out chest that makes me thankful I'm sitting down.

"You do look beautiful, but you still didn't fool me."

My heart stutters at the compliment, because these are things we don't say to each other. I collect myself before speaking. "Clearly."

When they call out our number, Beau retrieves the food, breaking up our conversation before we dive into the mouth-watering burgers I've been craving all day.

"Mmm, this is so good. I love this place," I say after my first bite. I venture a look at Beau, whose face still shines with glory. "Since you seem to know what I like, what are some of the other things you've noticed, Big Guy?"

"I've learned a few things about you over the years, Squirt. Your favorite burger is one of many." Beau drops this like it's nothing, but to me it feels like everything.

I tuck my hair behind my ear, questioning if I'm the only one with growing feelings. I really like being with Beau, and there's something about the way we are together that heightens my curiosity.

But it's just attraction.

My mind is still trying to process how much Beau knows about me when he fills the silence. "Tell me more about your family. You mentioned you had a brother."

I pause, wondering how he knows to ask this and now—of all times—hours after calling Monica and leaving her a jumbled message that I'll probably have to clear up with another call tomorrow. The change in topic has me momentarily reeling, so I take a bite of my burger to gather my thoughts. I don't often share about Jacob on purpose. It's not that I don't want Beau to know but finding the words is difficult.

Could I share this with him? I think to myself, wiping my hands on a napkin and taking a sip of my milkshake.

I look down at the white cup with its pattern of red palm trees circling it. "I don't talk to him…" I start, testing my ability to continue. "I think about him, though." I can't *stop* thinking about Jacob, I almost add. "We were separated ten years ago when we were both put into foster care. I haven't seen him since."

I pause, watching Beau twirl a french fry between his thumb and pointer finger. Could I share more than this? It would leave me vulnerable but maybe, just maybe, it would feel good to talk about things with him. I knew it felt that way when I told Andrea and my therapist, and Beau is one of my friends.

I focus on the busy street beyond Beau's shoulder, finding something to anchor me. My voice is weak when I start, but I continue anyway. "I promised I would never leave him." The levity of the night is replaced by the weighty reality of my broken promise.

Beau doesn't say anything. Instead, he picks up another fry and trains his eyes on my face, but I avoid looking at him. If I'm going to get this out, I can't look at the compassion lining his features; it would be my undoing.

I take a few bites of my french fry, trying to tamp down the regret. "Yeah, I, uh, told him I'd protect him and keep him safe. I didn't do that, and now I don't know where he is."

Beau looks at me with astonishment. "You've really been searching for him for ten years?"

"Yeah."

He straightens. "Have you made any progress? Any clues in finding him?"

I shake my head slowly. "Not enough."

Beau wipes his mouth with his napkin. "The job fair would be a great spot if he's still in the system."

"If he hasn't been adopted and is still living in a foster home," I reply, looking straight at Beau's drawn brows, "it's like trying to find the back of an earring after dropping it on the ground."

I enjoy another sip of milkshake, but seeing his confusion, I shake my head. "Never mind. What I'm trying to say is that it's an impossible mission."

"I don't think it's impossible." His eyes hold me captive as he reaches across the small table to cover my hand.

I nod slowly, feeling hopeful and terrified all at once. I stare at his large, all-encompassing hand, reminded of how small I feel in a world so big. I've been swallowed by it before and couldn't handle it happening again, especially when there is so much at stake. The weight of his hand feels like a weighted blanket, calming my nerves and settling my anxious body. I don't want him to ever remove it, not when it feels this comforting.

Beau exhales slowly, pulling his hand back, and I shiver from the loss. "I remember you saying that your mother died of alcohol poisoning, but what happened to your dad? You've never talked about him."

I peer around the sparsely occupied patio and picture my father's face. Dark hair and dark eyes, like me. He's there as he always is, haunting and dark. "There isn't a whole lot to say about my dad. He worked hard to earn money for our family." I choose my next words carefully. "He left us. Well, not while my mom was alive. They were both happy for a while, I think."

Beau grabs his cup and takes another drink. I wish he would reach for my hand again, but having done it once already, I don't expect him to again.

My body isn't tense and rigid like I expect to feel after sharing so much. He makes it easy to want to share the stories that make my heart beat, while simultaneously making it stop. So, I decide to continue. Sitting up straighter, I clear my throat. "It was after she died. He started working more, coming home less, and forgetting to give me money to pay for the basics. A neighbor must have noticed how much time Jacob and I spent alone. I tried to keep things quiet by avoiding direct questions about where he was all the time, but it didn't work. The next thing I knew, a CPS worker was picking us up, and I haven't seen my dad since." I let my shoulders sag, aware of my stiff neck and the weight of that day's memories.

The story is a permanent scar, ingrained in my memory like carvings in wood and impossible to remove.

"Hey, you okay?" Beau says, chasing my gaze.

I allow myself to be caught. "Yeah, I'm good. It's just…hard to talk about."

I'm grateful when he moves the conversation along. "I know not all siblings get to stay together, but did the agency even try to keep you and your brother in contact? What about visits?"

I clear my throat, recognizing how shaken my revelation has left me. "The CPS worker told me I'd get Jacob's number and he'd have mine. They either forgot or it wasn't important. Likely both." I push aside the empty container of fries. "I moved homes a lot in the beginning and wondered if Jacob did, too. It's hard to keep the thread of connection intact when it's constantly being handed to someone new. The social workers couldn't keep track of my history, much less that I had a brother, and it got to the point that I stopped asking them to. I'd figure it out on my own when I aged out."

"So you never saw each other after that day?" he asks in a quiet voice.

"Nope." I shove the memories aside and continue. "When I started working at the Journey Center, I realized how common this is. If there isn't a foster family willing to take a sibling group, we're split up. That's why I wanted to work there, to help the teens that slipped through the cracks. Maybe they lost a sibling along the way, or maybe they didn't have anyone on their side."

He's slow to speak, digesting my story. "That's rough, Kit. I'm so sorry."

I don't hear pity in his words, and I'm glad for it. Pity won't find Jacob; I learned that a long time ago. "Thank you," I manage to say.

"What can I do to help?"

I'm not sure what to make of his question, but I consider his determination as he leans his forearms on the table.

I wave him off. "Oh, you don't have to worry about helping me. I'm working on it. Plus, there's already so many other kids that could use your help. Really, don't worry about it."

The deep sound of his voice reverberates off of the dome-shaped umbrella. "I *want* to help you. You've already carried this load on your own for years, Kit. Let me help you. I'll do whatever you ask."

His plea sounds sincere, but I keep staring, trying to figure out if he's really serious. "Honestly, I don't even know how you could help me. I've failed at every attempt so far. I don't know if it'll go anywhere."

I downplay my need, not because I don't need his help but because I don't know *how* to accept it. I'm scared by how much comfort I'm finding in him, and I don't want to discover more.

"We'll figure it out," Beau says, shrugging like this is possible, even simple.

A twinge of anger sparks within me, and I can't contain my next words. "Don't you think I would have figured something out by now?"

He considers the undertones of my reaction. "Look, I'm not saying you haven't been doing your best. All I'm saying is that I want to help. I want to be there for you."

I shake my head and cross my arms over my chest. I have to look away. I'm frustrated that I want him to want to help me and I'm annoyed at him for trying to swoop in and save the day. I've been the one doing all of the leg work, or at least trying to. He doesn't get how hard I've worked to earn money to support myself, or how I've reached out to local agencies only to be told I had to call so-and-so. I've been the one to make the calls that ended nowhere. I'll figure this out; I can handle it.

I'm biting the inside of my cheek to keep from responding when I feel his warm hand on my elbow. "You shared a lot about your family tonight, and that couldn't have been easy. I'm here for you, Kit, whatever that looks like."

Tears well in my eyes before I can tell them to go away, and my words, despite their truth, sound small. "I'm scared." A tear rolls down my cheek and I track it to my lap. "What if I don't find him?"

The question I've been most afraid of asking falls from my lips without much effort. I can't retract it, and I know Beau heard me. It's the most honest I've been with him, and I've never felt more vulnerable.

I feel a light squeeze on my elbow. "We can't let fear hold us back. One step at a time."

He's right. I want to skip to the end and figure out the answer, but I can't. One step at a time is all I've got, so when he hands me a napkin I take it. Beau's grip never leaves my elbow; he must know I need the support.

I wipe the liquid from my cheeks. "Okay."

"Okay, as in…I can help you?"

I nod, slowly but noticeably. I don't know if I'll regret this tomorrow, more than likely I will, but right now it's a relief to know I don't have to take the next step alone.

I hold up a finger. "On one condition."

"Anything. "

My mouth curls into a sly grin. "I'll let you know when I think of it."

CHAPTER ELEVEN
2010—Age 19

"You're late." Bobby's sharp words hit me like a slap to the cheek.

I sat shaking in the passenger seat, knowing his temper could erupt at any second. "I'm really sorry. I had errands to run."

He glared at me. "What makes you think I will accept that fucking excuse?"

The harsh lines between his brows made me sweat, and as if his features weren't dark enough, the faint light in the car made them even darker.

My resolve slipped. "I-I don't know, because it's the truth."

The window was cracked when I first entered Bobby's car, but it had since been shut, blocking off the noise of the busy street I was supposed to be working on. Instead, I'm holed up in the car, awaiting a punishment I'd take lying down.

His words leaked venom. "You think I don't know where the hell you are all of the time? I know where you were today, so I know why you're late."

Shit. That means...no, he can't know. If he knew I had spent the morning at a foster care agency trying to locate my brother, that means maybe he knows about Jacob. Damn it. He can't know about Jacob; that will only give him more power. My eyes widened but I didn't flinch. He would enjoy that too much.

"That's right. I know all about the kid you're trying to find, your brother, is it?" A laugh bursted from him, mocking my obvious disbelief.

I swallowed hard, grasping for composure. "I-I was just…" My voice faltered. I couldn't get any words out; I was trapped by fear.

"I was the one who found you when you were desperate and working that dead-end job. I can throw you back out there to fend for yourself if you'd like," he said with a counterfeit smile. "Don't tempt me."

I remembered all too well the help my pimp provided, and I regretted accepting it every day since. There were stipulations, agreements and non-consensual changes, but that's how this game played out. At eighteen, I left my assigned foster care agency, scared and fully aware of my lack of options. I could have gone to college, thanks to a generous offer from the state when teens aged out of the system, but I couldn't do that knowing I had unfinished business. I needed to double down in my efforts to find Jacob, and I needed money to do it. Bobby found me, offered me that money, and then remade me. I didn't look back, up, down or side-to-side without his permission.

"You will never go to one of those agencies again, do you hear me? You work for me now, which means everything in your past life is gone."

I skimmed his face when he paused. Wrong move. Bobby's eyes were dark but somehow still glowed.

Seeing my rigidity, he moved his hand from the steering wheel to my bare thigh. But he didn't stop there. He slid his hand up my leg until it was unnervingly close to the parts of me that he owned. I cringed at the contact, every one of my muscles tensing, but I didn't move, knowing that if I did, his hand would eventually find my throat.

He dug his fingers deeper into the tender part of my thigh, and I released a pained noise. "If I ever catch you searching for him again, I will make sure you fucking regret it, do you hear me?"

I needed this job and Bobby's protection more than I needed my self-worth. I was bought and paid for like the common goods I'd become. But I was torn. I couldn't forget about Jacob. If I stopped looking now, there'd be no one left to do so. It's not like we had any family he could live with in order to get out of foster care. Our mother's parents were dead and our Papa's family lived across the border. I was his only way out if he hadn't already been adopted. If I could make money, have a stable living situation, then get a better job, maybe a judge would look favorably on me. He'd find Jacob and then let me adopt him.

The only answer I could give Bobby, the only one that I felt safe enough to express for now, was a few quick nods. I bit the insides of my cheeks and held my breath to keep from making another sound. I feared Bobby but I feared life without my brother more.

He doesn't need to know.

"Good. That's all." He released my leg, leaving half-moons where his fingernails had dug into my flesh.

My hand shook as I fumbled for the door handle. Pushing it open, I filled my lungs with smog-filled air, grateful to replace the stagnant air of the car with anything else. Before I could fully escape, however, Bobby shot his hand out, gripping my arm like a snake wrapping around a smaller predator.

He lowered his voice, "I changed my mind."

He released me, but when I saw Bobby's hands move toward the zipper of his pants, I knew what was coming. I had a job to do, a person to be, and a name to live up to.

I LEFT ONE hell for another. But I'd much prefer this one than the confines of Bobby's car. He was long gone by now. Usually, his 'goons'—as I called them—would handle the dealings of a regular night on the blade. It wasn't long until someone stopped and inquired.

"How much?" he asked, rolling down the driver's side window.

Knowing how to play the game, I sauntered up to his vehicle, giving him a good look at my cleavage and exposed ass. They liked a sample. "Eighty for everything, fifty for foolin' around."

The man grunted. "That's a rip-off."

I knew his type. The kind that was after a bargain. It was my job to remind him what he would be receiving at the list price.

"Maybe if you were with someone else it would be a rip-off but not with me, sir." I leaned in slowly, letting the neckline of my shirt drop further and my tits grazed his arm that hung out the window. I touched my lips to his ear and whispered exactly the kind of experience he would get for my price.

The mood turned heady. "Alright, I'll pay. Get in."

The man appeared harmless and was probably in his mid-fifties, with salt-and-pepper hair and a wide gut. It was the middle of the night, yet he was still in his suit, like he'd gotten off of work and came straight here. I did a quick scan of his car, but aside from his discarded jacket, there was nothing or no one else there.

Rounding the hood, I climbed into the passenger seat, not even bothering to pull my mini skirt down. I extended my hand toward him, palm up, waiting for the cash. I always took money up front, especially when in direct visibility of Bobby's goons in case something shady went down. Maintaining eye contact, the man slapped the money onto my hand. It made me squeamish but I wouldn't relent. This money meant more than the fear this man tried to instill.

He didn't speak as we drove around the corner to a darkened side street, so I didn't say anything either. By now, I had seen it all. I had been working the streets for two years and the men I met were all the same. Most were hurried and spent little time on frivolity, and I learned quickly that sex was all about the customer's orgasm. It's what they paid for, so it's what they got.

When I peeled myself off of him and was preparing to exit the vehicle, he grabbed my arm. "Wait."

My voice shook. "Sir, you have to let go of my arm. You paid and I delivered." Rarely did scenarios like that one go any further. I had a pimp or his minions with eyes on me at all times. No customer in their right mind would ever risk doing what that man did.

Pure hatred reflected back at me making my skin crawl. But I was frozen in fear and he had an iron-clad grip on my arm.

He spoke through gritted teeth. "Give it back."

My body might not have been able to move but my mouth still worked. "Let go. I've given you what you paid for. You don't want any trouble, right?"

"What I want is my money back. You weren't even good."

A disgruntled customer was never a good sign. I could give him the money and be free, or I could fight and possibly lose my life. The in-between options were always shaded gray.

His steady gaze shifted from warning to danger. "I said, give me my money back, bitch."

Before I had a chance to react, a small knife was slicing through the air and diving into the soft flesh of my arm. The blood was immediate but my response was delayed. He held the knife under my chin while still gripping my other arm to the point it was hurting more than my fresh cut.

Where were Bobby's fucking goons when I actually needed them?

Seconds became minutes as I waited to be rescued, hyper aware of how much can happen in a short period of time.

"You think you can fucking outsmart me? You aren't worth the money I paid, and we both know it. I don't even like brown girls. Now, give me my money before I give you more to remember me by." The man yelled, his spit flying in my face. He tore his gaze away from me and reached for the small purse I had slung around my shoulder, digging in it with the hand that held the knife. He located the cash and finally released my arm, yet I couldn't move.

"Get out of my car, you fucking whore."

His words echoed in the small space and the door handle was hard to find in the dark, but I never allowed my gaze to leave the man with the knife and a pension for blood. Falling out of the vehicle, I hit the sidewalk and winced at the rough contact. His engine roared to life and he leaned over to snatch the passenger door closed before peeling away. I scrambled backward so I wouldn't get side-swiped, and it wasn't long before he'd turned the corner and was gone.

I sat there, sucking in air as pain traveled through my body, comforted only by the distant city noises and my own rapid breathing.

Cradling my fresh wound, blood dripped down my arm to color the sidewalk. My voice was ragged and muted but it didn't stop me from trying. "Somebody, help me."

But no one came to help.

CHAPTER TWELVE
July 2014—Age 23

It's early. So early that Olive isn't home from another night shift at the women's shelter.

Curled up in my bed with the soft glow of a lamp illuminating my sketchbook, I scratch out various shapes and angles as predawn darkness lurks outside the window. I can't sleep when I feel like this: when the memories haunt me and all I can see is Bobby's face when I close my eyes. Sleeping isn't worth the nightmares.

I didn't know what I was drawing at first, but now I see it clearly. It's a sketch of me. My hair is long, my face is…sad. I'm not drawing Kit; I'm drawing Mercedes. I add shadows beneath my eyes and catch the details of my lashes as they rest on my cheek.

If I knew I had been signing up for *this*—the kind of remembrance that never leaves you—I wouldn't have done it. I would have kept my job working at that rundown diner. At least my dignity would still be intact, and maybe my virginity, too.

The sketch is missing something, so I start outlining small droplets trickling down my face and neck. The tears aren't on my sketchpad anymore, though; they are running down my warm cheeks, leaving a cool trail in their wake.

When I look in the mirror, I like the girl reflected back at me. I didn't for a long time, but she needed compassion in order to grow. Mercedes needed to learn her decisions didn't break her. They refined her. The two parts of me have been slow to merge together, but the stories are beginning to create a fuller picture.

Rubbing my hand up and down my shoulder, I feel the raised skin beneath the thin cotton. I hike up the sleeve to expose the old wound. It's a scar now, like most of the experiences branded in my brain, reminding my body how far I've come.

Mercedes is as much a part of me as the skin holding my bones and organs in place. When I finally had enough and was handed a way out, I seized it like a greedy child, leaving a life that stole more than it gave.

My sleeve falls when I remove my hand and I set my sketchbook aside. I click the light off and nestle between the silky sheets in hope of a few, rough hours of sleep. Beau will be able to tell I didn't get much sleep. He always can, because he knows why I have trouble sleeping.

He rescued me from it—from them.

RIGHT AFTER I choose an outfit and head to the bathroom for a hot shower, I get a text from Andrea reminding me of our picnic with everyone later today. It's been on my calendar for weeks, but she knows a text the day of is a more effective reminder for me.

Setting my phone on my bed, it vibrates again so I pick it up. Beau reminds me to bring a blanket for the picnic. He told me this last night, too, and now I'm starting to think my friends will expect me to forget what's happening today after church.

I type out a sassy reply that I know will make him laugh then head for the shower. Our wager dinner was two days ago, and I can't help thinking of every single detail of that night. Did I say too much? Is he really going to help me find Jacob? Why did I agree to this? Not only are we spending tons of time together at work preparing for the job fair, but now I've held the door wide open for him to join me in my personal problems.

The more I try to convince myself of our friendship, the more I start realizing how unusual our friendship is. I don't tease, flirt, or touch *anyone* more than I do with Beau. I've never been in a relationship before—a real one—but this feels like more than friends and shy of labels. I had been *with* people but a boyfriend?

It's just attraction.

I groan, frustrated that these thoughts won't shut up. I can't entertain them when the sentences of my life are still unfinished. What happens after I find Jacob? I've never considered a future without him, yet I've never really envisioned a future with him, either. In my dreams, we just *are*. I've found Jacob. End of story.

But what comes next?

By the time I'm showered and dressed, I make the two-mile walk to church. I'm thankful for my holey jeans that let a breeze in on this already sweltering day as well as my tried and true ratty sneakers that don't make my feet ache. But they don't help my thoughts that are still swirling around like a tornado. Andrea hasn't been much help, either. Every time I mention my encounters with Beau, I see her arched brows and the questions within them.

I drag my feet up the front steps and push open the double doors, my anxiety lifting with the first "hello" and embrace. I'm struck by the kindness every time I walk into this place and see the faces that make up my community. The beauty of acceptance is that it doesn't hinge on the *what ifs* or the *how comes*. It starts and ends with love.

Walking into the sanctuary, I spot Andrea and Jordan in the middle row. I slow the pace of my feet when I notice a dark head of buzzed hair sitting next to Jordan and a foot above everyone else sitting down. My stomach drops at the sight of him.

Beau, my heart reminds me, as if I'd forgotten.

Taking a deep breath and letting it out, I move closer to the group.

"Hey, over here," Andrea calls when I make it to the edge of the row. It takes no time at all to realize there is only one seat available, and it's between where Beau is sitting and where I'm standing.

Andrea's broad smile tells me this is not an accident. "We saved you a seat."

Jordan waves. "Morning, Kit."

"Morning everyone. Thanks for the seat." I sit, lean forward to place my shoulder bag on the floor, and tell myself I need to appear calm when I stretch back up. My heart rate is fast beneath my chest and the combination of flutters in my stomach aren't helping.

Beau grins at me, and it's like a light has been turned on in this dimly lit space. His smile is brilliant against the backdrop of his dark skin. "Hey, Squirt. How was the walk?"

"It was brisk, thanks for asking, Big Guy." I wink at him and immediately regret it. *Since when do I wink at people?* Since Beau, apparently. "I thought you'd have been at the earlier service?"

"Nope. I'm goin' to a picnic after this. You are, too, remember?"

Before I can give a snarky reply, I hear a familiar cheer filling my other ear.

"Hello!" Aunt Cindy is standing next to me, so I jump up and embrace her. "It's so good to see you, sweetie."

"You too," I say, inhaling her Wisteria perfume. The familiar scent automatically causes my shoulders to relax.

When I release her, Andrea waves her aunt over. "Aunt Cindy, you can sit over here with me."

"It is so good to see you. Beau, you are taller than ever, son." Aunt Cindy laughs, giving him a hug in passing.

Beau shrugs. "My Mama makes sure I never skip a meal, maybe that has somethin' to do with it."

The shuffling and welcoming hugs continue as I swallow the lump in my throat. I know Beau is incredibly close with his family, so this normally doesn't come as a surprise, but something squeezes my heart hearing him talk about his mom. Aunt Cindy is as close as I've come to a mother, but even still, she isn't my mom.

The concern in Beau's voice registers in my mind. "Kit?"

"Yeah, I'm good," I say, shaking my head.

The music picks up and Beau has to raise his voice. "You look deep in thought."

I force a smile that I hope convinces him I'm fine, then motion toward my ear and mouth, *I can't hear you,* as the drums add their beat and the singers lean into high-pitched vocals. The room fills with a soft melody, and I'm grateful for something else to focus on.

The pounding of the music ricochets between the walls of my chest as a harmony of voices—young, old, sick, healthy, rich and poor—fill the space with unity. I sing the words along with everyone else, but my mind travels to times before. The times where I had a family, regardless of how broken we were.

We had one family photo in our apartment growing up. It hung on the refrigerator door, so that every time I opened the fridge, I was reminded of how fake it was. Everyone was smiling, even me, but I knew what came before and after that photo was taken.

It was a Saturday morning, and we'd been on our way to the farmer's market, even my father, whose presence was rare. But that particular morning, my mother had already been drinking, and her morning binge collided with whatever was in her system from the night before, which resulted in her throwing up all over the sidewalk. I don't know if the headshots' vendor had seen it, but when we passed his booth and my mother begged him to take our photo, he did. I've always felt like his generosity was due more to my mother's garbled speech, our wide eyes, or my father's blank expression, but whatever the case, something tugged on his goodwill enough to result in the only real proof that we were a family.

I left the photo behind when we were taken from that apartment. My mother died, my father forgot about us, and I didn't give two fucks about a stupid family picture. Now I wish I'd kept it, if only to have another picture of Jacob's smile. I'm banking on being able to recognize him when I find him, despite the fact he's an adult now.

I close my lids, allowing Jacob's face to take shape behind them. I would recognize his youthful features anywhere, but in truth, that boy doesn't exist anymore. The picture in my mind changes, and I'm startled by what I see.

While the music continues to play, I bend down to retrieve my shoulder bag. My sketchbook and pencils are tucked safely inside, and I clutch them tightly in my hands. Drawing and sketching came into my life when I needed an outlet, and it has stayed with me ever since. I picked it up during one of my stays with a foster family. The mother was an art teacher who loved sharing her knowledge like it was a physical part of her herself she was handing out. She gave me power in the form of a pencil and paper. I'll never forget that, or her.

Relaxing back, I flip to a blank page, my hands itching to draw the new picture of Jacob in my head. I move my hand across the page with an increased fervor as the eighteen-year-old I haven't met yet comes into focus.

I highlight his face with furious movements as I alternate between drawing and shading. This vision of Jacob shows him with a mop of curly brown hair, caramel-colored skin, like mine, light brown eyes, a full mouth turned up in a big smile and two dimples. I do my best to capture these details on the page but a pencil doesn't do him justice. In my vision and my drawing, I can see him as an adult, but I can't ignore the defining, child-like features I have memorized. The sketch has both versions of him, and though I don't know this adult Jacob, I want to.

Does he have facial hair, a girlfriend, or can he drive? The sketch doesn't tell me these things, so I cross my legs and assess what it is trying to tell me. It must mean he's safe, happy even.

"That's him? That's Jacob, isn't it?"

I hadn't noticed my audience of one, and looking into Beau's face, I nod, feeling too fragile to speak. The shadows of the room hide his face, and I can't see his full expression, but there's enough light to know that he sees it, too. He notices what makes Jacob and me siblings. I see it so clearly and have to bite my bottom lip to keep from crying.

Beau reaches for my hand and I squeeze it back, clinging to every unsaid word in his supportive gesture.

I don't understand why, but when I look at this sketch of my brother, I know this is what Jacob looks like…now.

CHAPTER THIRTEEN
2003—Age 12

"I want these ones." Jacob pointed to the wallet-sized photos. The ones that were too small to fit in any frame but he wouldn't be deterred.

The school sent a packet home in his folder so we could choose which size photos we wanted to purchase. We had never bought them before, and I didn't know why he wanted them. There were no other pictures of us or our parents on the walls of our apartment, but the real problem was that we didn't have money to buy them.

I laughed at the tiny pictures. I'd need a magnifying glass in order to see his smile.

"Jacob, these are too small. If we're going to splurge on pictures, I say we go big. They don't make picture frames this small."

He shook his head. "No, I want the small ones."

"You planning to pass them out or something?" I asked with a laugh.

He shrugged as his only response.

I could tell something was working in his seven-year-old brain. "What is it?" I prodded. "You can tell me."

We had each other and no one else. I was the only one Jacob had to tell these kinds of things to. I was the only person he had for a lot of things.

He released a quick breath. "Maybe Papa can put one in his wallet, so when he's working, he can look at my picture."

I turned my head away from him and back at the photo packet in my hands. *This is why he wanted the small photos? To give to our dad?* My heart wasn't made of stone. I knew that feeling of wanting our parents to notice us, yet I also knew what it felt like when they didn't.

"You can have one, too, Kit, and Mom, if she wants," he added in a small voice.

Tears pushed forward, but I blinked them back before responding. Jacob knew our father was busy working, but that's all I let him know. There are things a boy his age shouldn't have to know; our father's blatant neglect was one of them. I wasn't willing to crush him. "I think that's a great idea. Let's get them, buddy."

I didn't tell him that I thought it was a waste of money to get those minuscule photos so a man who barely spoke to us could carry it around. And I never told Jacob that I had to trim our grocery bill down just to afford copies of those pictures. It wasn't possible when I saw so much desperate hope in his eyes.

Jacob was so confident those photos of him would mean something, and they did, but not to our father. Jacob's wallet-sized photo meant the world to me.

CHAPTER FOURTEEN
July 2014—Age 23

The park bench is uncomfortable, but the warmth of the sun on my upturned face makes up for it. It isn't unbearably hot as we wait for the rest of Andrea's family to arrive and my black t-shirt is thankful for that. Ever since I drew that picture of Jacob, I can't shake his face, so I need a minute to gather my thoughts.

Dropping my chin, I spot Beau, who's been talking to Jordan, or so I thought. I squint to see him more clearly, and there's no denying it, he's watching me—though for how long, I can't say.

My attention shifts from Beau to the eager figure running in our direction.

"Cici!" Allison screams before leaping into Aunt Cindy's arms.

Aunt Cindy catches her in an embrace and plants a kiss on her head. "Allison! Oh, it is so great to see you darling."

Allison, Andrea's birth daughter she placed for adoption as a baby eight years ago, wraps her arms tightly around Aunt Cindy's neck. "Andrea told me you were coming today!" She turns and spots me standing from the bench. Releasing Cindy,

Allison barrels toward me, knocking me off-balance with the strength of her hug. "I didn't know *you* would be here!"

A small laugh escapes along with the air in my lungs as she squeezes me tighter. "I can't miss another chance to play tag with you and Peter, now can I?"

I discovered their love for the game soon after meeting them last year, and it has quickly become *our thing.* Every time we get together, the kids ask to play, and I'd be lying if I said I don't look forward to it, too.

"Yes!" Allison says, pumping her fist. "Today is going to be awesome. Come on, my mom and dad packed a bunch of sandwiches and want me to eat first." Allison flips her hand in the air with a hint of sass in her voice.

"That sounds like a smart idea since you're going to need a lot of energy to beat me," I tease, tickling her sides and filling the space around us with her giggles. I wish I could bottle up this sound and listen to it every time my world looks and sounds a little gray.

We move closer to the group of people greeting one another. Three-year-old Peter is walking circles around Andrea's legs when Allison rushes forward and starts chasing him. Weaving in and out of the bodies, she tickles Peter like I had done to her.

I risk a look at Andrea to see her wide smile. She looks comfortable with her hip pushed out and arms loosely crossed. She tilts her head and studies the family she's inherited.

Walking over, I lower my voice and nudge her shoulder with mine. "You have a beautiful family."

The moisture tugging at her lower lids speaks volumes. "I can't imagine it any other way. I love them all."

When Andrea got pregnant at fifteen, it changed her life. She surrendered Allison to an adoptive family and did the same for Peter years later when her life was still in a rough place.

Lifting a hand, I rub her back. "I do, too."

It isn't long before Aunt Cindy calls out, "I am sure all of you are hungry, I know I am, so let's eat!"

We settle on multiple picnic blankets in the shade and enjoy the homemade sandwiches, fruit, and veggies. I'm barely finished when I get coerced into a few rounds of tag with Allison and Peter. I can't say no, and they know this.

Sweaty and exhausted, I settle down on one of the blankets a while later and reach for a water bottle. I guzzle it and focus my attention on Jordan and Beau who are chatting with Allison and Peter's parents, Sarah and Anders. Allison is sitting cross-legged in front of Aunt Cindy as she braids her hair, and Andrea and Peter are next to them reading a picture book. It's so normal, how a family should interact with one another.

Lifting the water bottle to my mouth again, I swallow to keep my emotions in check.

Will I ever have a family like this one?

I haven't called Monica since I left the message, but it's in her voicemail, so I'm expecting a text or at least a return message to be waiting for me when I return to work on Monday. And if there is, I'll have at least one path to finding the family I want so badly but has been out of reach. It's hard seeing others with what I want most in life.

Peter nuzzles his head further into Andrea's chest, her words lulling him to sleep. The moment is so tender as she brushes the hair away from his forehead and rubs her hand up and down his back. It makes my heart constrict, and I wonder if my future includes kids. A growing desire strengthens in my chest, but I earmark that page in my story to come back to another day, a day when I have a family to offer a child.

Beau moves his large body toward the blanket I'm occupying, and I cap both the water bottle and my daydreaming.

His voice carries a sing-song lilt to it, making it hard not to smile. "Penny for your thoughts?"

"You'll need more than a penny, that's for sure." I nod once, proud of my quick response.

A muscle in his jaw works as he thinks. "How about, if you tell me, I'll add dessert to my next dinner tab?"

I look off into the distance. "What makes you think dessert wasn't part of the original dinner offer?"

"Dinner is dinner. Dessert is on another level."

I purse my lips and try to decipher his words. "You're right, dessert does kick it up a notch." I take another sip of my water, suddenly feeling parched, and watch Beau do the same. How long can we sit here like this before one of us speaks? But the real question is, how long can I play this game—our game—before getting hurt?

"Dessert it is. So, what's on your mind?"

I don't feel as hesitant as I'd expected. Is it because I've already shared so much about my family with him? Setting my water down, I lean back on my hands. "Family."

He smiles. "Alright, alright. That sounds like a conversation I can hang with."

His smile does something weird to my brain, like a short circuit or blip on the radar screen; it's offline and back in one breath.

I laugh to hide the effect it has on me. "Is that so, Mama's boy?"

"I'll wear that title proudly. I love my Mama."

A breeze passes through and changes the air around us. I know all the basic information about his relationship with his mom, but there are gaps in my knowledge concerning the rest of Beau's family, and I'm desperate to fill them. "I knew you were a Mama's boy, but what about the rest of your family? Tell me about them."

"I have an older brother who's married with a couple kids. My two sisters are younger and still live at home with Mama."

He pauses, turning to look at me, then he lowers his voice. "I have a lot of respect for my Mama who raised us all as a single mother. We didn't make it easy on her but she handled it."

"Your brother and his family, are they close by, too?"

He leans back on his elbows and nods. "They live a few miles away."

Reaching for the carton of fresh strawberries, I pick out the juiciest one I can find. "What about your dad?"

His smile drops and he presses his lips into a firm line. I don't say anything to fill in the silence that follows. Instead, I nibble around the edge of the strawberry stem and stay quiet.

My question eats at him, and I'm three strawberries deep when he peers over at me. "Wanna take a walk?"

I look around and everyone is talking and pecking at the leftover food. They likely won't notice if we slipped away. "Sure."

We stand and meander down the path that leads around the park. It's busy today, full of families, runners, and people walking their dogs. I stay quiet, grateful for the distraction so I won't thrust meaningless words between us. But, it's awkward since I obviously hit a soft spot asking about his dad.

He rubs the back of his neck. "I don't talk about my dad," Beau starts. "Ever since he left, Mama doesn't like to."

I don't know anything about his dad, but I guess I've never really asked. Thinking back, it's been a conversation that ended before it ever got started.

Beau drops his hand and shrugs. "He wasn't around much, because he was a thug."

I whip my head to look up at him. "Wait, what? Like, a real thug?" As opposed to the fake ones, of course.

"Yeah, the runnin' drugs, poppin' people who cross you, and hustlin' at all hours of the night and day kind of thug. My Mama hated it, so when my dad got her younger brother in the game, she finally snapped and kicked him out."

I tear my gaze away from Beau and focus on the path in front of us. "What about your sisters? They must have been so young."

"They were. Jada was two and Serenity wasn't even one. Of course, they were too young to remember him, but my brother and I do. It was hard, but Mama was adamant that it was for the better." Beau mimics the high-pitched sound of his mother's voice. "She told me once, 'baby, I feel safer now than I ever have before.'"

"I imagine being married to a thug makes it difficult to feel safe," I say. "You never saw him after that?"

Beau shakes his head slowly. "Nah. Mama wouldn't let him come around until he got his act together, which hasn't happened. He tries sending her money to help out, but I don't think she's ever used any. Says it wouldn't feel right not knowin' where it came from."

I swallow hard, considering the kind of fathers Beau and I had. We didn't have a choice, and their unwillingness to change cost them their entire family. "I'm so sorry, Beau. That your father was a thug, sure, but more so because he never got to know you."

He stops walking and turns to face me, shoving his hands in his front jean pockets. "Even though he wasn't there, my brother and I had other men to look up to. There was always someone there to teach us things that our dad didn't."

I have to squint to look up at him, but I do in order to see the sorrow I hear in his voice. "Why didn't your mom ever remarry?"

"I don't know. I have my guesses. I think she's hopin' one day he'll turn himself around. It's been seventeen years, but I still see the hope in her eyes. It kills me sometimes."

I don't know what comes over me, but before I can stop myself, I'm wrapping my arms around Beau's waist like it's the most natural thing in the world, like I do this all the time and not just in my dreams. I cling to him, tightening my grip as I rest my cheek on his chest. The rush of his heartbeat beneath my ear is fast, and the delicious smell of his spiced scent is embedded into every fiber of his shirt. He's stained by cinnamon and it's delicious, smelling like the only contentment I've ever felt.

My swift movement catches him off guard at first, but when he settles his arms around me, their comfort surrounds me. I don't pull away, even though I should before my compassion morphs into something else. Something more than *just attraction*. A feeling that will steal my attention away from my brother. It'll distract like Bobby distracted me and every other man I slept with for money did. Though when I heard the distress in Beau's voice, it sounded familiar.

We are so close, I can feel the heat radiating off of his skin, yet I don't pull away. Instead, I whisper into the folds of his t-shirt. "You should have had a father, and I'm sorry you didn't."

"We both should have."

I need to pull away, but I can't because I've discovered something about Beau's arms today: they feel like my new home.

CHAPTER FIFTEEN
2004—Age 13

Getting home from school, I flung my backpack onto the couch and headed to the kitchen to make us all dinner, Jacob close on my heels. A candle was burning on the counter, which meant our mother was praying again and then likely forgot about it.

My mother was the religious stakeholder in the family. She grew up Catholic and knew all of the prayers, customs and traditions that went along with it. We had all the beads, candles, and pictures of various saints hanging in our rundown apartment in Santa Ana, too. All of which were a constant reminder that we must be doing something wrong.

"Jacob, blow out that candle, will ya?"

He strode toward the counter. "Are you sure we should? What if…" his voice trailed off.

"What if…what?" I asked over my shoulder, already busy pulling out ingredients.

Jacob stood at eye level with the candle. "What if it's bad luck or something?"

Our mother often prayed to St. Jude, the saint of hopeless causes, and I would find her murmuring her prayers every night, rosary beads in one hand, a bottle in the other. "Most holy apostle, St. Jude, faithful servant and friend of Jesus, help me in my struggles. Please pray to God for me and the suffering I am trapped in." Her words often came out garbled, having already drained a bottle of wine while she lay sprawled out on her bed or sometimes on the floor. I have nothing against the rituals and prayers that Catholicism offers, but I grew up believing God cared little to nothing about us. Religion worked for other people, but not for my mother and definitely not for me.

I suppressed a laugh. "I think we'll be okay."

He leaned in, pursed his lips, and blew out the candle. Looking up at the ceiling as if to judge whether a lightning strike would hit, Jacob backed away slowly to fetch his homework.

The liquid gold in a glass bottle is what my mother knew, so it's what she did. God was an afterthought, a means to her end. "Kathryn, don't ever drink. You'll be hooked for life; it's in our blood," she would say, warning me against finding comfort in the bottle like she did. It wasn't hard to avoid alcohol when I was the one to clean up her puke and help her change her clothes most nights. Addiction is a needy bitch.

I don't remember my mother as a woman, a mom, or a friend; I only remember her as a glass filled with alcohol. When the drink was gone, all that remained was a limp body in the back bedroom.

Jacob's voice rang out from the living room. "Kit, I need your help with my homework. It's division this week and I don't get it."

I sighed, setting a pot of water on the stove to boil noodles. I hated division. "Alright. I'll help, give me a minute."

It was Jacob who was the first to call me Kit. I never saw myself as Kathryn, the name my mother chose and the good little helper she's glad she had. I found myself only wanting to be Kit—the one Jacob needed.

Scooting a chair out at the dining table, Jacob collapsed into it, shuffling papers around and sharpening his Ninja Turtle pencil in preparation for the division I'd have to figure out. Our mother was in her room, door closed and quiet, which meant she had likely had a long day of drinking and was either asleep or passed out; I could never tell which. Everything was in usual working order, for our family.

Sliding the pasta into the water bath, I focused on our dinner preparations. There was a half-full jar of spaghetti sauce in the fridge that I added water to in order to make it stretch. No meat to speak of and only a wilted salad I packed up and brought home from school when someone at our table was about to throw it away. It was simple but more than we had most nights.

Jacob's seven-year-old voice pulled me out of my thoughts. "Will Mom be okay?"

I was used to that question and already had my standard answer prepared, "Yeah, she'll be fine. She just went to bed early."

"No. I mean…" Jacob paused. "Do you think she will ever get better?"

I was placing a strainer in the sink when his question stopped me. My mind blanked. I was only thirteen, but I had tried my damndest to protect him from all of it, to protect him from our mother. His question made my heart sink because, apparently, I wasn't doing a very good job. Jacob was a sensitive kid. He didn't understand that our mother was sick—so sick that she couldn't be healed. I tried my best to stay neutral whenever we talked about them, because I didn't want him to worry, but it was hard when they were obviously screwed up.

After stirring the noodles, I moved to the rickety dining table where Jacob sat. Pulling out the chair beside him, I allowed the reality of my mother's addiction to settle on my shoulders. "I don't know, buddy, I hope so." Lies. I didn't care.

He stared at his lap, his next question coated in fear. "What happens if she doesn't?"

I cleared my throat when I saw the uncertainty etched on his young face.

"Nothing. I'll keep taking care of us, and Papa will keep working. We'll be okay, you'll see, bud." I needed to reassure him more than I needed my mother to get healed; that would be great, but it was also unrealistic.

His lips dropped into a frown, chin quivering, and tears slipping down his cheeks.

"Hey now, what are those tears for?" I moved to kneel in front of him, my hands cradling both of his.

"I…I can't lose you too, Kit. P-Please don't leave me."

Emotion welled up in my chest as pressure built behind my eyes before I could scold it for showing up when I needed to be strong. I swallowed, the taste of my own skepticism burning my throat. "I will never leave, Jacob. Ever. Got that? I will never leave you." My blurry gaze pierced into his glistening eyes as I tried to convince both of us that we would make it out of this in one piece. He looked so small at that moment, which was exactly how I felt.

"You promise?" he asked, voice feeble but hopeful.

I pushed aside my own hopes of seeing my mother get better, of wishing my father was present, and the belief that I wouldn't break under the pressure. "Of course. I promise I'll always be in your life no matter what happens. Come here." I pulled his small body into the circle of my arms. He was the reason that I kept going, and I would do whatever necessary to see my promise through.

Holding him at arm's length, he wiped the tears from his face. "Dinner's almost ready. What do you say we play cards now and do homework later?"

His face lifted. "You mean it?"

I nodded. Sometimes, rules are meant to be broken, like blowing out prayer candles that don't even smell good.

CHAPTER SIXTEEN
July 2014—Age 23

"Okay, so you aren't crazy about restaurant jobs," I say, staring at my computer and looking up at Stella every so often. I'm trying to find a job she'll apply for, and it's turning into a search-for-a-pot-of-gold-at-the-end-of-a-rainbow situation.

Stella smooths her hands over her long blonde hair. "No, I was so nervous every time I worked, it made me sick. Most nights, I actually got sick, you know…bleh," she says, pretending to throw up.

I switch to a hopeful tone. "Alright, restaurants are out, but there are plenty of other places. What about a retail store?"

Her fair skin pales while her lips tremble. "I can't. When I'm on the spot, it makes me so freaked out that I'll screw up," Stella sighs. "I'm not good at anything."

"Don't say that. There is a job out there for you, and we'll find it. It's normal to be nervous about doing something new."

I review the options on my computer but can't help watching this dejected eighteen-year-old girl out of the corner of my eye. A low self-confidence will spread any lie to stop a person from growing. Stella's confidence started out even smaller than it is now, if that were possible.

"Hey, I want you to know that I'm here to help you." Crossing my arms, I rest them on top of my desk. "It can be intimidating to enter the workforce for the first time."

I search Stella's face for a reaction, but she's looking at her hands, spinning the few rings she's wearing to avoid eye contact. But I know she can hear me, and while my words may sound trite, they're from a place that's recognizable to me.

Stella opens her mouth to speak but it's like she's lost her voice.

I wait patiently, knowing this moment means more than helping another street kid fill out job applications.

She clasps her hands together and her thumbs start chasing one another. "I wish I didn't have to deal with all of this shit."

I tap a finger on my crossed arms, feeling tears swell at the corners of my eyes. Working with foster care kids means tears are part of the job. For me and for them. The stories are endless and the needs are great, especially living in L.A. county, which has the most foster kids in the entire state. It's sobering to constantly be reminded that the work is never done but always beginning.

I'm looking at this young girl and calling her Stella, but she's also an eighteen-year-old Kit, too. What's more shocking is that she's also an almost eighteen-year-old Jacob. My posture stiffens causing my muscles to tighten at this realization.

I'm talking to Jacob.

I drop my head and stare at my folded arms. Where are the magic words? The ones that will knit her together again and confirm that she is whole and not broken. I wish they existed but compassion is all I have.

Lifting my head, I straighten. "I want to tell you this will get easier, but I can't."

With downturned lips, Stella focuses on combing the ends of her hair.

"I want to tell you that since you chose this path, you'll forget the one you were on before. You won't forget," I lower my tone, "but you will heal." I know I'm talking to Stella, that the person across from me is a blonde teenage girl. But I can't help seeing a curly-headed little boy who I may never see again, and who may or may not be afforded these same opportunities. "You may feel lost but know you will be found in all of this. Now doesn't mean forever."

Her eyes are misty and her fidgeting has stopped. "Thanks."

I give her a half-smile, reaching across the desk to settle a reassuring hand on her arm. "Let's keep looking, okay?"

"Alright."

It isn't much, but I have to trust that my words will be enough.

"HELLOOO, KIT?"

Beau's large hand comes into focus as my brain comes back online. "Oh, sorry. I was thinking. What's up?"

He takes the seat across from me, relaxing into the stiff wooden chair like it's the most comfortable thing in the world. "I walked past your desk and said 'hello,' but you never answered me. I thought you were giving me the cold shoulder or somethin'."

"No, nothing like that," I start to say before realizing that was too easy. A smirk tugs at my lips. "I mean, you did forget my coffee this morning."

"I see how it is. I forgot your coffee *once*, and now I'm cut out?" Beau slaps the center of his broad chest like I've wounded him. "You're killin' me.

I lean on the arm of my chair. "It's a pretty extreme offense. If I hadn't come prepared with a spare, I don't know if anyone would have survived me this morning, let alone you."

We exchange amused looks. "I was gonna take my chances," he says.

"Mhm."

He waves a hand at me. "So, you gonna tell me what's got you all distracted?"

I look past his shoulder at the wall. "I was talking to Stella this morning, the young foster girl who has been living here for the last couple of months, and I've been trying to help her find a good job."

Beau's eyebrows scrunch together in question. "The girl with blonde hair who never looks at anyone?"

"I mean, can you blame her when you're that tall? She'd have to crane her neck like I do." I laugh. "But she also has a good reason for that. She's had a rough time."

Beau nods. "I believe it."

"She reminds me of my brother," I say in a hushed tone.

He rubs his jaw. "That's actually why I came by."

"Oh, yeah?" I gulp as my pulse quickens.

"Yeah. I was planning to ask you for a picture of him so we could send it out to some of the agencies we've been callin'. Maybe we'll get a bite." He crosses his arms, highlighting the prominent muscles and veins bulging beneath his skin.

I pull my gaze away from his hypnotic effect. Clearing my throat, I try to respond without revealing too much. "That'd be great, but I don't have a recent picture."

He tips his head to the side. "You sure 'bout that?"

"Positive. The only picture I have of him is this one." Pulling open my desk drawer, I locate Jacob's tiny school picture. "He was only seven at the time."

Beau reaches across the desk and grabs the photo. "He looks just like you."

"He does," I say in a low voice. "We both look a lot more like our dad than our mom."

He glances between the small picture and me. Each time our eyes meet, longing rolls down my spine, and I only hope he won't notice. "This one's good, but I wasn't talkin' about this picture. I was thinkin' about the one you drew yesterday in service. Could we use that one?"

I blink rapidly and wave a dismissive hand. "No, that was just a sketch. I don't really know what he looks like now. That picture could be totally wrong."

Beau nods slowly. Then, he leans forward and drops the picture on my desk. "It's probably the best we've got. It'd be worth a shot." He folds his hands and waits for my response.

I scoot forward, laying a palm on top of the picture and sliding it toward myself. Monica hasn't called back yet, and I don't know what my next move is. The picture I drew could be way off, but it could also be way accurate. "Alright," I say, pushing back and bending down to retrieve my sketchbook. "Here." I flip to the right page and hand it to Beau.

He takes it carefully in his hands and glances over it, tipping his chin up to look at me. "I'll scan it and send you a copy, too."

"Thanks," I say, wondering if I should tell him about Monica now that he's helping me. His gaze is unwavering as he licks his bottom lip. I try not to stare, but it's impossible. "What?"

"You look tired. Again."

My mouth drops open, and I playfully kick him under the desk, thankful for a distraction from his lips. "Beau, didn't your mama teach you how to talk to girls?"

"Ouch," he says with a grunt while rubbing his shin and smiling. "Of course she did, that's why I'm sayin' somethin'."

I cross my arms and shake my head, holding back a laugh.

His smile drops slowly, and the mood begins to shift. "For real though, you gettin' by?" He waves his hand in circles. "All this with Jacob, it's a lot. I want to make sure you're doin' good, too."

I'm not surprised he noticed how tired I look after another long night. Even two coffees deep and concealer couldn't erase the dark circles. Among the nightmares, the sketching, and memories, I'm hanging by a thread. "I didn't sleep well, but I'll get by. I always do."

He lowers his eyelids and purses his full lips before saying, "I got your back, Kit. You'd let me know if I could help more, right?"

I rush to reply. "For sure."

He studies me for signs I'm not being all the way truthful, but I school my features and add a smile for good measure. The more he helps me, the more I'm tied to the imaginary string weaving us together, and that scares me. Searching for Jacob feels awfully intimate since it's the most tender area of my heart, and now I've welcomed Beau to join the party.

I'll have to tell him about Monica another time. That's another story with layers that I will need to explain, and I'd rather have more information before opening that door.

"So, when are you going to make good on that second dinner you owe me?" I ask with a teasing smile.

"And dessert," he adds, pointing a finger at me. "How about tonight?"

"Oh. Tonight?" My mind races to remember my schedule, and a rush of excitement pulses through my body when I realize I'm free. Completely free. "That works."

"Cool. We can keep talkin' about more ideas to find Jacob."

"Sounds great," I say, still unsure how I feel about him helping me out. I'm not used to cluing other people into my plans. Hiding them is more my speed.

"I'll pick you up at seven in our street clothes?" he asks, standing to leave.

I bite my cheek, the only effective way to keep me from smiling. I think our ideas of street clothes are a little different.

His lips part and I recognize that look. He's surprised by the words that just fell from his mouth.

But I'm amused. "To clarify, street clothes as in…jeans and a t-shirt, not the *other* kind of street clothes."

He pulls at his shirt. "Yeah, t-shirt, jeans… "

"Maybe some shoes?" I add.

Nodding his head, he says, "See you at seven," and then winks before walking out.

A flutter dances in my chest. "Definitely shoes."

I'm still smiling like a fool when I check the time. I mentally count the hours until seven this evening, and it already feels too far away, but at least I have work to get lost in. I pick up Jacob's small school photo from my desk and study it once more, even though my eyes are familiar with every color, angle, curve, and story that belongs to it.

It tells the story of the boy I remember most; the one I fiercely miss.

Instead of putting away the photo, I grab a piece of tape and secure it to the corner of my computer monitor. It may not help us find Jacob, but I like looking at it. He was so naive at that age. Some days, I wish I could have stayed that way, too. Innocent. Unaware. Hopeful beyond understanding. Seeing Jacob's photo makes me feel this way, too. Hopeful, not necessarily innocent.

I exhale, dropping my shoulders and reaching for the phone on my desk. Monica never called me back, and as I punch in her digits again, I wonder how many more tries it will take before I can admit it's a dead end. Today isn't that day, and now isn't that time.

I cradle the phone between my cheek and shoulder and pull up my email as the phone continues to ring, and ring, and ring. Opening a new email from Candace, I start to type out a reply when Monica's voicemail picks up.

"Hello, this is Monica."

I pause, waiting for the rest of the recording to tell me to leave a message. It doesn't.

"Hello?" she repeats.

I grip the phone and sit up straight. "Monica?"

"Yes?"

Clearing my throat, I ignore the rush of adrenaline that surges through my entire body. It's really her. "H-Hi. I, um, I-I called. Did you get my call?"

"I'm sorry. Who is this?"

I run a hand over my forehead and realize I never said my name. "It's me, Kit."

"Kit!" Monica says without pause. "I thought it might be you. Wow, yes, I got your message this afternoon. I was on vacation, so I've been swamped." Her jovial tone is tangible. "Tell me, how are you?"

I lean back, straightening the coiled phone cord that keeps me tethered to her familiar voice on the other end of the line. "I'm doing good. Gosh, it's been forever. I wasn't sure if this was still your number."

"Oh yes, I'll always have this number." There's a smile in her voice. "Are you still in Cali?"

"Yeah, I'm living and working in L.A."

"Where do you work, sweetie?"

"The Journey Center, with the foster care youth program." I'm so glad we're talking today instead of a couple years ago, because now I can tell her I have a good job, friends, and clean money instead of the dirty kind that I had to sell my soul for.

"You don't say. I know the place, pretty amazing spot."

"It really is," I say. "I, uh…" I shake my head, wondering if I should tell her how I got here. "I was part of one of the programs a few years back, and now I'm working here."

Her silence is short but noticeable. "So you truly know how awesome that place is, then. That's great, Kit, I'm so glad you called. I've thought of you over the years. And your brother, too."

Monica entered my story when Jacob and I hadn't been in contact for two years. I ran away from the latest foster family, because no one else cared about finding Jacob like I did.

"That's actually why I called," I say. "It's about Jacob."

"Oh, yeah? What is it?"

I drop my chin to my chest. "I still can't find him," I admit in a quiet voice. "He turns eighteen in a month and you know what this birthday means."

It's not like I haven't called every agency in and around L.A. county, I'd even visited a few, but Jacob's name never came up. Did he get adopted? What if they gave him our mother's last name, not our father's? He'd be a whole new person if that were the case.

Monica exhales long and slow. "I do. Oh, honey, I sure do. Have you really not talked to him since we tried to locate him?"

My response is even quieter than before. "No, I haven't." This shouldn't have happened. There should have been people or structures in place to make sure of it, but there wasn't. Papers get lost, details get missed, and pretty soon, siblings get split.

"I can't imagine what you've been feeling all these years, Kit. It couldn't have been easy. I'm so sorry this all happened," Monica says.

I hold back my tears, not wanting to lose myself in her empathy. "Thanks, it's been really hard, which is why I have to find him. Now."

"Of course. I'm here. What can I do to help?"

When she asks this question, my mind goes blank and my mouth runs dry. How can she help? She was never his social worker. She'd never even met him. Add all of that to the fact she already tried to find him once and came up short. What if there's nothing she can do?

My words come out jumbled. "I...I have no idea, actually. I'm not really sure why I called, other than the fact that I found your business card the other day and thought...well, I don't know what I thought."

It's all hitting me. The hopelessness, the inability to locate Jacob, and the impossibilities I'm asking of others. I rub the back of my neck and stare down at my desk.

Without hesitation, Monica fills in the gaps I feel are too wide. "Why don't I check the database again and see if his name comes up. He was non-viewable last time, for reasons we can't see on our end, but maybe something has changed. I can also reach out to other social workers, and maybe they'll know something. We'll figure this out together this time. And Kit?"

I swallow the lump in my throat. "Yeah?"

"I'm here for you. I can't promise we'll find him, but we're going to do our best to try." Her confidence screams louder than any of my doubts.

"Okay," is all I can manage to say while still staring at the lump sum of this problem.

"I'll get to work on my end and call you by the end of this week. Alright, sweetheart?"

Monica's words of endearment hold me together. "Alright. Thank you, Monica. I've missed you."

"I've missed you, too. You have no idea how good it is to hear your voice."

Closing my eyes, I cover my mouth to keep the sobs in until I can end the call.

We say our goodbyes, and I set the phone on the cradle before both of my hands hide my face. My eyelids are so heavy with tears that they spill over and drench my face and hands, leading a trail down my neck.

I don't know how someone like Monica can believe the impossible and yet, in light of her certainty, I believe it, too. Again.

CHAPTER SEVENTEEN
2004—Age 13

Three days of playing cards to pass the time.

Three days after our mother died.

Three days since we left our home.

And three minutes to break my heart.

A worker walked over and shook my shoulder as I lay asleep on one of the cots. Sitting up, I rubbed my eyes and peered at her through the dimness. "What's going on?"

Her tone was quiet, probably not to bother the other kids. "We found a placement for Jacob."

I nodded slowly, yawning and rubbing a hand over my face. "So, are they going to pick us up?"

The woman frowned. "No, we'll have a driver take him."

Swinging my legs over the side, I planted my socked feet on the floor. "Do you want me to wake him up so we can go?"

She cleared her throat and bent lower. "Hon, the placement is only for Jacob. We still have to find a home for you."

Panic pounded in my chest, beating faster with every breath. "What? No. Jacob needs me. I can't let him go without me."

"You have to. This foster family can only take one child."

"But…he's my brother. I told him I wouldn't leave him." Tears jammed my throat as defeat crept up my spine. I wanted to argue, to talk some sense into her, but her expression said this decision had already been made. I clenched my fists, realizing my fears were coming true. Jacob was leaving here today, but I wasn't.

"I'm sorry. It isn't ideal, but it will be better for Jacob to be in a home," she said. "We should do this quickly so it doesn't make it harder."

I looked back at Jacob, asleep on his cot and unaware of what was about to happen. What was I supposed to tell him? How could I protect him from this? I couldn't, and I hated that. These people were supposed to help us stay together, but instead, they're tearing us apart.

The woman stared down her nose, placing a hand on my shoulder. "You have to be strong. For him. We'll get you his number and you can talk on the phone."

Tears trailed down my face. We had no choice, but I didn't think she did, either. We were at the mercy of the system, and it was brutal, unforgiving, and unpredictable.

This was so wrong but right didn't exist.

The woman dropped her hand and backed away, giving me space to talk to Jacob. I twisted on my stiff cot and stared at him for a moment, absorbing his rumpled curls and soft features. No kid should have to go through this: abandoned by their parents and taken from their family. He was only a kid but me? I had already become a parent.

Reaching over, I tousled his curls like I had done thousands of times, but that time felt different. That was the last time. Jacob blinked, and an innocence was in his eyes when they slowly opened. It broke me. Tears streamed down my face, and I cupped my hand over my mouth as a gasp escaped.

"Kit?" he whispered, propping himself up.

I shook my head, the need to comfort him was in my bones, but I couldn't. Not that time.

He inched closer, wrapping a hand around my wrist as he pleaded for answers. "Kit, what's wrong? What's happening?"

"Jacob," I started to say through my pained cries. "I-I'm sorry. I–I'm so, so sorry." I choked on a sob building in my throat.

He tried to pull my hand away from my mouth. "What's going on? Tell me. Kit, tell me!"

I reached across the gap between our beds and wrapped my arms around him, burying my face in his shoulder as I repeated my apology over and over, hoping it would cover what's about to happen. It won't change it, but maybe it could coat the inevitable. How was I going to leave him, like our mom and dad did? I'm not like them, but I sure as hell didn't look any different by leaving Jacob. I was shaking and struggled to breathe. All of my air was being used to cry.

A light hand settled on my back. "It's time," the woman said. "Say goodbye to your brother, okay?"

"Kit!"

I pulled back from our embrace and dropped my heavy arms. "I'm sorry, Jacob."

All of my senses were dull. Tears fell into my mouth, but I couldn't taste their saltiness. The lingering smell of diapers in the room was gone and the only thing I could hear were Jacob's growing sobs. My own had been drowned out by his.

"You have to be strong. Your brother needs you to be strong," the woman repeated over his wails.

But, I wasn't strong. I really was just a kid.

I had experienced the pain of loss before with my parents but with Jacob it was different. That kind of pain felt like my heart was being torn in half. You can't survive without a heart, and I didn't have one afterward, at least not one that worked like it should.

The woman tried to speak over the noise. "Jacob, Mr. Gray is going to take you to your new home."

Jacob's voice took on an identifiable terror. "What about Kit? I don't want to go without Kit," he shrieked.

The woman sat on the cot beside me and reached a steady hand to Jacob as I fell apart. "Kit will be going to a different home."

"Where?" Jacob yelled, waking up a few of the other kids and creating an audience.

"Sh-sh-shhh. We'll get you her number when she's placed."

I watched the hurt cover Jacob's face. He needed me. I had to be strong like the woman told me. He needed to have hope that we'd be together again. "I'll see you soon, okay?" My words caught in my throat. "I–I love you."

"Kit, I'm scared to go by myself," he whispered through his tears. "Don't leave me."

His plea broke something in me that couldn't be fixed.

The woman stood, reaching out to help Jacob do the same. He didn't fight her, and I was glad. It wouldn't work. The powers we were up against were too strong. I was too weak.

I wiped the hot tears from my cheeks and stared at the floor, swallowing all emotion. "I'm so sorry, Jacob. They don't have a bed for me. But, there's a place for you, so you have to go. Don't worry, we'll be together soon. I promise."

Jacob nodded, his tears doing most of the talking as the woman walked him into the hallway and the waiting Mr. Gray. Every step he took away from me made the cracks inside of me open wider. By the time he stood on the other side of the glass window, the cracks were permanent fractures.

I forced myself to watch, despite wanting to hide beneath the covers. He nodded at something the woman was saying to him, tears still wet on his cheeks. He was trying to be strong, too. It was a strength I didn't know existed and never thought I'd have to tap into. My mother could die, I could forget a father who forgot me, but I'd never forgive myself for losing Jacob.

He isn't lost, only misplaced.

You'll be together again, soon.

Even the voice in my head sounded robotic and fake, causing me to doubt every word that wasn't helping anyway.

He peered in my direction, giving me a small, hesitant wave, and within seconds, disappeared down the hall and out of sight.

I didn't know then that those seconds would turn into years.

CHAPTER EIGHTEEN
July 2014—Age 23

"Hey, Big Guy," I say, walking outside to meet Beau. I'm not taking the chance of having him come inside again. He raises too many questions for Olive and Dina that I don't have answers to.

His eyes roam the length of me before landing on my feet. "Nice shoes, Squirt."

I peer down at my scuffed black sneakers, the opposite of sky-high heels. "Thanks. I like yours, too," I say, pointing at his feet.

"I'm just glad I remembered them." He balances on the heels of his black leather sneakers. "Are these *street* enough for ya?"

That pulls a laugh out of me. "They'll work."

He follows me to Olive's car, but I don't miss the grimace he makes before bending to sit in the passenger seat. I smile but hold in my laughter. "It's my turn to drive. Remember?"

Adjusting the seat so it sits all the way back, he glares at me.

I buckle up. "I swear I'll be on my best behavior. No speeding, no road rage, nothing. It's not like Olive's car can break sixty miles per hour anyway."

He buckles himself then tests the strap. "I'll believe it when I see it."

Resting a hand on the back of his headrest, I look through the rear window as I reverse. "Oh, you'll see it."

He grips his thighs and stares out the window, but I see his smile and feel mine.

WE TAKE THE freeway south to Seal Beach, a beach town with a few fantastic food trucks. It's a drive, but we hardly notice between the playful jabs and consistent conversation. As we near the water, the smells of grilled food and sticky sauces best cleaned off with your mouth instead of a napkin are irresistible and make my stomach growl in hungry protest. There are so many food options: teriyaki, tacos, pupusas, gyros, burgers. I am good and hungry, so every option sounds better than the last.

"How am I supposed to decide?" I ask, waving a hand up and down the lineup.

"Who says we gotta choose just one?" He grins and grabs my hand. "Come on."

We order a little bit of everything, because I can't narrow it down, then lay out our smorgasbord on an open picnic table.

"I am so dang hungry," I express with zero chill.

Beau's half-grin is lost behind a burger as he takes a large bite. "So good," he murmurs through a full mouth.

The sun is well on its way to setting, and though it's warm outside, the temp isn't stifling. We eat in comfortable silence as I peer around at the bustling groups of people enjoying the last leg of the daytime heat.

I take another bite of teriyaki chicken, watching a group of boys riding their bikes and skateboards past an elderly couple. They're trying to avoid the couple, but it's hard to be chivalrous when you're also trying to impress girls. I snicker. "Boys."

Beau follows my gaze. "They're just tryin' to get a girl's attention."

"There are safer ways to do it."

He levels me with a serious expression. "What, like rescuing a lady from her pimp and goin' on a wild car chase? Mhm."

I smile as my heart beats out of rhythm. Me. He's talking about me, or getting my attention. I ignore his rhetorical question and spend the time decoding what it could mean.

It's just attraction.

At least, it is for me, but what about him?

He shakes his head and takes another bite of his burger. Swallowing, he asks, "How is it?"

I pick up my own and take a slow, mouth-watering first-bite. "Delicious, as I thought it would be." I pause before eating another bite and consider Beau's family again, thoughts I can't stop having. "I've been thinking about you," I start to say when he looks up quickly and tilts his head. "I mean, I've been thinking about your family. Your Dad, actually."

Both are true, but ever since he shared about his dad, I've been hungry for more.

His shoulders relax. "Yeah?"

"Yeah. So if he's still in the game, do you know what he does? Drugs, robberies—*cough*—prostitution?"

Beau grabs a napkin, and I monitor every movement like it will tell me more than the last one. "I don't know. I haven't talked to him in years." His attention lands somewhere behind me, but I keep my eyes trained on him. "I don't think he ever got into prostitution though. If what my Mama says is true, he wasn't that kind of guy. But, then again, what kind of guy leaves his family to be a gangster?" Beau shakes his head in disbelief.

"If your Mama says he isn't that kind of guy to exploit women, then he probably isn't."

Beau's dark eyes turn flinty as he stares into mine. "He better not be."

A chill runs down my spine, and I shiver. His expression could kill, and it might if given the chance. If I've learned anything about Beau over the years, it's that he's wildly protective.

I'd been in that world, the one where sex, drugs, and rock-n-roll are a reality and not just song lyrics. Beau's father still lives in it, making me wonder how a man like Beau comes out of it all being the kind of man he is. He said there were always other men in his life, and he's obviously close to his mom, so I guess they made up the difference. All I know is that his dad is missing out. Beau is every bit of the man his father isn't.

I extend my leg under the table and playfully nudge the inside of his calf. "Thanks for dinner tonight."

He locks my foot between his legs briefly. "Which one? We ate five." He laughs, and I can't help but join him.

"You're right, but I think the burger took home the gold."

"You and your hamburgers." Beau shakes his head and asks, "Did you leave any room for dessert?"

I place a hand over my satisfied stomach. "I'm going to have a rain check on dessert. I'm stuffed."

"Alright, how about a walk on the pier?"

Looking at his hopeful expression, I'm caught in the realization that I don't want this night to end, either. Not yet.

"Yeah, I haven't been out there before."

This surprises him. "You haven't?"

"No, I've only been to the Santa Monica pier."

Beau claps his hands. "Let's go then."

He adds a wink for good measure, and I roll my eyes, acting as if it doesn't send warmth rippling through me.

We trash our to-go containers and walk to the promenade, where the pathway and rugged wood meet. The expanse of water in front of us stretches into forever as we shuffle side-by-side in comfortable silence, the energy of the pier doing all of the talking for us. Everywhere I look, people are walking, talking, fishing, and laughing. Beau leads us farther down, away from the bustling groups of locals and tourists, where the pier stands hovering over the ocean. The wind is stronger when we reach the end, so I tuck wayward strands of hair behind my ears then lean my forearms on the railing.

Beau stands beside me, resting his arms on the edge, too. Then, he breaks the cocoon of silence we find ourselves in. "Thanks for hearing me out tonight…about my Dad."

I raise a shoulder. "I can't say I wasn't curious. You've never really talked about him before, but you're always so, I don't know, put together? Easy-going?" I try to find the best description but each of them falls short. He is so much *more*.

He turns and leans against the railing on one elbow, body and attention facing me. "Maybe that's what everyone sees on the outside, but on the inside…" his voice drops as he looks out at the ocean, "I'm just a man doing his damndest to prove himself."

He's somber but not dejected as he shares this, his eyes trained somewhere far off and his expression fixed. I want to know his story, his pain, his past, everything. I rarely see this edge to him, but I suppose we all have parts of ourselves that, if bumped, reveal what we rarely show people. And right now, I'm finding out exactly what growing up without a father has done to Beau, and it breaks me.

It happens in the flash of seconds that lines are crossed.

I'm looking at him, he's staring at me, nothing else exists. I take a swift step toward him and cradle his cheek with one hand, running my thumb along the jagged creases that have developed through time and solidified by trauma. His face is softer than I imagined it would be, and as my fingers glide across the surface, I wonder what the rest of him feels like.

A rush of warmth stirs within me, filling my belly where my wants and desires live. I lick my bottom lip as my breathing becomes rapid like I've been running, but I'm completely still, curious about what comes next.

It's just attraction.

That's it.

Nothing more.

Beau's mouth is parted in shock over my boldness like mine is. I shake my head and go to drop my hand, but he doesn't miss a beat and captures mine in his. He blinks slowly and waits. I wish I didn't see that look, the one that encourages me to keep going, but I do and immediately translate it in light of my own feelings. It was only a matter of time before we ended up here, right? Before I'm holding Beau's cheek in my palm and a tingling sensation climbs the length of my body. I can't remember why this isn't a good idea. Why have I been pushing him away? Why are we only friends? There's a reason, and I'm sure it's a great one, but I've forgotten it as I stare into his impassioned eyes and hold contact.

I step closer to him, his gaze hooded with a look of expectancy and awe written in his sharp features. The same curves, lines, and creases I've memorized and have become more familiar to me than my own. Because, *it's just attraction.* My body is moving in slow motion, but every step I take is reeling me in like a hooked fish. I can't get away, and I'm not trying all that hard, either.

I need to try harder.

I reach my free hand up to caress his other cheek, intent on smoothing away the hard lines that tell the story of his pain. It's the same brand that has seeped into my own DNA only to tell its nasty lies that I'm not worth the time, effort, and patience to love.

I'm not worth more than friends or more than attraction. I'd mess it up. I have messed it up. Shit, I'm messing it up.

I retract my hand, but he still holds the other, waiting. His patience is off the charts.

I'm beginning to doubt the truth of those lies when I'm staring at the truth reflected in Beau's desire. How could I believe them when he's staring at me like that?

A boldness bubbles up from the depths of me and I can't stop it, so I don't. I succumb to the forcefield drawing us together, the *just attraction,* and I pull Beau's face closer to mine, rising onto my tiptoes and inching closer to his mouth. Hesitantly at first, I taste the breath passing from his lips before I stop it with mine. I test out the temperature of the water and find it feels just fine. More than fine. Why would I fight this?

He cradles my face like I cradle his, claiming the empty space between us and hating any distance that dares to keep us apart now that we're together. If this is our only moment, I'm going to take it. The truth rings loudly, screaming at me, and rebounding off my previous experiences that tried to tell me something different. But, that's the thing about truth, it rises to the surface like ice floating on water.

Beau drops a hand to grip my waist, tugging my hips closer to his and inciting an unquenchable heat within me that shoots lower in my body. It fills every one of my pores until I am fully consumed. Until the lies are hushed, the questions don't exist, and all that's left is us and this moment. Nothing else.

I slide my hands down his neck, over the width of his shoulders, and back up again to feel the smooth skin at his nape. Matching the quick tempo of his lips, I explore the curves and dips I've been less familiar with. I release a soft sigh of pleasure. He grasps me tighter, closer, angling my body until I'm pressed up against the railing and leaning further into me as his hands take the journey from my waist up my back. They claim me, clinging to me like I might slip through his arms and disappear.

His finger sweeps across my cheek, tickling the delicate skin it touches before his hand settles beneath my jaw, spanning the distance into my hair and making me momentarily lose myself. I'm lost. Gone with the wind still rustling around us. I tilt my head back, overcome by everything Beau is, but he chases my mouth with his, holding me up when I want to melt. I offered him comfort, wanting nothing more than to be the strong footing he needed. Instead, he's become that for me.

Our mouths dance in unison, bending, twisting, tasting one another as if we've been deprived for years, which we have been but didn't know it. *This* was waiting for me on the other side of yes. My body is jolted by my bold maneuvering and shocked by the pure delight of being in Beau's arms and savoring the flavors of his mouth. They aren't subtle. They're bold and bright and consuming. It's as if my body has been woken up after years of being asleep. Every one of my hairs stands on end when Beau's tongue plunges into my mouth, pursuing mine. My lungs are on fire, inhaling and exhaling to match the pace of my heartbeat.

Attraction tastes delicious.

He rests his hand where my collarbone meets my neck as he breaks contact with my mouth, leaving a path of kisses and hot breath along my cheek with such gentleness, a well of tears begins to fill my eyes. Why are they here? What is happening? It's the severing of our lips that does it for me. Emotions begin to pile up faster than I can process them, and before Beau drags his mouth to the tender spot near my ear, my hands are on his chest and pushing him backward with a force that surprises both of us.

His breathing is heavy, mouth agape. "You okay? What's wrong?"

I look up, trying not to notice how full and wet his lips are. "No, I–I...sorry. I don't know why I did that." Closing my eyes tightly, I shake my head, considering all of the ramifications of what I'd done. I can't tell if I'm more shocked that I pulled him in for a passionate kiss or that I pushed him away from one.

He closes his mouth, letting his breathing even out as he inhales and exhales through his nose. When he speaks, a breathy laugh escapes with it. "Don't be sorry, please. I was clearly cool with it."

I let my gaze fall to my feet and can't help but feel the regret creeping into my gut as I remember every reason why I shouldn't have kissed him. I'm ruining our friendship, and while attraction is there and stronger than ever, I'm met with the real reason I pushed Beau away.

My future hopes and dreams don't exist outside of finding Jacob. He's the only future I've ever seen and entertaining whatever *this* is with Beau is fleeting and won't change the fact that Jacob isn't here. He's missing, like I am. "I'm sorry for pushing you away. I'm sorry for…for…" my voice falters and I wave a vague hand, "*that*. I wasn't thinking."

Our heavy breaths become louder than the crashing waves, and his shoulders rise and fall as he studies me. Closing my lids for the briefest of moments, I envision a reality where this didn't happen. I could have been dreaming; I've been known to do that. But the cold slap of wind on my warm cheeks tell me that isn't possible. The brand of his hands all over my skin won't lie.

I drop my chin to my chest and open my eyes. He's silent, but I can see his leather shoes standing across from me as he shifts from one to the other. But I can't look up and see the waiting expression on his face. Whatever it is, I already know I'm too weak. I reached for what I couldn't have, and I don't trust myself not to do it again.

A gull pipes up, though I can't see it in the darkening sky, and it chastises me for acting on my attraction for Beau. This is why it can't be trusted, because eventually, attraction acts out and the next thing you know you're making out with your friend.

Unable to meet his eyes and completely aware of where this decision has landed us, I rub my chilled arms. Around us, the waves crash one on top of the other, the wind howls in my ear and creates an unrelenting soundtrack that should fill the silence but doesn't. Instead, it grows and thickens until it's so stifling I can't breathe. Beau doesn't say anything, but what words can fix this? I need to get out of here; I can't handle hollow sentences or explanations about what took place. I don't have anything else to offer outside of my embarrassment.

I side-step Beau, giving his body a wide berth. "I have to go," I whisper, which is all my vocal cords can manage.

I continue walking, fully aware that I'm his ride, but I need to give my mind and body the space it craves so I can sort through the choke-hold of my emotions. I don't know what just happened, other than the fact I kissed him and he kissed me back. I'm not sure how we'll recover our friendship after this.

What I do know is that everything changes.

CHAPTER NINETEEN
2011—Age 20

"Make sure you shower first, Mercedes." Bobby pulled off his necktie and undid the top few buttons of his dress shirt. "I don't want to see dirt under your fingernails like last time."

I nodded, struggling not to sound snarky as I walked into the small hotel bathroom and locked the door behind me. I cranked the shower to the hottest heat setting and waited for the steam to overwhelm the room. Stripping down, I stepped into the shower, allowing the biting intensity of the water to scorch my back. I scrubbed my hair, my arms, my legs, every inch of myself so that Bobby wouldn't find a speck of dirt on me. I knew he'd be looking.

We were in the hotel room that he used to conduct business. It wasn't anything fancy, but it was better than the rundown apartment on the outskirts of the city that I shared with a couple of other women. Bobby picked it out for us and said it would be fine—livable, even—yet it was anything but. There's no way we'd be able to afford the rent otherwise. He didn't care about the peeling laminate in the bathroom that exposed mold, the oven that didn't work, and the water that was never hot enough. He didn't like to be bothered with trivial things like that, and his goons sure didn't care either. Bobby wanted hard workers. The kind that overlooked some things in order to climb the ladder to his bed. He was looking for someone like me.

We all took turns with Bobby. Warming his bed while his wife and family were tucked away in the hills—Beverly Hills, that is. I'd get a hot meal delivered via room service when it was all said and done, and then I would be on my way to work my assigned blade for the rest of the night. There was an order to things, like clockwork, that we never veered from. We didn't get paid more or less than any of the other women hustling the streets, but Bobby's girls came with a notoriety that I never understood.

But really, it only came with loneliness. Not the standard kind, but the flavor that changed depending on Bobby's moods.

Bobby liked luxurious things, which meant he needed money to maintain his lifestyle and prostitution was only one avenue he made his cash. Drugs were another way, but his day job in banking sealed the deal, indicating he was a normal man with an unsuspecting way of paying for his fancy toys and flashy women.

I turned off the water and grabbed a towel, dabbing gently at my now-seared skin. There is no amount of washing that could clean off the stories my body could tell. I never let it. I shoved it aside like it didn't grate on me in order to make it through another night. I didn't use drugs or alcohol to numb the truth I was living. My motivation to find Jacob was all I needed.

Wrapping the towel around myself, I quickly brushed out my long hair. Bobby was waiting, and I knew he was counting every minute that passed and every minute I was wasting.

He glanced up briefly as I walked out. "Done? Come here," he said, slapping a hand to his lap.

I walked toward him, my towel clinging around me as I clung to it. I knew how to play the part; I'd done it enough times, but it didn't mean I enjoyed it. There were times I thought I did.

Being in Bobby's good graces had felt something akin to nice at times and it was preferable to the alternative.

He pulled me onto his lap, sitting me sideways so that my bare legs dangled over his thighs. His eyes became hooded and his smile devilish as the cigarette hung from his lips.

I leaned in and started kissing my way up his neck.

A groan escaped him. "You didn't think it would be that easy, now did you?" His pleasure quickly changed into something else. I reared back as he tensed and straightened, his jaw clenching down. He tamped out his cigarette and before I could ask, or even blink, Bobby threw me off of his lap. I landed on the floor in front of him, clambering for my abandoned towel and clutching it in front of my naked body.

Short, pained breaths came from my mouth. "What's wrong?"

He stood to his full height, jaw still clenched and the veins in his neck standing to attention. "Where is it?" Bobby yelled through gritted teeth.

The red hue climbing his neck made my mouth run dry. "Where's what? What are you talking about?"

He reached down and grabbed both of my arms, yanking me up to stand in front of him. My towel was gone, left somewhere on the ground with my composure as his fingernails dug into the soft flesh of my arms.

"You've got one chance to tell me the truth."

I shut my mouth, breathing so heavily through my nose that my nostrils shook with each exhalation. Someone was lying to Bobby, but it wasn't me. "I-I don't know–"

Spit flying in my face he yelled, "Tell me!"

His voice ricocheted off the floral wallpaper and pointed an accusatory finger at me. I could barely speak through my trembling lips. Voice quiet, I replied through my confusion. "I don't know what you're talking about."

He shoved me hard, the bed catching my fall. "Don't fucking mess with me, Mercedes. I know you've been taking an extra cut of the money you get. Did you think you could play me like that?"

Fear slithered its way through my body, causing me to lay limp on the bed. Closing my eyes, I pretended to be anywhere else: in the foster homes that only wanted me so they'd get money, the limbo of being between homes, even under the same roof as my parents. Anywhere but there.

He leaned over me, fists planted on the mattress to either side of my head. "You're fucking lying to me. You know I don't like liars. They have to be punished." Lifting a hand, he caressed the soft skin beneath my chin.

I swallowed and kept my eyes closed. I didn't want to see the hate in Bobby's expression and guess at the punishment he would enact. At that point, I didn't care. He already owned too many parts of me, what was one more piece?

He stretched his hand around the width of my throat and began constricting my airway. Eyes flying open, I stared at the evil grin tipping one side of his mouth and scratched at his hands to pry them from my throat. I kicked and thrashed to no avail. I was at his mercy and only he could decide when enough was enough. Dread pumping in my veins, I tried clawing free, but my efforts weakened with every second that passed without air. If I had a voice, I'd yell that I'd done nothing. But I didn't have one; he had stolen it.

Finally, he released me and a sputtering cough left my mouth and clung to the air I was desperate for.

Bobby had always been forceful. He took what he wanted, and he always knew what he wanted. I lay curled on my side, chest rising and falling, lungs hardly believing they had air again. If that was his plan, I had to tell him. He had to know the truth.

My voice was hoarse, but I had to explain. "I didn't take any money, Bobby. I would never do that. It must be one of your guys. It has to be."

"You don't think I've talked to everyone else, Mercedes? Do you consider me a fool?" he asked, but I wasn't dumb enough to answer. I already knew his questions were rhetorical.

I raised a surrendered hand while lying defenseless beneath his scrutinizing gaze. "I swear on my life I didn't do it. I didn't take anything."

In a split second, Bobby's expression morphed from villain to victor. The performance was over, cooling off like the water in my shower. He leaned over me again and I shrank back, expecting another death grip but his fingertips gently traced my cheek, jaw, and lips. He ran them gingerly down my neck and my shallow breaths prepared me for more. I didn't fight it, because I'd be no match for Bobby's strength. Even in his mid-forties, he was spry.

Seeing the shift in his demeanor, I did exactly what I'd been taught to save myself. I sprawled my hands above my head, lifting my bare breasts in invitation. Sinking further into the comforter, I circled my legs around Bobby's waist to pull him closer. He watched me like I was watching him.

Eyes full of lust, he moved his hand up my thigh and lowered himself down until every accusation he made was soon being thrust into me. My only thought as he took what he wanted was that I wished I had a knife to drive into his side. I wanted him to feel the pain I felt. I had never been that person, and I hated myself even more for thinking that, but that didn't mean the thoughts weren't there.

Later, while I ate the chicken and potatoes that room service brought up, I considered my options. I could bring my knife next time. I could try to get back into Bobby's good graces; I knew what broken trust was like in this line of work and it would be hard to recover from, if not impossible. Or, I could leave. It was always the question of how, since he had eyes on me at all times. But I needed to do something. I wouldn't be like my mother, who drank in order to forget. Or my father, who worked in order to avoid his family. I would be the sister who fought to live another day knowing her brother was out there somewhere.

I stood and ambled to the window. Not knowing where the words came from, I spoke them out loud as if there were someone else in the room with me.

"God, I don't know what to do next, but I could use some help. Please, help me."

That was the night I met Beau.

CHAPTER TWENTY
July 2014—Age 23

His hand lingers on my waist, squeezing gently and pulling me closer.
The look on his face as his lips drop to mine.
His hands cradling my face, angling my mouth toward his.
My arms drawing his body closer, a guttural sound of pleasure escaping our locked lips.

I groan and toss my head back to look up at the kitchen ceiling. The coffee is brewing, my bread is toasting, and my mind is reeling. I can't stop replaying every detail of my kiss with Beau. It's seared into every fiber of my being, threatening to stay there forever.

I peer at the red numbers on the coffeemaker, which taunt me. I will see Beau in an hour and that doesn't feel like enough time to freak out. I'll have to shove all this deep into the recesses of my memory bank if I'm going to face him again. Will I be able to look at him without jumping into his arms? The way my temperature rises as I think about it, I'd say no. Every part of me felt so alive when he held me, until it didn't.

I slap my hand to my forehead and cringe. I can't believe that happened. What was I thinking? I pulled him in for a kiss as quickly as I pushed him away. I can't go around kissing Beau. He's my friend. *But that wasn't a friendly kiss,* my brain reminds me. *It's just attraction.*

My toast pops up, causing me to jump. I pull it out and immediately regret it when it burns my hand. "Dang it." Waving my seared hand, I use the other to smear the bread with avocado. I'm too distracted. I kissed him like I had forgotten we were friends, like we didn't have history together. And he kissed me like it's been the only thing on his mind for years. Has it been?

Last night, we drove home without a word, offering a weak and awkward goodbye as we slid out of Olive's car. He wanted to talk, but I told him I needed space. What I really needed was a cold shower and to think. I knew what happened last night—the lips, the touching, the hunger—would change things between us, but I wasn't sure how. Now I know. I want more than anything to do it again and that's a problem. We kissed our friendship goodbye.

Taking a bite of my avocado toast, I pour a full cup of dark roasted coffee into a mug and sit at the small bistro table by the window in our tiny kitchen.

"Morning," Dina says, walking straight to the coffee pot. "How was your date?" She raises her eyebrows on the last word.

I don't wait to finish chewing or swallowing. "It wasn't a date."

She points to her ear with a smile. "What did you say? I can't hear you?"

"It wasn't a date," I say, spewing bits of toast. Detecting the start of a smile, I glower at her.

"Okay, fine. How was your *not* date?"

I consider holding back the details that have been making me sweat all morning, but this is Dina, one of my best friends. I need to tell someone, or this is going to eat me from the inside out.

"It was…hot," I say, widening my eyes and lifting the steaming cup of coffee to my lips.

Dina looks at me curiously, adjusting her glasses. "What do you mean? Like, the weather?"

Bless Dina. She's not on the same page as me, because I've never given anyone a reason to think I'd cross this line with Beau. These dates, or "wager" dinners, were as close as it got.

I speak into my coffee mug, "We kissed."

Dina, in her shock, jostles her cup and spills some coffee on the counter. "What did you say? Kissed? You and Beau?" She snatches a hand towel to wipe up her spill.

I test out how the admission feels coming out of my mouth. "Um, yeah. Beau and I…we…kissed."

Dina's mouth falls open and she pushes her glasses up. "Like mouth-to-mouth kind of kissing?"

"Well, more like the tongue-to-tongue kind." I scrunch my nose as I lay out the details.

"Oh. My. Gosh," she mouths. I know how she feels. This is basically what I've been thinking since I fell into bed last night.

Olive's footsteps echo loudly down the hallway as she heads our way. "Hey," she says with a yawn.

Dina's eyes are still wide. "Olive, did you know?"

"Know what?"

"That Kit and Beau *kissed?*"

Olive shakes her head and fetches a cup from the cabinet. "No way. I don't believe it. Not Kit and Beau. I mean, they for sure have something going on," Olive pauses and looks over at me. "Sorry, no offense, but it's obvious."

I shrug. "None taken."

Olive pours her coffee then pins me with a questioning glare. "But kissing?"

"It's true and not a sweet peck on the lips at the end of the night kind of kiss. We're talking *full on*, according to Kit." Dina offers this information as if this is her story and not mine.

Olive sits across from me. "Is Dina right? Did this really happen?"

I nod, admitting to both of my roommates and myself that I did something I can't take back.

"Oh my gosh," Olive says. "So are you guys like a thing then?"

"What? No," I reply too quickly. "We can't be. We're friends."

Dina leans against the counter and crosses her arms. "Um, I don't think friends make-out with each other."

Amused, Olive leans in on her elbows. "She's right. Even if you wanted to be friends, I don't know how that's going to work now that you've both become *acquainted* with each other's lips."

I set my mug down, cover my face with my hands, and groan loud enough for the neighbors to hear. "What am I going to do, you guys? What am I supposed to say to him today?"

"This conversation could go a couple of different ways," Dina starts to say. "He may ask you to talk and then—"

"Then, you'll say, 'yes I'd love to chat, let me grab my lip balm in case we decide to make out again,'" Olive says, cutting in before Dina can finish.

I drop my hands and shoot them a warning look.

Dina wears a sultry grin. "Or, he might ask to talk so he can tell you how much he likes you, how much he's *always* liked you and wants to be more than friends—way more than friends."

"*Way* more," Olive adds with a whistle.

"And what if he doesn't say that?" I ask. "What if he wants to talk and then tells me that there is no way this could ever happen between us?"

Dina sucks in air through her teeth. "Yeah, that's the other way things could go down."

My voice, like my heart, is small and fragile. "I've really screwed things up. I shouldn't have kissed him."

"You won't be able to guess how he responds, Kit," Olive starts to say, "but you can decide how you will. What do *you* want?"

Eyes on Olive, I draw my legs in and rest my chin on my knees. Her question is so simple, uncomplicated and without repercussions. She doesn't know the full story about Jacob. The part where I'm against a literal time clock to find him. I don't have time for a relationship. It'll distract me, like it already has. I feel guilty over the joy of a first kiss when my brother is out there in conditions I'm not aware of.

But this is Beau, the man my body clearly wants and my heart is drawn to. If only this happened at a different time.

"I don't know…" my voice falters. "I don't know what I want." And it's true, but one thing I'm absolutely positive about is that I can't lose our friendship. I need to hang on to us before the kiss.

I'M SITTING AT my desk an hour later sweating at the prospect of seeing Beau. He isn't here before me, which is weird because he always is. He's always here first. *Why isn't he here first?* I need air. I only just got here, but I already can't take the stifling temperature in this building. It's sucking out all of the oxygen and blocking my ability to take a full breath, and I need breath in my lungs if I'm going to face things.

I rush down the steps and power walk outside, refusing to stop until I round the edge of the building and press my back to the cold brick wall. Why is this rattling me so much? I didn't think it would happen, first off, and second…second, I'm not ready for it to happen. This wasn't supposed to happen. Leaning my head back, I close my eyes and take measured breaths.

You got this, Kit. Relax.

You can talk to Beau and set him straight.

It's just attraction.

"Hey…uh, what are you doing out here?" Beau asks as my eyelids fly open and I jerk my head in his direction.

He's feet away from where I'm trying to not look like a frazzled mess, but I know it's not working. Beau will see my distress and know something's up.

"Oh hey, I'm…" I stand ramrod straight and curl my hair behind my ear, keeping my back flush against the wall for support. He doesn't say anything, but the tension between us is thick with unsaid words.

He's walking toward me, holding a to-go thermos of what I know is black coffee and looking too intent on the air I'm occupying. It's as if he needs to inhale it, too.

I have to get the words out before he gets closer. "Look, Beau–"

He's standing in front of me now, and I can't move. My brain has shut down; my body is in control and it doesn't want to move away anymore. It wants to stay and see what happens next as if I don't already know. I'm waiting for him to say more words; I need him to say something or else I will surely pull him in for another edition of last night's kiss.

The air around us thins with the rise and fall of our chests. The words in my brain have apparently gone on vacation, but I have to fill this space—the space in between our bodies and hearts. "Beau, I–"

My plea is cut short when Beau lifts his arm and spreads his hand on the wall next to my head. I'm frozen. Waiting. Wondering. Watching. I part my lips to breathe and begin panting with need, feeling winded with his face so close to mine.

"You okay?" he asks, breath hot against my skin. Notes of cinnamon fill my senses, and I have to close my eyes. I can't smell him, feel him, and look at him all at the same time. It's too much.

I suddenly don't want to miss a thing, so I open my eyes and nod. But I'm not okay. My heart is going to burst out of my chest and my hands are itching to grab and touch him. I'm the most okay person not being okay.

My mouth runs dry as my gaze fixates on his full bottom lip. Hadn't I started to say something? I can't remember now that my lips tingle in anticipation for how he'll taste today. The spiced concoction swirling around us gives me a clue, but I need to know for sure.

His eyelids are at half-mast, studying parts of me I can't hide when we are this close. It says so much about his own desire for this, *for me*, and there isn't a trace of regret. None. Does he see it in my eyes? Or only the tangible craving I have for him filling me like a slow drip in a cup?

Moving his face slowly toward mine, he gives me every chance to shove him away again, but I don't, because I am okay. So okay that I want everything that comes next.

Beau's lips drop to mine and his kiss is so much softer than the one we shared last night. Our bodies were frantic and eager then, but this is like the brush of a feather on bare skin. So light, gentle, and slow. He pulls his lips from mine and touches them faintly to my top lip, then teases my bottom lip before pressing a kiss to my cheek. I want to grab his face and kiss him back hungrily, but I'm too engrossed in the feel of his mouth on my skin that I can't. It sends longing coursing through me, making my reaction delayed, or simply unimportant.

He pulls back, only slits of his eyes available for my consumption. "It was real," he whispers against my mouth.

I smile, though my head is in a fog. The slow drip of desire becomes a faucet turned on full blast, and once again losing all inhibition, I reach for the neckline of his shirt and grab a fistful of his soft t-shirt and pull him closer. When our lips touch again, I release his shirt, allowing my hands the freedom to trace the ridges of his biceps and tug at his broad shoulders, not to push him away but to draw him closer. I don't want to run or shove him off; all I want is this right here. Savoring a kiss that is longed for but forbidden, sought after, but lacking the right timing. It's everything I want and nothing that I need in my life right now. But here we are, again.

We both plunge into one another, allowing our bodies to mesh and removing any stretch of space. Our kiss continues to build in intensity, that is until I feel the sharp bite of hot liquid against my skin. "Ouch!"

Beau lurches back. "Shoot. I'm sorry. I forgot I had your coffee in my hand."

I pull my shirt away from the tender skin, trying to relieve the burning sensation, a laugh building in my chest. Both the burn and laughter startling me from the intimate moment.

He steps back, eyeing me with concern, studying every twitch my face makes. His tight smile loosens into one that makes my knees weak.

"I'm sorry, wait, did you say…" I try to speak through my amusement, "did you say 'it was real' earlier?" I stand up straighter, locking my knees and flattening both of my palms on the wall behind me.

Beau rubs the back of his neck slowly and takes a sip of the coffee in his hand—*my* coffee. "Gross. Here." He hands it over and a relaxed look steals across his features. "Yeah, after last night, I thought I dreamed the whole thing up."

I grip the thermos tighter at the mention of last night's kiss. I start shaking my head. "I'm sorry Beau, last night was…I'm really sorry. It won't happen again." I say these words at the same time I'm trying to get my heart to believe them. "And, well, after today too." All of the reasons come back to me in one punch. The reasons we shouldn't be entertaining whatever *this* is. Good reasons that I thought were logical and honorable this morning. Now, they all pale in comparison to the rush of sensation rippling through my body.

He stares at me, confused, while I clear my throat. The space between his brows scrunches in confusion, and I feel even worse. What is wrong with me? What am I doing? Why can't I keep my tongue out of his mouth?

"Why?" he asks.

I stare at him with equal amounts of confusion. "What do you mean 'why?'"

His gaze drills into me. "Why are you sorry?"

My eyes drop to my feet. "I'm sorry because well…I kissed you last night and then today…we," I point between the two of us, "are friends and I'm sorry for crossing that line." I am so embarrassed that we're here having this conversation, because I did something forbidden—twice—and want to do it again.

"Kit. I kissed you, too, and I'm not sorry about it."

I look up at him, unable to locate the regret that's been dogging me. All I can spot is a determination that I really wish I hadn't seen. But I'm just as determined. I can't have this kind of attention right now; I need his help finding my brother, not making my heart beat faster.

"Yeah, but…we're friends, Beau, and right now, I really need a friend. That's it." The weight of my admission hits me with every piece of truth it holds. I do need a friend, more than I thought. "I need *us* to be friends. You know how much I'm focused on finding Jacob. I can't get side-tracked right now."

"Side-tracked? Okay, so you want me to forget that we kissed like *that*?"

"Yes," I say, still conscious of how his savory lips felt pressed to mine. "I think it's for the best."

Beau considers the building, then me, then the ground. The soft pink of his lips contrasts with his dark skin, and I want to rub my fingers across where my mouth was, but I don't. I hold back, convincing myself this is for the best.

He exhales. "If that's what you need, I'll respect it."

Our eyes meet again, and I nod as my only reply. His response surprises me, because it's exactly what I asked of him.

"I'll see you inside."

Beau quickly pivots on his feet and walks away, disappearing around the side of the building and leaving me with every feeling, thought, and thirst I've been navigating all morning. Plus, I'm cold now. The sizzle emanating from Beau kept my body temperature stable. If only he'd come back, wrap me in his arms, and ease every one of my doubts, but he doesn't; he can't because I told him not to.

I tear my eyes away from the empty space Beau had occupied and stare straight ahead, tipping my head back so it rests on the building. Closing my eyes, I realize he is absolutely right.

How am I supposed to forget a kiss like *that*?

CHAPTER TWENTY-ONE
July 2014—Age 23

I'm experiencing the midday slump. That time in the day where I've sunk so low into the chair that my back aches something fierce. I haven't blinked in hours and staring at this computer screen hasn't helped any. The walls of my cubicle are closing in on me and the hungry growls in my stomach are getting louder.

Call it avoidance or protecting my heart, but I can't go out there. I refuse to leave the protection of my three-and-a-half walls to chance a run-in with Beau, not when he could be wandering around the break room ready to talk, or kiss again. I'm still rattled by the amount of passion we packed into this morning's kisses. They were even hotter than last night, and when I woke up today, I didn't think that was possible. Dina and Olive are going to die when they find out it happened again. How did I let round two happen, exactly?

I'm shaken from my thoughts by an aggressive ring coming from my desk phone. Fumbling for the phone, I pick it up and pretend like my pulse isn't yelling louder than my voice.

"Hi, this is Kit," I say.

"Kit, hi. It's Monica."

I let out a long exhale. "How's it going?"

"It's going well. And you?" she asks.

I'm a mess, I think but don't say out loud. "I'm good. Did you happen to get my email?"

"I did. Thanks for sending the information about the job fair. You can count me in."

Doing my best to multi-task, I pull up the mega-spreadsheet Candace sent me and type in Monica's name. "Awesome. We'll be glad to have you there." I punch in her name as another confirmation. This event is shaping up to be huge, which makes my hopes dwindle. It's finding one person out of hundreds or thousands that has me doubting if it's possible.

"Sounds great. I'm sorry it's taken me so long to call you back. You know how it goes though, as social workers, we're in the field more than at a desk," Monica says with a small chuckle.

I'm reminded of the last social worker I had who used to say her office was a storage closet and nothing else. Her car was more of an office since she was always on the road visiting foster homes, picking up kids, and dropping them off with new families.

"No problem, I get it. I'm happy for the callback. Please tell me you have some info." I don't mean to sound desperate, but I have a lot riding on Monica's update. And, without being overly dramatic, *a lot* meaning my entire future.

"I've put a call out to a few different social workers I know who may have been assigned to his case at one time or another. Can you confirm Jacob's birthday again?"

"August tenth. Just over two weeks from today," I tell her, working myself up in the process. *Two weeks.* Time is closing in on me, and I feel the pressure start to build in my chest. "This is impossible, isn't it? There are too many files to wade through, too many people to call." My voice sounds rushed and frantic as every word trips over the next.

"Kit," Monica says gently, but I ignore her.

"It's a dead end, right? We don't have enough time. "

"Kit."

"What if he doesn't even want me to find him? Maybe that's why it's so hard."

"Kit!" Monica finally yells.

I grip the phone tighter and look at my lap. "Sorry. This is all–" I let out a heavy sigh, "so much."

"Kit, I have a lead."

I slowly lift my head as a jolt of hope courses through my veins. "What?"

"Yes. I looked in our state database for a Jacob Lopez since we don't know his state ID number. The file has been inactive. Looks like it could be a runaway situation since there is a police report number. But, here's the thing," Monica pauses and my hopes pause, too. "When I started looking further, I found another boy that has the same name. Different birthdays but I don't know Kit, it could be something. I hate to admit it but some of the paperwork isn't always accurate. Errors happen."

"So you think this boy could be Jacob then?"

"I'm saying it's worth meeting him. I could call the family listed on the file and see if they'd be willing to come to the job fair this weekend?"

My mouth hangs open as I try to process all that Monica is telling me. When she first called, I hadn't blinked in hours, and now I can't stop. My aching back is no more, and the need for food has vanished. I've gone completely still.

I wanted to believe something would turn up from Monica's efforts, but I know better than to set my expectations too high. Help comes at a cost and usually gives payouts of disappointment.

"Wait, a family? He has a family?" I press, realizing this *other* Jacob has a backstory. A recent family history that doesn't include me.

Monica's words are slow and hesitant. "He does."

"And he'll be there this weekend?" I look at my hanging calendar. "In four days?"

"I can ask."

My thoughts kick into freak-out mode, simultaneously trying to process all of this information and produce new questions. In four days, I could be staring at Jacob's face. I could hug him and apologize.

Shit. I'll have to apologize. What if he doesn't accept it?

"Kit? You still there?"

I nod like she can see me, and then I realize she can't. "Yeah, yeah. I'm here…trying to absorb everything, I guess."

"I hear you. It's a lot to take in."

All of my emotions are charged up. The tears well behind my eyes, my heart pounds wildly beneath my breastbone, and I can't stop bouncing my leg. All of these feelings live inside of me, and I don't know which to choose. I'm on the edge of my hope with the possibility of seeing my brother.

Monica's melodic voice comes through the receiver. "Do you remember what I told you all those years ago when I first gave you my card?"

I don't tell her that I remember every single word as if she said them today. "I do." I close my eyes and picture the two of us sitting on the bed. "You said you'd be here for me."

"That's still true. I'm here for you today, and I'll be there for you on Saturday. Whatever happens. I'm right here with you, Kit."

The tears that rose up are heavier now, pushing to be let loose. I open my eyes and let the first one fall, knowing the others will be right behind it.

Switching the phone to my other hand and wiping the tears from my cheeks, I whisper, "Thanks, Monica. I can't believe I found your card when I did."

"Oh, I can. God is always working, sweetie, even when we can't see it. He always is."

"That He is, Monica."

We say our goodbyes and make a plan for meeting up on Saturday. It's seconds after putting the phone down that I search for the email that Beau sent me containing the scanned file of my sketch. I need to send it over to Monica for reference, even though I'm not sure how helpful it'll be.

When the email is sent, I sigh and stare at the blank cubicle wall. I envision the picture I'll get to hang there soon. The one that hasn't been taken yet but will show Jacob and I smiling so wide at the camera that our eyes crinkle while our arms are slung around each other. I don't know if the photo will reveal the glossy coating in both of our eyes, but I'll know the tears are there.

I can't believe it, Monica has a lead and I could be seeing my brother in a collection of hours. Or, rather a few days worth of hours, but I'm giddy at the thought and also terrified. Would he forgive me? Does he want to see me as much as I want to see him? A lot can change in ten years. My life is evidence enough that a lot can change in *one* year.

Turning back to my computer monitor, I jostle the mouse and navigate back to the picture file. I double click and the sketch of my brother opens up and fills half of the screen. I wish I didn't have so many doubts, but mistakes do that to a person. Every mistake from Jacob's school photo until this sketch tells me I am going to be disappointed. That I should be let down, because that's what I deserve. I left him. Then, I aged out of the system and took a job that destroyed me. One that I had to rebuild from and took more time away from searching for him.

I pull open my desk drawer and shuffle things around that don't have a permanent home but have somehow found solace amongst the random collection of items. When I find a sharp push pin, I hold it up in front of my face. Fitting between my pointer finger and thumb, it's noticeably small, but when I sink it into the cubicle wall, it's purpose becomes larger than life.

I can't get any of the time back that I lost with Jacob, but that push pin will hold the vision of our future: a photo of *us*.

CHAPTER TWENTY-TWO
July 2014—Age 23

"Did you get the chairs from the office already?"

Beau lifts his brows. "Yeah, they're leanin' on the wall over there."

I follow the path of his finger to the stack of chairs. Wasting no time, I move toward them and start unfolding a couple. It's Saturday, the day of the job fair, and I'd be lying if I said I'm not a freaking mess. It doesn't help that I stayed up way too late sketching, listening to music, and pacing my room. Now, I'm a ball of nerves running on way too much caffeine and barely any rest.

"Uh, Kit, you doin' okay?" Beau asks.

Sliding the chairs over to the table, I glance at him. "I'm fine. I'm good. All good here. I need to go grab a few more–"

Beau rests both of his hands on my shoulders and forces me into one of the hard metal chairs. "I can get the rest of the things from the office. You sit here, and I don't know, drink some water."

I wince. "Right. Good idea, I may have had too much coffee this morning."

"I didn't know that was possible, but now I do." Beau's face lights up with his smile, revealing straight teeth. They're stunning. He's stunning. I need to find something else that's stunning.

Opening my water bottle, I take a sip and then decide to chug half of it, staring at anything other than Beau as he leaves. Did it just get hotter in here? It's the first time we'll be around each other for more than a handful of minutes since our set-things-straight conversation. And it's only adding to the noose of tension I feel around my neck. I didn't know *just attraction* felt like this. All-consuming in thoughts and feelings, but I guess it is.

I scan the room, seeing folding tables and chairs, and people milling about preparing for visitors. We've all been working tirelessly to make this event happen, and now it's here. Kind of like how I've been searching for Jacob all these years, and now the day that I might be staring into his eyes is here. God, I hope I'll be staring into his eyes soon.

Lowering my water, I watch Candace approach the table. She's wearing a giant smile. "Morning, Kit, how's it going?"

"I'm…" I pause, filtering through the range of emotions inside me. "Fine. I'm feeling fine."

"I couldn't have done all of this without you and Beau." Her expression is as warm as the hand she rests on my shoulder.

"Thanks, Candace, " I reply with tears in my eyes. Blinking them away, I drop my head so Candace doesn't notice. Wow, my emotions really are all over the place.

"Hey, Candace," Beau says, approaching the table again. When I see him, I let my shoulders sag and my body sink further into the chair, a mix of relief and anxiety coursing through me.

"Hi, Beau. I was telling Kit how grateful I am for everything you've done to help get this event off the ground."

He crosses his arms and looks between the two of us. "For sure, it all came together nicely."

"I'll swing by and check on everything later, but for now I'm going to make the rounds. See you later." Candace waves and begins meandering around the room to greet others.

Beau pulls out the chair beside mine and sits. "Have you heard from Monica this morning?"

An email yesterday was how I told Beau about Monica. A freaking email. I didn't have the guts to talk to him in person. It's weird being distant with him, like we're miles apart but still in the same room. And that distance has made the solitary morning walk to my desk feel longer, too. This is exactly what I didn't want to happen. I knew kissing him would change our friendship.

"No. I haven't," I confess. "She told me she'd be here at ten." I check my watch: 9:24. There's still plenty of time before she shows up and enough time to work myself into a frazzled mess.

Leaning forward, I straighten the flyers, pens, and swag we have decorating our table. I feel my skin tingling under his intense gaze.

"Are you nervous?" he asks.

I don't look at him. I can't. "Is it that obvious?"

When he doesn't respond, I turn my head and see him nodding.

"Okay, so it's obvious." I exhale and lean back in my chair again. "I don't know what I'll say. If Jacob's angry, and he has every right to be, I don't know what I'll do."

Beau reaches over and wraps his hand around my forearm, giving me a few strong squeezes. "The truth is usually a good place to start."

My whole body tenses. That's all he says, but it's enough to render me silent. I don't know how to reply to that, because deep down, I know he's right. The truth is all I've got, regardless of how ugly it looks.

I open my mouth to say something but Andrea and Jordan approach our table so I clamp it shut.

"Hey, Kit and Beau—wow look at all of this, you can't even tell it used to be a gym," Andrea says.

Jordan peers around. "Apart from the basketball hoops and bleacher seats…"

Andrea nudges Jordan with her elbow.

"Hey, man." Beau stands, grips Jordan's hand, and leans in, both slapping each other on the back.

I can't tear my eyes away from them, well, one of them. For a moment, I consider what it might be like to take back the words I said to Beau, the ones that created this awkwardness between us. I saw the hesitation in his eyes earlier and know that I'm the one who put it there.

Andrea clears her throat, effectively interrupting my focus.

What? I mouth to her with a shrug.

Andrea crosses her arms and gives me a half-smile. "Kit, let's go grab a cup of coffee before you get swamped."

Beau tips his chin up toward me. "How about tea for Kit. She's been hittin' the coffee pretty hard this mornin'."

I scowl at him. "You know I hate tea."

"Maybe today's the day you change your mind." He winks at me, and my heart stops.

It's the first friendly jab he's made today, which hopefully means we're on our way to finding our footing again; that the kiss is in the past and we can move forward, as friends. My heart doesn't like this prospect, but it's the best I can do.

I smile in reply. Moving around the table, I intertwine my arm with Andrea's.

She glances over at me a few times as we walk, but she doesn't say a word.

I sigh. "I know what you're thinking."

She leans in so our heads are close to touching. "Are you going to tell me about the kiss?" This is the problem with sharing every detail with your best friend: they know too much and ask even more.

I pause. "Which one?"

Andrea stops and pulls me behind the nearest booth, whispering fiercely. "What? You kissed *twice*?"

I press a hand to my forehead and realize I never told Andrea about our second kiss. It wasn't on purpose, but then again, maybe it was. I've hardly been able to process everything myself, and after telling her about the first kiss, it's all she wanted to talk about.

"Sorry. I should have told you."

"Yeah, probably, but now I want to know what happened," she says.

"It was a few days ago. The morning after I kissed him the first time, and he may have pinned me against the wall and kissed me."

"Wow." Her eyes widen and she blinks rapidly. "That sounds…"

I raise my eyebrows and finish her thought. "Hot. I know." Like I'm not already aware. "It was."

"So, what did you do?"

Awareness prickles my skin as I remember Beau's touch, so I cross my arms. "First, I kissed him back."

Her mouth curves into a small smile, but she doesn't let it get out of control, thank God.

"Second, I told him we're just friends. Not friends that kiss." The memory floods my mind like it's been doing ever since the second Beau took his hands off of me. I know it's the best decision, but it leaves a bitter taste.

She steps forward, pulling me with her as we continue our journey to the coffee cart. "Look, I know you want to wait until you find Jacob to start anything. I get it. It's been a long time coming, and I can imagine all the angst you're feeling."

"I sense a 'but' coming on…"

She squeezes my arm. "But don't let the questions you have about the future stop you from living in the present. You can't know what comes next, though by the sound of it, right now it is looking pretty good."

"Thanks for that," I say, digging an elbow into her side and she squirms. "But Beau and I have time to figure things out, yet Jacob and I don't."

She exhales loudly but doesn't reply. Instead, we approach the cart and she orders her drink as I look back at the table. Beau is still casually chatting with Jordan, hands tucked into his pockets, a relaxed smile hovering at the corners of his perfect mouth. The soft cream of his crew neck hoodie contrasts with the depth of his brown skin and makes me inhale sharply at the sight of him. This would be so much easier if I weren't attracted to him, or if we weren't spending so much time together, but I am and we are, making the task in front of me impossible.

Andrea tugs on my forearm. "You know your happiness and search for Jacob don't have to exist separately. You can pursue both."

I shake my head as we move to the other end of the cart. "I don't think I can."

My life has hinged on the moment I'm about to experience today. For years, a part of my soul has resided with Jacob, and I don't feel right only giving part of myself to Beau. He doesn't deserve that. He deserves all of me, and all of me doesn't exist right now.

Choosing to stay silent, Andrea steers us back toward the table, where I notice a short woman standing next to Jordan as she speaks with Beau across the table. Her back is to us, but I would know that woman anywhere.

My emotions are pure glass today, apparently, because when I see her, tears spring to my eyes and I want to embrace her. I want for her to hold me and tell me things will work out, with Jacob and with Beau.

I pick up the pace, and Andrea's stride grows longer as she attempts to keep up.

"Here's Kit," Beau says as I approach the table.

Monica turns around and her eyes crinkle as her smile grows. "Kit." She opens her arms, and I step into them without hesitation. "It's so good to see you."

Closing my eyes, I savor a moment I never thought I'd have, nor one I thought I'd need.

A tear escapes the corner of my eye. "It's good to see you, too."

Monica holds me at arm's length but doesn't let go. "Are those tears, hon?"

I laugh through the waterfall originating in my eyes. "Maybe."

She tilts her head and studies me. "Look at you, Kit, you're a beautiful young woman."

I wave a dismissive hand but not before heat slinks up my neck at catching Beau's smile.

"Are you ready? The family is outside waiting."

My stomach drops, and I place a steadying hand over it. "Right now? This is going to happen right now?"

She nods. "If you're ready."

I glance at my friends, who encourage me with smiles and silence. But when my gaze travels to Beau, the importance of this moment feels weighty. My future is being held in an open palm and could be crushed or set free depending on the outcome of these next few minutes.

The invisible tether that connects us is being tugged closer when Beau says, "Go for it. I'll be here when you get back."

I nod my thanks, emotion thick in my throat and nerves arresting my pulse.

Turning back to Monica, she smiles and beckons me forward. "Follow me."

Sweat gathers on my hands and the pattern of my breathing becomes stunted.

I run through the rehearsed words in my mind, the ones that will bridge the gap of broken promises, as my feet carry me forward. I will shoulder every foul word, hurtful look, and angry tone if it means that he is safe, alive, and thriving. It's these very thoughts that have kept me going all these years, believing he is living his best life and waiting for me to join him.

Monica pushes through the gym door, and I'm immediately blinded by the bright sun. Just as quickly, I blink away the piercing light, because I need to see the boy I haven't laid eyes on since he was a child.

The boy who holds the other half of my heart and always has.

CHAPTER TWENTY-THREE
July 2014—Age 23

"Well?" Andrea tries to lock eyes with me, but I don't let her. "Was he your brother?"

I rest one hand on the edge of the table to stabilize my shaking legs and raise the other to my chest. My lack of sleep is catching up with me.

Eyes focused on the ground, I close them and answer. "It wasn't him."

The noise in the gym is louder now that more people fill the space, and it's creating a buffer for the silence that follows my reply.

Andrea's words are hushed, "I'm sorry, Kit."

She moves in to hug me, and Jordan pats my shoulder as I swallow back my disappointment. Beau stays where he is, and I'm thankful for it, because I wouldn't be able to hold back my plague of tears if he touched me. Not when our future snapped along with the last hope of reuniting with Jacob.

After Jordan and Andrea say their goodbyes, I sulk behind our table, standing there, unmoving and refusing to make eye contact with Beau. I don't know if I can handle his pity or his kindness right now. Both might be my undoing.

And they are. "I'm still here," Beau says quietly, rubbing my shoulder with his hand.

I'm no good at pretending his words don't impact me. His encouragement is like an invitation to draw me closer to him. But I don't allow myself to take that step. Instead, I say what I feel, because why the hell not? "Will I ever find him? This was my best shot. *Monica* was my best shot, and if she doesn't know where Jacob is, I'm not sure anyone will."

The sinking sand of this impossible search is pulling me under with every day that passes. I'm drowning in a pit of my own making. If I could have been better, done more, Jacob and I might still be together or in contact, at the very least.

Unable to face my mistakes and my losses, I retreat to the back of the gym and let myself fall apart. I should have demanded Jacob's phone number, clawed and kicked when they tried to take him from my arms. Instead, I'm here: pining for a brother who vanished into thin air.

Covering my face with my hands, the hot tears fall, retracing well-worn tracks. A light brush of fingers trace the channel up and down my spine making my tears only grow bigger and fall faster. Beau squeezes my shoulder, unintentionally grazing the skin at my neck. His actions are all the words I need.

Dropping his hand, he returns to the table, but not before branding his touch into every cell of my body. I pinch the bridge of my nose to stop the flow of tears. I'm breaking under the pressure that's been building since I was thirteen. At what point do I give up? Cut my losses and the heartache that comes with it.

As soon as Monica and I stepped outside the gym, she turned around and looked straight at me. My expression told her everything, but mainly, that this boy wasn't my brother. My face fell, disappointment so obvious it was impossible to hide. The black hair, brown eyes, and lanky figure that this kid had were all wrong. But when I wanted them to be right, I tried to envision a scenario that this kid was Jacob and that it had been too many years since I saw him last to know for sure. Yet, it was clear I was a stranger to this boy, too. He didn't have a sister, he'd told me, but he supposed his birth mom could have been lying and agreed to meet me. Unknown siblings turn up all the time but apparently not mine.

My sobs slow, not by choice but by force, and I relax, taking a few steadying breaths. I check my reflection in one of the windows, hoping my mascara isn't streaked across my face, and walk back to the table with a practiced smile. I am the hostess after all.

The person talking to Beau leaves as I sidle up to him. I want to say something to acknowledge every part he has played in this whole mess."Thank you," I say, voice thick from crying and trying not to.

His penetrating gaze causes me to look up. He's looking straight through to my heart, seeing the hole that only Jacob can fill. I stare back at him, watching as he licks his lips and reaches a hand to hover over my cheek. He doesn't lean in, he knows he can't, but I wouldn't stop him. There's something about his touch that grounds me, and I need that kind of reassurance, even though it scares me. I wish he would cup my cheek and tell me it will all work out—with my brother and with us.

He caresses my cheek with his thumb, running it over the trail that my tears had made. But he doesn't linger long. Dropping his hand hastily, he swallows once, clears his throat, and looks forward, breaking the eye contact I crave.

"Anytime." His voice is above a whisper and made quieter by the swirl of activity around us. "I, uh, still owe you dessert. Tonight might be a good night for it. Whadya say?"

Battling the tides of desire and loss, I peel my eyes away from his face and into the clutter of people weaving in and out of the table displays. "I do like frozen yogurt."

He cracks a smile when I look at him, and my world looks a little less dim.

"MMM. CAKE BATTER froyo with bits of strawberries and chocolate drizzle—*perfection*." I roll my eyes in satisfaction before closing them. I enjoy every burst of flavor that explodes in my mouth and when I open my eyes, Beau is staring at me with amusement. He hasn't even taken a bite of his frozen yogurt yet. "What?" I ask through a mouthful.

He smiles at his frozen treat. "I can tell you're enjoyin' it, that's all."

Despite today being a total bust, the job fair was better than any of us expected. My mouth never stopped moving as I helped teens figure out what comes next. For many of them, one small step can feel like ten.

This ice-cold treat makes it even better. "I haven't had frozen yogurt in a really long time."

I asked—scratch that—*begged* Beau to drive us to West Hollywood where this spot sits nestled among a strip of businesses, some that are open and others that are boarded up. It's in a rough part of town, but I've never had better tasting frozen yogurt. Ever. I'll make this drive every time. Or make Beau drive me, in this case.

"It's good." Beau plunges his spoon in for another bite.

"See, I told you it was worth the extra few miles."

"It isn't that far, but we did pass a few other places that had me wonderin' what was so special. Now I know."

"It's the only one I know of that's open really late, too." What I don't share is that a couple of the girls and I would come here in between clients or after long nights of working the blade. It was the best kind of pick-me-up.

Beau fumbles to trap another bite of the cheesecake topping with his spoon, and when he looks up and catches me staring, his brown eyes see through me. "Did you want to talk about it?"

The shop is small, and apart from the single employee, Beau and I are the only occupants. Still, I lower my voice. "No, I don't, but it's also hard to pretend like it didn't happen when there were so many witnesses."

He scrapes at the dregs of his bowl, then whips his head from side-to-side, as if searching. "What witnesses?"

I glower at him. "Try everyone I know and love."

The words fall out as naturally as they felt on my tongue, but I still try to skim past them.

Sticking my plastic spoon into my dessert, I let my hands do more of the talking. "That was the only real lead we had going for us, and now we're back to square one."

"What did Monica say?" he asks.

Disappointment floods me. "That we'll keep looking."

"You said the only other Jacob Lopez she found with that birthdate had a police record?"

I shake my head. "Not a police record. His file had a police report indicating he was a runaway, but he hasn't been found." If that was *my* Jacob, then our search got ten times harder.

He polishes off his frozen yogurt and pushes it aside, folding his hands in that carefree way he wears like a second skin. "Maybe that's him. You said you ran once or twice."

"I tried every time I was in a new home." Licking my spoon clean, I drop it into my empty bowl. "I don't know about Jacob running, though. He was always such a good kid. I can't imagine him leaving even if things were hard."

"We all do things that don't make sense when we're desperate and afraid, Squirt."

The nickname causes a pang in my chest. It's different hearing him say it now, like the punch it carries is that of friendship and nothing more.

Beau slides out of the booth and I follow suit, tossing our bowls in the garbage before walking to the swinging door. Beau stretches an arm in front of me to push it open, and we're met with the warm, night air. It isn't until I'm reaching for the passenger door handle that I hear the shrill voice behind me. "I knew that was you."

The familiar voice sends a jolt of fear down my spine as if someone dumped a bucket of ice down the back of my shirt.

Bobby.

I'm in shock and not only does my face reveal this, but my body does, too. I whip around, expecting him to grab me, but he doesn't since he's perched in his car. I press my back up against the unopened door; my heart rate all over the place.

"One of my guys thought he saw you walking in here, so I had to see for myself."

Smoke exits the window of his Cadillac two parking spaces away from where Beau's car is. I'm trying to stay calm but the memories freeze me, and everything else, in place. I'm trapped in a world where time stands still and all sound becomes muted.

I swallow the horror climbing up my throat as the voice in my head keeps screaming at me to run, but my terror is too strong. I never thought this would happen, maybe because of everything that has changed since then, yet here I am, my biggest fear playing out in real time.

The fear of facing the woman I was through the eyes of a monster.

CHAPTER TWENTY-FOUR
July 2014—Age 23

"I didn't think you'd run from me only to get new… representation." Bobby's gaze scours over Beau.

My mouth is sewn shut, however, and I can't reply. Beau gathers quickly that this isn't a friend from my past. He's a foe.

Beau crosses his arms and widens his stance. "Can we help you with somethin'?"

Bobby keeps his eyes glued to mine. "Just catching up with a friend." The words make my skin scream in remembrance. "It's been too long, Mercedes."

The smirk on his face, mixed with his bewitching tone, have my legs locked, unmoving and unresponsive. I can't wake myself from this nightmare.

Beau's gaze swings from Bobby to me. "Mercedes?" The question in his tone tells me that the realization of who this is has hit. Beau knows who Mercedes is, but Bobby is a character he's never met face to face. He directs his words at the man who feeds on the fears of others. "We're leaving. You should, too."

Bobby's eyes are pitch black in the dim light of his vehicle, contrasting with the bright lights of the frozen yogurt shop that create shadows across his smooth features. Every hair is slicked back and his olive skin is a few shades darker.

"Oh, that's no way to treat an old friend now is it, Mercedes?" Bobby leers at me, undressing me with eyes that never leave my face.

He flings his cigarette butt and it lands on the pavement between us, a tail of smoke rising from it. I follow it, but only briefly, not wanting to take my eyes off of the sleeze who's made his living as a con.

I feel exposed in his presence, more than I thought I would and more than I ever did. Beads of sweat rest on my upper lip and forehead, and I'm thankful for the hand that Beau has splayed on the small of my back. He must know that my legs are not long for this world.

"I won't keep you, but I have some news that I thought you'd want to know." Bobby finally severs the cord tying our gazes together and pulls out another cigarette. He puffs out the first inhale of smoke and looks at me for a reaction.

Every muscle in my body clenches at the memories. After sex, he would always light up a cigarette, puffing the smoke out of his mouth slowly while I dressed. It disgusts me that I can still recall every detail as though we are in that room together instead of a rundown parking lot.

I don't know where my words come from or how confidence appears inside of me where there was none before, but I open my mouth and hurl my disgust at his smug face. "Fuck you, Bobby!"

Beau's hand tightens on my waist, and he places another stabilizing hand on my trembling arm.

"Watch it, Mercedes," Bobby grinds out. "Your boyfriend might be able to protect you now, but I've got a lot of allies that will do my bidding at the snap of a finger."

I wish this were an empty threat, but I know it's not. Bobby runs multiple businesses on the streets aside from prostitution. I was always just a small paint stroke in the bigger picture.

"I thought you'd be happy to see me after learning I've got information on Jacob." Bobby deepens his voice as he says my brother's name, making my stomach churn.

Beau's arms are the only things holding me upright. He's angling me closer to him so he can open the passenger door. "We don't need the information you've got," Beau says. "Come on, let's go."

Bobby isn't another face from my past—he was my pimp. The one that Beau helped me escape from two years ago. *If Bobby only knew it was Beau, he'd kill him on the spot.* Damn it. I can't let that happen.

"You're in a hurry, like last time," Bobby's tone is angrier than before. He must notice it, too, because he stretches his neck and softens his voice. "I want us to be on the same team again, Mercedes, that's why I'm willing to give you the information I have."

I don't recall how I got into the passenger seat, but Beau is standing by the open door, doing his best to get the rest of me inside. I don't want to be in a position that places me below Bobby, to be the one staring up rather than down, because that's how I've always felt around him: small.

Beau grips the top of the door as he glares back at Bobby. "We're good man, we don't need the information."

I want to shake him for saying this. *Of course* we want this information. I'm desperate for it. But I didn't know I was Bobby-level desperate to hear it.

"That's too bad. If you change your mind, you know where to find me."

I don't nod or say anything further, but I do tip my chin up like this meager act of defiance will deter him. He clutches the top of the steering wheel with the hand holding his cigarette, his knuckles turning white with the pressure.

He stares at me, one brow arched. "I'm sure you still remember where my offices are located, right Mercedes?"

Even though I don't answer, I know exactly where they are, which is why I have avoided that part of the city like it doesn't exist. It went up in flames when I set fire to that period of my life.

I hesitate to reply but feel my lip twitch and chin tremble, the fear wreaking havoc on my weaknesses. This man knows every one of my dirty secrets. He witnessed my greatest mistake in life, because he was my greatest mistake.

Bobby flicks his cigarette out the open window and shifts his car into reverse. "I'll take that as a yes." Then, with a screech of tires, he's peeling away, leaving nothing but the smell of burning rubber and my shame.

What's left of my composure slips and my breathing becomes hard and fast, pounding for release yet begging me to hang on.

"Kit, I'm here. It's okay, I've got you." Beau says in my ear. He's kneeling beside me, one hand on my shaky knee. His presence drapes over me, and it's the only thing keeping me from bolting. I wish I could run and not look back, but I know I can't, because there's no place I could go that Bobby wouldn't find.

Hunching forward, I fight against the rising panic. "I…I…" my voice falters, but that doesn't stop me from trying to explain. "It…he…"

"Sh-sh-shhh, don't worry about sayin' anything right now. Just breathe. I'm right here." His touch is warm as he rubs my back, and I focus on that. I have to focus on something, anything but the claws on my throat.

Bobby was here. So close that he could've been breathing air that had been in my mouth. The thought makes me sick and I cover my mouth. Every time I'm ready to move forward and continue my life, the past inserts itself into my plans. This is why dreaming up a future that hasn't happened is false advertising. What's the point?

When my heart rate slows, I lean my head back on the headrest and take measured breaths, completely drained of energy but still trying to find some.

"You alright?" he asks.

I let out a deep breath. "Yeah I'm good now, but I need to stand up." I need to prove to myself that my legs still work. That I'm not a broken, wounded creature like Bobby makes me feel.

He grasps my hand tighter and helps me out of the car. When I'm standing in front of him, his towering height provides a security that I want to drown in. Before I can, though, he drops my hand and gently reaches to cradle my face. Lost in the safety of his touch, my adrenaline wanes, leaving a quiver in my chin and opening me up to the emotion pushing against the backs of my eyes. With his thumbs, Beau wipes away the remnants of terror from one eye and the panic from the other. I step closer, wrapping my arms around his waist and sinking in further.

"That's him," he whispers, and I nod. "I hate him." He rests his chin on top of my head. "So much."

I borrow some of his strength. "I know." I want to say more but my throat is raw and scratchy, products of the hysteria that was choking me for far too many minutes.

Beau pulls his forehead away from mine but keeps his hands on my face. "He won't touch you again. I won't let him get to you."

Believing these words would keep me tucked into the hedge of protection that Beau has created but hiding won't fix this. It won't deter Bobby, and it sure as hell won't deter me. He'll keep hitting rewind on the disc until he gets what he wants, and I have to figure out how to stop it.

He settles me into the passenger seat and shuts the door. When he gets into the driver's seat, his jaw is clenched and he wraps his fingers around the entirety of the steering wheel. The ride to my house is silent. Neither of us speaks, because both of us know Bobby is back in the picture. I try not to notice the countless times Beau looks out his rearview mirror, but it's impossible not to. Pulling my gaze from him to stare out the windshield, I'm barely able to merge the two halves of this evening together. One moment I'm laughing and enjoying myself, and the next, I'm chin-deep in cigarette smoke and nightmares.

"Do you feel safe bein' at your place tonight?" Beau asks over the soft hum of his car.

Panic flutters in my chest. What if Bobby followed us? What if he already knows where I live?

"No." I can't even pretend otherwise.

He glances at me before training his attention back on the road. "It's pretty late. Why don't I stay at your place tonight? Are you cool with that?"

My thoughts begin to wander and it's only producing more worry. I'm afraid that I'll never feel safe, or normal, in my own home again, that I'll always be looking over my shoulder or needing Beau to rescue me. Yet, he's the only one I feel safe with right now. I need Beau more than I've ever needed anything, and for tonight, I'm going to let myself lean into that. Tomorrow, I'll become the strong one again. The woman who shoulders things twice her size. "Okay."

"I'll sleep on the couch."

I nod as Beau reaches over the center console and covers my hand with his. He doesn't intertwine our fingers or keep his hand there for long, but the comfort it provides travels through every part of me.

He's protecting me like he's done since day one.

WHEN WE ARRIVE at my place, my roommates are already tucked away in their rooms. The clock claims it's close to midnight, but that can't be right. How can you fit days into hours? Whatever the time, I have to set Beau up for the night, so I sluggishly move about the house, gathering pillows and blankets.

"Sorry I can't offer you pajamas. We aren't exactly set up for male guests." I release a small laugh, but my attempt at levity comes out forced.

"Don't worry about it. This is fine." Beau sets the blanket and pillow on the couch and turns to face me again. "Are you going to be okay tonight? I can post up on your floor if you need."

I bite my bottom lip, knowing I want him closer than the couch, but that's not a good idea. "Nah, having you on the couch is helpful enough."

We stare at each other, longing and desire mingling with our waning restraint.

He reaches out and brushes a piece of hair from my face, sending desire shooting through long-neglected areas of my body. "Night, Squirt."

I exhale and smile up at him. "Night, Big Guy."

Leaving him to set up his bed, I hesitantly walk to my room. Having him this close fills me with all sorts of feelings that I am no good at trying to sort out tonight. I've been teetering on the edge of sanity all day, and I need sleep so I pull the door shut and quickly change into my I'm-cool-wearing-these-in-front-of-

Beau kind of pajamas. Then, I slide my weary body between the cool sheets, and tug my comforter up to my chin, releasing a long, tension-filled sigh.

Not ready to close my eyes, I stare up at the blank ceiling. It holds no comfort that I need, but the man in the living room does.

I could ask him to sleep on my floor; he did offer. And knowing how protective he's been, I could ask him to sleep in my bed, too, and something tells me he would. Is it because that's what I want, too?

Closing my eyes tightly, I convince myself it's time to sleep and ignore the thoughts running through my head. This is why entertaining things with Beau isn't a good idea. Our relationship might as well be labeled "unknown" at this point since we are situated somewhere between friends and *not* friends. Sleeping together, even if it were only to share the same bed for comfort, would only complicate things even more than they already are. Besides, it's *just attraction.* These feelings won't last.

Flinging my covers off, I pad to the door. Holding the knob, I hesitate, but only for a second. When I pull it open, I can see Beau, his long form barely fitting on the couch. It can't be comfortable, but his sacrifice means the world to me, so I stand there, watching him until my dizzy thoughts ease up enough that I might be able to sleep without him right next to me.

Keeping the door open, I shuffle back to bed. My body is sore from past memories coming out to haunt me, and my eyelids are heavy from the truth of my present, but I let them close and start to pray, because in moments like these, I need a friend closer than the man on the couch and closer than the fear in my bones.

CHAPTER TWENTY-FIVE
July 2014—Age 23

"Kit?"

"Mmm."

"Hey, wake up."

Am I dreaming?

"Kit." The voice in my head repeats, louder this time with a shake to my shoulder. "Kit, it's Dina, wake up."

I startle awake and sit up so fast my head spins as I scan the room for the voice that I've convinced myself isn't actually Dina. When my eyes land on her face, I can tell I've freaked her out, too. "What's going on?" Thunder banging in my chest, I place a hand over it to stop it's racing.

"Sorry to surprise you like that. That's kind of how I felt this morning." Using her thumb, she jabs it toward the living room.

Shoot. All of the events from last night come flooding back. Blinking rapidly, I rub a hand over my forehead. "Oh no. Beau."

"I walked into the living room and *surprise!*" Dina waves her jazz hands. "I jumped back and hit the wall, almost knocking the frame off, too."

With my heart beating in my ears, I say, "Sorry Dina, really. I totally meant to text you a heads up last night, but I forgot." I drop my hand, wondering how many times I've said sorry and how many more will suffice.

"So, why is he here?" Dina asks, putting her hands in the pocket of her sweatshirt.

I slump my shoulders and try to gather my wits. "It's uh…" I pause. There are far too many details to try and explain at this hour. "It's a long story. What time is it, anyway?"

"After seven. He's still asleep and didn't even twitch when I hit the wall," Dina says.

A laugh escapes me as I picture the scene. "Sorry, Dina, again. I didn't mean to startle you by bringing a guy home without warning you first."

"So…" Dina starts.

"So…what?"

She lowers her voice, even though I'm positive no one else can hear us. "So…did anything happen with you two last night?"

"No, nothing," I say so fast that my words trip over each other. Actually, everything happened, but I don't tell her this. "I'm not looking to get involved with anyone right now, you know that." I don't mean to sound harsh, but I am.

Dina lifts a brow. "You could've changed your mind. At least that's what Andrea thinks."

Great. Now everyone is discussing my love life. I release a pent-up sigh. "Beau is a friend. I was kind of losing it last night, so he offered to stay. That's it, I swear." I rub my temples.

"It isn't a big deal, Kit, really. But a heads up next time would be fantastic." Dina gives me a thumbs up.

"You got it, but I highly doubt there will be a next time." Unless I don't do anything about my fear of Bobby.

Dina's nod is hesitant but accepting. She leaves my room and I watch her tiptoe past Beau, who I can see from my vantage point on the bed. He's still passed out and makes our couch look like doll furniture. He's all limbs. The adult-size blanket I gave him to sleep with is draped over his chest, barely covering him, and looks like it belongs to a child. I shake my head and lay back on my pillow, rubbing the last remnants of sleep out of my eyes.

I still can't believe last night was real and not another one of my nightmares. Last night was the first time I didn't wake up from a bad dream and other than being startled awake by Dina, I slept soundly. Yet, I still remember everything Bobby said and didn't say.

Clutching my stomach, I run a shaky hand through my hair, pausing at my throat. I left Bobby in order to save myself, but I know how it must've looked to him. I looked guilty, like I really had stolen something. This is why I shouldn't be interested in the news he has about Jacob. I should stay far away from Bobby like Beau encouraged. The information that he has can be figured out another way. I shouldn't entertain the help Bobby is offering.

But I do.

"MORNING," BEAU SAYS with two quick raps from the other side of my door.

I set the hairbrush back on my dresser. It hadn't done much to tame whatever was happening on my head, but it was worth a shot. "Come in," I say before running my hands down my tank top and yoga pants and opening the door. He's looking far too fresh in yesterday's outfit than I care to admit and definitely won't. I better not.

"Hey," he says, casually leaning against the door frame.

I smile tentatively. "Hi, how'd you sleep?" I point my finger at him. "And be honest."

His eyes light with playfulness, but he keeps his smile under wraps. "I've slept on worse."

I drop my hand to my hip. "Seriously? Worse than a couch that's too small and a blanket that doesn't even cover your legs?"

Beau finally releases his grin and a throaty laugh. "Alright, it was pretty bad." He reaches a hand to rub the back of his neck. "I'm glad I stayed, though."

I wish I could live in the days before running into Bobby. The ones where my safety wasn't threatened and my choices weren't strapped to bombs. "Yeah, I'm glad, too."

My mind begins to race with the thoughts I had last night. Not the ones that couldn't stop picturing him kissing me again fully and completely, but the other ones that are confusing. "Beau, we should talk."

He slides his hands into his front pockets. "I know, you're right. Bobby had no right springing up out of nowhere like that. He's so–"

"No, not about Bobby. About…us."

"Us?"

I nod, crossing my arms. "Yeah, *us*."

I don't know where this is coming from, but we can't keep touching, because touching will lead to kissing and kissing will lead to more attraction and more attraction will put us into a territory I'm not ready for.

A smile grows on his handsome face, crinkling the corners of his eyes. "I was kind of hopin' we wouldn't, considering it didn't go so well last time."

I tilt my head to the side and glower at him.

"I'm kidding. We'll talk, but let's eat first." He rocks back on his heels. "Does this bed and breakfast come with breakfast or is that false advertising to get people in the door?"

I relax, dropping my hands from my back as my laugh softens the charge between us. "I don't know. Are you planning to cook it?"

He leans in, closer to my eye level. "Point the way to the kitchen."

Standing up straighter, I attempt to brush past him, jabbing an elbow into his hard stomach, but he doesn't move. Instead, he slips one hand around my waist as the other curves behind my knees to swing me up into his arms.

A small scream pushes past my lips. "I haven't forgotten how to walk!" I slap his chest with the hand that isn't gripping the back of his neck for dear life.

"I know, Squirt."

He doesn't explain himself, and based on how I feel pressed up close to him, I don't fight it either. I relax into the strength of his arms as he carries me through the living room and into the kitchen.

"Hey, Olive." Beau shuffles past her and sets me down in one of the kitchen chairs.

Olive does a double-take. "H-Hey." She lifts the glass pot. "Um, coffee?"

I shift as if to stand when Beau points at me. "Stay. I'll get it."

His bright morning face coupled with his attentiveness is doing things to my insides.

Olive shoots me a questioning look behind his back. When he moves to pour us cups of coffee, I reply to her by widening my eyes and mouthing, *I don't know.*

And I don't. My mouth says one thing while my heart says another. What I do know is that Beau held me together last night when I fell apart. Maybe I should let him get a little closer.

Beau opens the cabinet above the pot and shuffles cups around, spending far too many minutes choosing a mug. He smirks at Olive who doesn't even try to hide her laughter at the mug he chose.

"She'll love it."

I immediately regret letting Beau pour my coffee, knowing he's had full reign over Olive's crude mug collection.

I drop my chin to my chest and groan. "Oh, no."

"Oh, yes," Olive says.

Beau pours two mugs full of coffee, then carefully carries mine, trying not to slosh any over the edge. The wait is agonizing. Whatever's on that mug has been handpicked by Beau and approved by Olive, a terrifying combination.

Setting it in front of me, I let my chin hover over the steam drifting up and close my eyes. "Mmmm. Thanks."

Maybe if I keep my eyes closed, I can save myself the embarrassment of reading what's plastered on the side of the mug cradled in my hands. I've seen Olive's collection; it's extensive and oddly impressive.

"The first sip is always the best."

"You mean, the first *slurp*," I correct.

"Yeah, that too, and don't forget to open your eyes," Beau says.

I reluctantly peel one eye open and peer at Beau, who's holding a carton of eggs and a small basket of strawberries and blueberries in his hands. "Do I even want to look?"

Olive gives a closed lip laugh. "Absolutely, you do."

Fluttering my eyelids open, I focus on the black, unforgiving lettering wrapping around the side of the mug as I lift it in front of my face.

Fresh outta Fucks.

I purse my lips to hide the smile forming after reading the lewd phrase. Olive and Beau don't hide their laughter like I try to since they are laughing enough for me. "Very funny you two."

Beau's generous smile has me catching my breath. "Where are your pans?" Is all he asks, my words getting stuck in my throat.

"Oven," Olive answers when I'm unable to speak. "I'll leave you both to your breakfast. I have to get ready for church. You guys coming today?"

Beau looks over at me with lifted brows. Last night was a mess of emotion, and I'm not ready to face the questions. "Nah, not today."

"Me neither," Beau adds, setting the pan on the stove.

Olive grabs a few strawberries as she walks out of the kitchen. "Alright. See you later."

"Bye." I lower my head to take another slurp of coffee, ignoring the words plastered on the side. The pan sizzles with every egg that Beau cracks and drops onto the hot surface. "Need any help?" I ask.

He glances over as he extracts a couple of plates. "I got this. Stay put and enjoy."

The view of him making breakfast for me causes a satisfied smile to erupt behind the rim of my mug. He shuffles barefoot around the kitchen, a permanent crease between his brows as he searches for utensils hidden in plain sight. I could get used to this. A terribly normal existence between a man and a woman who wake up together, cook breakfast, and fill the space in between with laughter and a whole lot of love. A pang erupts in my chest as I realize how much I want this.

After a few minutes, he plates our food and arranges the berries delicately in the middle. He delivers them to the table for two with a smug grin and sets our plates down for the reveal. The berries smile back at me, truly, since they're arranged in the shape of a smiley face. "You didn't."

Sliding into the chair, he treats me with another one of his full smiles. "I did."

"How'd you even know I like my eggs cooked over easy?" Shaking my head to mask my delight, I take the first bite, savoring its perfection.

His squared jaw moves steadily as he chews, the hints of stubble already visible on his usually smooth cheeks and neck. "I told you. I pay attention."

I'm aware of the stutter beneath my breastbone hearing him admit this, and I almost choke on the blueberry I have in my mouth.

"You all good?" he asks.

Coughing then clearing my throat, I manage to choke out a, "Yup."

Mimicking my earlier question, he points his fork in my direction. "Did you sleep well? And tell me the truth."

I take a sip of coffee to clear the food and desire I have lodged there. "Good. Really good. Probably the best night of sleep I've had in awhile."

"No nightmares?" he asks, furrowing his brow.

"Other than the one where we ran into my former pimp and he lured me in with information on my brother? Nope. That was the only nightmare I can remember. Oh, and I was awake for that one." I try to make light of the sickening circumstances I'm right in the middle of, thinking it would work, but it only reminds me of how much things have changed and how much they will.

He avoids my eyes. "You don't have to take the bait."

I bite my tongue to keep from responding right away. He doesn't know what it's like to be desperately determined for information.

"Kit..."

"Mhm?" I look up to meet his lowered gaze.

"You're not going to take him up on his offer, right?" he asks, which is more of a confirmation than a question.

I set my cup down with a thud neither of us are expecting and cross my arms over my chest in defense. "I don't know."

Concern and warning flashes across his face. "Kit, you can't. This is Bobby. Whatever info he has isn't worth knowin' if it could cost you your life. There are too many questions."

He's right, of course, but it doesn't stop the fury from climbing my throat and settling on my tongue. I tense, clamping my mouth shut in order to keep the words back I want to hurl at him.

He presses. "How do we know he has any legit information on Jacob? What if he's lyin'? You know he plays dirty."

I clench my hands, pressing my nails into the pad of my palms. I've asked myself these questions. But the rope is getting shorter, the leads are drying up. Monica made her shot, Beau has been emailing local agencies with no leads, and I've been sending up prayers faster than God can hear them. As painfully difficult as it is to admit, Bobby is my only option.

Beau's eyebrows pinch together. "Are you really willing to risk everything, even your life, in order to find out what he knows?"

I stare out the window, where birds are flitting about in search of seeds, cars pass in monotonous regularity, and the colors of summer scream with vibrancy. How is it that life can continue with such normalcy on the outside while our conversation has caused time to stop on the inside? It's all so unbothered. That isn't how I feel, though. My words come out hushed. "Beau. You don't know what it feels like to lose someone you love."

Once the harsh words laced with a soft tone fall from my lips, I want to call them back.

He flinches and leans back in his chair, the distance between us even greater than a table. "I think I do."

I swallow my pride and droop my shoulders. "I'm sorry, you're right. I wasn't thinking about your dad when I said that."

Breakfast churns in my stomach knowing I hurt him. "But I couldn't live with myself if I didn't consider every option to find Jacob. I'm not saying I'm going to seek out Bobby, but I need a chance to think here, okay?"

His eyes are downcast, mouth open as if he'll say something, and I wish he would put me out of my misery. Set on groveling, I start again. "Beau, I–"

"I'm not talking about my Dad, Kit." He clears his throat and looks directly into my soul. "I'm talking about you."

CHAPTER TWENTY-SIX
July 2014—Age 23

Andrea gasps. "He said what?"

"Nothing. He was saying he wouldn't want to lose me, that's all," I say to Andrea and Aunt Cindy at our regular Sunday lunch date.

I wipe my mouth and toss the napkin on my empty plate, trying to brush off what this conversation is stirring in me.

Andrea gives me an incredulous stare. "It sounds to me like he was admitting he loves you, Kit."

I choke on my water. "What? No. That's…crazy. And too soon. If you remember, we kissed for the first time last week. How can he love me already?"

It's just attraction.

When Beau told me he didn't want to lose me, and maybe, possibly, kind of said he didn't want to lose someone he loves (also me), I cut him off and changed the subject. We needed to talk about *us*, but when it came time, I froze. I couldn't decipher what he meant, and I surely wasn't about to analyze it right there in front of him. So I shut it down, and instead, when Andrea texted to see if I wanted to come to lunch, I didn't hesitate. I needed to process all of this with someone, and now, I'm analyzing it with her and Aunt Cindy and wishing I hadn't brought it up.

Andrea sips her iced tea. "I'm going to pretend like you didn't ask that."

Poor Aunt Cindy is hearing most of this for the first time, but she appears unfazed, sipping her water and nodding at the appropriate times.

Face tightening, I give her a hard stare. "What do you mean?"

"I mean, nothing about the two of you is too 'soon.' You've been friends, sure, but there has always been attraction there." Andrea pushes her plate away and sits back.

I lean forward, ready to protest, but then stop myself. I can't deny the attraction part, that's why we're here, in this situation. Attraction did this and now it's asking for more. But I can't give more. "Okay, maybe some attraction but love? I think I would know if I'm in love."

Both Aunt Cindy and Andrea are quiet, but I know one of them will jump in to agree with me. They have to, because we all know how ludicrous the idea is. Yet, for some reason, neither does.

"I'm not in love with Beau."

Silence.

Crickets.

"I swear. I don't love him. We're friends."

More silence.

More crickets.

The loudest kind of quiet there is in the middle of a crowded restaurant.

Seeing the seriousness on their faces has me questioning my previous answer. Beau has always felt like more than a friend, but it's because he was also my rescuer. He's the person I lean on when my life is in shambles. He's the guy I trust to treat me like I'm not just a body but a person worth knowing. There is love, but it can't be the kind they're talking about, right? Even as I mull this over in my head, I don't believe it and understand why Andrea and Aunt Cindy aren't buying it either.

I drop my forehead to my folded arms on the table. "Oh no. I'm in love with Beau."

It's not just attraction.

A soft touch tickles my arm, and I meet Aunt Cindy's bright eyes.

"How did this happen?" My question may be directed at them, but it's really for myself.

Aunt Cindy squeezes my arm. "Falling in love is one of the sweetest things, Kit."

I sigh. "Yeah, maybe, if I knew I was falling in love."

Aunt Cindy's laugh lines pucker when she smiles. "If I know anything about Beau, it's that he's honest. If he says he loves you, I believe it. It doesn't surprise me to see things developing with you two."

"But they aren't developing. They can't," I say, slamming my fist on the table. I wince and apologize to Aunt Cindy with my pained expression. All of my words are coming out rough. My filter is broken and clearly my judgment is as well. I knew I should have run far away from the man that plagues my thoughts, but instead, my appetite won out.

"You've been pushing these feelings away for a long time, but they're still there." Andrea leans in. "Why are you pushing them away?"

"Because…" I close my eyes to ward off the influx of emotion, but no matter how tightly I squeeze them, tears still multiply behind them. One tear escapes, and the others aren't far behind. Opening my eyes, I look beyond Andrea and Aunt Cindy, past the restaurant wall and somewhere only my dreams have been able to transport me: the face of my brother. My lips start quivering. "Because of Jacob."

No one says anything for a beat. They know my *why*; the reason I do anything and the reason I don't.

"Maybe I love Beau, I don't know, but I love Jacob more." The warm tears trickle down my face as I try to catch them with my paper napkin.

Andrea strokes my arm, catching me before I can hide behind my walls. "I believe you, but why can't you love them both? What is really causing you to push Beau away?"

Slumping further into my chair, I wring my hands in my lap. If Jacob weren't needing to be rescued, would I be jumping into a relationship with Beau?

I inhale sharply. "I've always done things on my own. I was the parent, sister, friend, caretaker, *everything*, for my family. When Jacob and I got split up, it's like I was tagged with a big "failure" sign that I haven't been able to take off. I'm not sure I know how to be in a relationship with someone, and I'm scared. What if Beau gets taken away, too?"

The confession is made through my slow-rolling tears and from the voice of a thirteen-year-old girl trying to keep everything together. She is scared of losing more people and has blocked herself off from being anything other than "the helper." It's a shield, a mode of protection that worked for a time but is losing steam.

This young girl is scared to open up again and as much as I don't want to admit it, this young girl is still me, like Mercedes is. They are all parts that make up the whole of who I am. I've made peace with Mercedes, now I need to accept the teenager who couldn't hold it all together but shouldn't have had to.

"Oh, sweetie, you've had to carry so much," Aunt Cindy says, but I can't see her through my blurry vision.

Andrea moves to the chair beside me, laying her arm across my shoulders and pulling me closer. I didn't mean to break down in the middle of the restaurant or fall in love when I've tried not to. I didn't think my heart would be able to after all that I've put it through but here I am. It's somehow still beating and still capable.

I want to learn to love again, even if it feels like it could kill me, or the ones I love.

CHAPTER TWENTY-SEVEN
July 2014—Age 23

"Olive, can I borrow your car tonight?"

"Sure, no problem." Olive plucks the keys from her desk and tosses them to me.

"Are you running errands? Maybe seeing that hunk that slept on our couch last night?" She wiggles her brows.

My laugh reflects my nerves. "Only errands tonight." Stepping backward, I wave and make for the front door. If I stay too long, I know I'll tell her what I'm planning.

Guilt settles high in my chest knowing I'm lying to Olive, but she'd try to change my mind, like Andrea would have if I had told her at lunch. There's also an unread text from Beau that I can't bring myself to look at. Not yet. Not until I'm back home.

I'm still not sure what I expect to find as I drive Olive's car deeper into the heart of L.A.

The idea struck me sometime between Beau's confession and mine. Now, I'm lying to my friends and only miles away from Figueroa street: my old stomping grounds.

Twisting my hands around the steering wheel, I dart my gaze between the abandoned buildings, struck by a rush of recognition that has me breathing through my nose slowly. The brick structures are shorter in this part of town but still hug their neighbor closely, sharing a wall or more. The bars, wooden boards, and warning signs on the windows remind me of the danger I'm willingly driving into. Maybe I'm taunting my own fear, but I need to face the shadows of my past, real or imaginary. It's time.

Women of all shapes, sizes, and colors come into view, scattered along the sidewalks in a kaleidoscope of sequins, neon colors, and flashing lights. I get held up by the line of cars ready to drive down the street like it's a drive-through, ordering a woman like she's a combo meal. My hands start to sweat as I recall how it felt to take the money. It paid well—though Bobby took most of it—and on this side of things, money wasn't worth the parts of myself I had to sell. There are plenty of women out here doing their damndest to try and earn cash to support their families, but it's only because there's a demand. There are people who want to pay for sex, and they'll pay cash for it. There are expectations though—strings you don't see but are part of the culture out here. When an exchange happens, the person paying holds the power, like most customer service jobs.

The rise and fall of my chest quickens as the women saunter along the street in g-strings, heels, pasties, bras, and other forms of skimpy lingerie. I stare at them until I no longer see them, rather, I see myself. I see my entire history play out in front of me as memories flood my system. I didn't think it would be like this. To have a visceral reaction I can see, taste, smell, and hear. I had moved on, or I thought I did.

Pulling out of the line of cars with a jerk, I park perpendicular to the street, rubbing the ache rising higher in my chest. The smell of car exhaust from stalled vehicles and the muffled chatter of deals being done has me trembling uncontrollably. I can taste the flavor of nicotine on my tongue from the occasional cigarette I'd smoke, or the ones Bobby did. I can't close my eyes, too afraid that if I do, I'll open them and find that the last three years of my life didn't happen. Beau, Andrea, the Journey Center—all of it—would go up in smoke in the time it takes to blink.

I release my next words on a sharp breath. "What am I doing here?"

This is Bobby's world, not mine.

I'm not expecting to see Bobby tonight; I hope I don't, but there is a part of me that needs to know that this was real. I was a prostitute. The title alone reminds me of the reality I clawed my way out of. I also need to see what my brother might be tied up in. Bobby didn't say how he knew about Jacob. He could have found him, living with an adoptive family, finishing up his senior year of high school. Or, he could have met him out here, picking up a woman or selling her body to someone else. God, I hope that isn't the case. Just the thought makes my stomach roll over and a burn rises in my throat.

Placing both of my hands on the wheel, I look around once more. I need to leave before I'm seen. Vehicles lurk but never for long. A new wave of fear crashes over me, and I reach to fling the gear into drive, trying to get out of here fast before the darkness closes in. Sweaty, shaky hands cause me to slip when I clasp the wheel, giving the passerby a chance to tap on the window.

The clicking sound on the glass pulls a piercing scream out of me, and I clutch my hand to my chest. Holding my breath behind sealed lips, it takes a second for my mind to register that it's a woman rapping on my car window rather than a man pounding on it.

I push a button to lower the passenger window. The woman with straight, jet black hair and full red lips leans down and rests her forearms on the window frame. Freckles dance across her cheeks, using her nose as a bridge to connect them. There's something familiar about her. It's probably the flashbacks of being a woman like her on a street like this.

"What can I do for you tonight?" At a loss for words, I look at her, then glance around, wondering how much attention we've garnered.

When I stare back at her, it's like her name is on the tip of my tongue, but I can't place her.

Her eyes widen. "Kit?"

I narrow my eyes but my mind still can't produce a name like she apparently can. "I'm sorry, I don't recognize you. Do I know you?"

She tugs at the edge of her black-haired wig to reveal her fiery red hair beneath. "It's me…Ruby."

"Ruby?" The memories all but slap me in the face and realization flips on like a switch. "Ruby," I say again with a sigh of relief. "Holy shit, you scared me." A whoosh of air leaves my lungs as I relax into the seat.

She's wearing a pink lace bra, a wrist full of bangles, and shorts that are riding up every time she breathes. I brace myself by holding the steering wheel, keeping my body in the present as my mind and Ruby's presence take me back in time.

"What the fuck are you doing here?" Ruby asks, bending ungracefully to lean inside the open window.

Even from where I sit, I can smell the alcohol on her breath and see the glaze coating her eyes. "I, well…" My mouth runs dry at the shock of seeing her. Apparently being here is taking longer to bounce back from than I'd anticipated. Shaking my head and diverting, I ask, "How are you, Ruby? It's been a while."

"Three years," Ruby says, as if she's been counting.

Remorse floods me. "You've been out here all this time?"

She bites her tongue and nods slowly.

When I got into the van three years ago, I cut off everything in my old life. I had to, or at least I thought I did. It's not like friendships are common out here. Ties are nonexistent on the blade, but that doesn't mean we didn't look out for each other. You need people watching your back between the nightly fights and kidnappings.

Ruby tips her chin up. "You want to give me a ride around the block?"

Looking out every window, I straighten in my seat and check the pulse of the street.

"He isn't here. Just the dipshits that work for him," she says, rolling her eyes.

I sigh in relief knowing Bobby isn't here tonight. "Hop in."

Ruby falls into the passenger seat, and we head straight, weaving through neighborhood streets. She pulls out a flask from her purse and takes a swig, leaving the cap unscrewed.

I bounce my eyes between her and the road. "So, how's life been on the blade since I've been gone?"

"It's the same…and different." She shrugs and looks at me. "You know how it goes." Adjusting the slim purse slung across her shoulder, she takes another drink before continuing. "Some of the girls still talk about it, you know, the night you both left."

I lift my brows. "Really?"

"Oh, yeah. Two street girls leaving, a car chase, and gunshots all in one night gets people talking," she says, releasing a strained laugh.

"I didn't think of it that way," I murmur, more to myself than to Ruby. Andrea and I hadn't met before that night, and now I can't imagine my life without her. She knows things about the world I came from that not many people understand.

I crank the steering wheel—and really crank it since Olive's car has something against right turns—as we meander through houses and businesses nestled in the action of street life.

"Not like Bobby would let anyone forget, either," she says.

She caps the flask and exchanges it for a pack of gum, offering me a piece, too. I shake my head and hold my hand up. "What do you mean?"

Looking down, she adjusts her top. "He threatened every other pimp who operates their business out here. Spooked everyone so much that they kept a tighter leash on everyone more than they already did. They assumed it had to be tied together somehow. What happened?"

I swallow hard, hoping words will form where there aren't any. I can't bring myself to say it, to admit why I left Bobby, not when I made her life a living hell afterward. "I'm sorry, Ruby. I never meant to make your life harder."

She waves me off. "I'm not mad at you, girl. That's why I don't have a pimp and choose to represent myself. Sure, it has its own risks but nothing like being controlled by a man." Clearing her throat she says, "It was your time to go and look at you now. Looks like you're doing good."

I pause at a stop sign and gather my thoughts. "Honestly, I wouldn't be here if it weren't for the people who rescued me and the facility that took me in. I owe them my life."

I remember how it felt to leave that night: heavy with desperation and longing for a world outside of the one Bobby created for me. The one time I asked God for help, He showed up. Sure, He looked like two men and a former prostitute, but I saw them for exactly who they were: my angels.

As I approach a stoplight, my mind is still in my memories. "If I could find my brother now, then maybe everything will feel worth it."

"Your brother?"

I stare at the lights, waiting for them to change along with the solemn mood hanging in the air. "Yeah. I lost him in foster care and still can't find him. We can't locate him in the system, so

I thought maybe he'd be out here," I say, pointing to nothing in particular. "Or, at least some trace of him."

Ruby flips the visor down and opens the mirror to check her reflection. "What does he look like?"

The light finally turns green, and I press lightly on the gas pedal, making the car creep forward and creep it does. "Tall-ish, curly brown hair, light eyes, and tan skin."

She huffs. "I don't really know why I asked. Every face runs together for me."

I look between her and the road. "It's mostly a guess. I haven't seen him since we were kids."

"Shit. And you really think he's out here? On the streets?" Ruby asks before swiping more red lipstick on.

"I don't know. I have to look everywhere though, even if that place leads me back here." Or to Bobby.

Ruby tucks the tube back into her purse and rubs her lips together, smoothing the color evenly across her mouth as she flips the visor shut. "Be careful, Kit. If you poke around too much, they'll find out."

"I will." I have to.

"Can I do anything?"

I take another right down the next street to start the ride back to Fig. It gives me a few minutes to think as I focus on driving. Involving Ruby may not be the smartest idea, in fact, I know it's not. I've already put pressure on her and asking her to poke around could put her life at risk. But, I need more information. Something that could tell me what Bobby knows.

"Maybe you can find out if anyone knows a Jacob Lopez." The words taste sour as I say them. I know Ruby is the only one who can hear me but asking for help out loud sounds like I've just announced it through a loudspeaker.

"I'll ask some of the other girls," she says as we pull up to the curb one street down from where she got in earlier. "I'll be discreet, don't worry." She squeezes my arm.

I've never been good at hiding my true feelings, despite being good at ignoring them, but a relieved smile stretches across my face. "Here, put your number in my phone. I'll text you and then you'll have mine."

She takes the cell phone and punches in her digits. Then, she exits the car, but instead of leaving, she leans down to peer into the open window again, a genuine smile lighting up her face. "I'll see you around."

I watch her cross the street, swaying as she goes and heading back in the direction of too many cars and not enough bodies. The shadow of time hasn't changed much about Fig. It's still as busy and as lonely even with all of the people. Seeing Ruby move to the beat of her own vice makes me want to gather her in my car once again and drive far away from here. Her black wig doesn't fool me, and even though her barely noticeable slurred speech is hiding the woman I know, she's still in there as fiery and lonely as ever.

Putting the car in drive, I take in my surroundings, telling myself I don't need to come back again. I know that I'm lying to myself, though. Now that I've been here, I don't think I can stay away but for different reasons this time.

One reason, actually. Her name is Ruby.

CHAPTER TWENTY-EIGHT
July 2014—Age 23

It's like any other Monday morning.

Running a few minutes behind, I grab a banana for breakfast and jog to work so I won't be later than I already am. When I finally round the corner to my office, my breath is still labored, and before I set my stuff down, Beau stalks in with fists clenched, mouth clamped tight.

"Can we talk?" His sternness makes me feel like I'm in trouble.

"Um, sure, let—"

"Now." His nostrils flare, and the searing heat coming from his eyes bores into me.

"Alright, why don't we go outside?"

Beau nods and follows me out the door. We wind up in the same place where we'd last kissed, but based on how Beau is acting, I'm not expecting a repeat performance.

I haven't fully turned around before words are flying out of Beau's mouth. "What the hell were you thinking, Kit?"

My mouth drops in surprise. "What are you talking about?"

Beau's curt laugh has me on edge. I've never seen him like this. Veins pulse and flex beneath his shaved neck, and the muscles in his jaw contract with every word he speaks and even those he doesn't.

Teeth bared, he answers in a cutting tone. "Going to Figueroa, alone? Does that jog your memory?"

About that. I sent Andrea a text when I got back last night and let her know about my cruise down memory lane, the real and the figurative ones. I knew she'd talk to Jordan, but I didn't think Jordan would get to Beau before I had a chance to.

I shift my weight ready to explain. "Well, I–"

His eyes are wild as he points to his head. "Did you even think to tell anyone you were going there last night? What if something happened to you? What if Bobby…" He doesn't complete his thought.

I try to speak again, needing to smooth things out and get him to understand. "Look, I–"

"I don't get you," Beau yells, folding his hands on top of his head as he paces.

I gape at the sheer nerve he has to confront me like this. "Do you actually want to talk about this, or do you want to keep yelling at me?"

He drops his arms and stops pacing, waiting for me to say something. His fists are clenched so tightly that his knuckles turn a shade lighter than his usual warm brown, and the fire in his eyes remains, inviting me to defend myself and change his mind.

"Yes, I did go to Fig last night, but I needed to go there, Beau. I don't expect you to understand all my reasons why."

His response is quiet but no less biting. "Bullshit, Kit. You didn't even give me the chance to understand because you never told me."

I cross my arms, protecting myself from Beau, the one person I never thought I'd have to defend myself against. "You think you're entitled to know everything I do or don't do?" I don't hide my clipped tone. He doesn't have the right to spring this on me and at work nonetheless.

"I'm yo–" Beau starts, then pauses, "your frien–" but he can't even get himself to say the word *friend*. It pains him to say it, and maybe I get why. "I'm concerned about you, Kit. I want you to be safe, but what you did…" Beau shakes his head, the fight seeping out of him. "How am I supposed to keep you safe?"

His fight may be waning, but mine isn't. "Right, it's my fault. Since when do I have to tell you everything?" Blood rushes to my face, and my breath is labored as I push back everything that Beau threw at me. "I'm the one with the past. I'm the one who has to deal with the shit ton of skeletons in my closet," I point to my chest. "I'm the one with the missing brother." My voice catches on the last word, and my speech ends as hot tears fill my eyes.

"Kit, I–" Beau starts, but I cut him off.

"No, you're my friend Beau, that's it. You don't get to make decisions for me or with me. I've already been controlled enough by a man to know that I don't like it. So back off." I make tight fists at my sides, ready to fight if I have to, but it's only my heart I'm daring to protect.

It's in the span of one beat that I remember the moment I told Beau he could help. "This is my one condition."

Beau puts his hands on his hips. "What?"

"The condition I told you I had if you were going to help me find Jacob."

I can see the wheels turning in his mind, but he stays silent.

I point at myself again, reclaiming my power. "My condition is that if you're going to help, I call the shots." The adrenaline coursing through my veins has me breathing like I just ran around the building instead of screaming my conditions beside it.

Beau dips his head, scrubbing a hand over his face.

When he tries to reach for my hand, I pull back. "Don't. I don't want you to touch me." I'm all too aware of what it felt like to be the bearer of Bobby's wrath one minute and caught up in his passion the next. And while I know that Beau isn't Bobby, Beau's anger caught me off guard. I'm struggling to decode any of my reactions right now.

Beau looks as if I've struck him, and I have. I know how cutting my words sound right now, but I don't give two fucks.

"I need to go," I say, because this time, I'm the one who's leaving first.

He doesn't reach out again as I brush past. After his failed attempt, he's taken the hint and given me the space I crave. But he does plead, even if only above a whisper, "I'm sorry, Kit."

Apologies mean little when actions say so much. We've never had a heated argument like this, and I have no idea how to fix it. What I do know is it won't be right now. Our fight has sucked the energy out of me, and I need space. I'm no longer in the work frame of mind, so instead of returning to the office, I go home. I'll text Candace when I get there and tell her I don't feel well, which isn't a lie. I haven't felt well since the moment Beau opened his mouth. In truth, I haven't felt well since running into Bobby. Fear has been worming its way into my thoughts, and after my fight with Beau, I know one thing for sure: fear had gotten to Beau, too.

"WHAT ARE YOU doing home so early?" Dina asks when she returns home and sees me posted up in my chair.

"Not feeling good." I pull the blanket further up my lap, hoping it hides more of my lies.

Her mouth moves so fast, I can't keep up. "Oh no, do you have a cold? Headache? Cramps?"

"None of those things." I curl my legs beneath me and pick at a stray thread. "More to do with matters of the heart."

"Yikes." She sets her bag down and falls onto the adjacent couch. "What happened with you and Beau?"

What didn't happen? I've felt every emotion under the sun when it comes to Beau.

Shaking my head, I slowly suck in air, and when I release it, I tell Dina everything. I'm halfway through the story when Olive shows up, at which point, she sits next to Dina and listens, too.

Olive scrunches her brows. "So, you used to work with Ruby?"

"Yeah."

I watch for their reaction. Olive worked the streets at one point, too. Different city entirely but with the same problems. Dina nods in understanding. No judgment, only acknowledgment.

I exhale. "She's not ready to leave the streets."

When I sent Ruby another text late last night asking if she wanted to leave, assuring her that I had a place for her to go if she wanted, she shot the idea down real quick. I can't say I'm surprised. Leaving the only thing she's known is no small feat.

"That's hard," Dina says, pressing her back into the couch. "Is she in danger?"

"That's the thing about this kind of job…you're always in danger. You never know what clients you're going to get," I say. "I want us to be friends again, but I don't know how to be one to her now. Our worlds are so different."

Olive nods but stays silent.

Smiling at me, Dina brushes her fingers through the ends of her hair. "There's something radical about challenging the way you think in light of someone else's differences. Maybe that's why Ruby came back into your life?"

She's right, though I'm slow to say it. An exhausted sigh escapes me. "I'm sorry I haven't kept you both in the loop. So much has been happening, and I don't know how to handle everything."

"You aren't meant to handle everything on your own," Olive says.

Dina nods. "Yeah, we're your friends and would have totally helped you, Kit. All you have to do is ask."

I continue picking at the fuzz on my blanket, my thoughts pulling me back in time and wishing I could have a do-over with everything that's happened in the last day. "I know. You're right, I should have shared everything with you both. I don't regret going to Fig last night, but I should have told someone."

"So, what are you going to do now?" Olive asks, sliding her hands between her knees.

"About Beau?" I search for an answer. "Hell if I know. I'm not the best when it comes to confrontation, hence all of the things I said to Beau today. I didn't mean half of them, but the other half I needed him to hear."

Dina reaches out to cover my knee. "I'm so sorry this is all happening. Has he tried calling you?"

I nod, pointing to the phone I've kept facedown all afternoon. "He's been blowing up my phone, but I haven't responded." I know Beau feels horrible; I feel bad, too. The anger fueled us in the moment, but as it's died down, the fear is still there, lurking in the shadows. My ability to think and act is stifling in ways that are detrimental and not productive.

"Well, I have faith you two will work things out eventually," Dina says. "The way you look at each other could melt a bucket of ice cream in the freezer."

Olive's smile tells me it's only a predecessor to laughter. "You're so right." She cups a hand over her mouth to stifle the predicted laugh, and we all join, helpless to keep it contained.

Later, when I walk to my room, my steps are lighter, shoulders less burdened. I thought it would be harder to tell them what has been going on, especially when it comes to Bobby, but it wasn't. Not when the power he had over me waned since I saw him. But his unnatural smile wasn't gawking at me in my own living room either.

Sitting on my bed, I decide it's time to text Beau. I'm not ready to talk to him as my heart is still too tender, but I can at least tell him I need more time. As I scroll through his texts, however, one stops me cold.

Beau: Look, I know you're mad. I get it. But I have news you're going to want to hear. Please call me.

News? Could it be that he finally got a response from one of the agencies? Maybe some more information on Bobby? It has something to do with Jacob, I'm sure of it.

Kit: Can you come over after work?

It's seconds before I see a response.

Beau: Yes. I'll be there.

My mind runs at warp speed, considering every possibility of what this news could be. Questions are asked faster than I can finish thinking them, and the beat that reverberates within the hollow space of my heart is loud in my ears. I don't want to get my hopes up, but when it comes to Jacob, that's impossible.

My hopes have been up since the day I said goodbye.

CHAPTER TWENTY-NINE
July 2014—Age 23

"I did something I never thought I'd do."

Beau is talking before I've opened the door, and now that we're facing each other, I'm far more worried about this conversation than I was when we were texting. Something is rattling him, and it's putting me on edge. "What did you do?"

Beau brushes past me and into the living room. I follow him and watch as he paces, hands in pockets, head hung low. This isn't the Beau from earlier, and like before, I haven't seen this side of him either.

"You're freaking me out. What's going on?"

He stops and looks up at me, staring for what feels like the first time since I answered the door. It's the endless expanse behind his eyes that causes my breath to catch.

"I tried searching for my Dad and…I found him." Beau curls his lips into his mouth and shakes his head.

I walk closer to him but stop short. My body wants to comfort Beau while my mind reminds me I'm still upset with him.

"You did what?" I don't mean to sound so shocked, but I am, considering all that Beau has shared about his dad. "How did you find him?"

He rests his hands on his hips, looking down and then back up. His eyes track somewhere past my head. "Turns out my Mama still has his number in her phone. I found it and copied it without her knowin'."

I'm not sure if he is more worried because he finally found his dad's number or that his mom will find out he took it. Either way, it's clear that he's trapped in the uncharted middle. He rubs his hands over his head and an uncertainty covers his face.

"Beau," I say to get his attention. He drops his hands, eyes on the floor. "Did you call him?"

He nods his head. "Yeah. I did. And…"

The air is charged with possibility, and I know whatever words he says next are going to change things.

"I called him today. I didn't think the call would go through. I thought it'd be an old number, but it wasn't. And when he answered, his voice sounded the same. He said 'hello' like it was anyone else on the other line and not his son." His shoulders sag along with his expression. "He didn't recognize my voice. Why would he though? We don't talk."

I swallow hard, absorbing Beau's pain as if it were my own. All of his old wounds are resurfacing like a scar reopening years after it's healed. I can't stand by and witness this kind of hurt and not do something. I'm tired of this metaphorical wall existing between us, the one I built and also resent.

Striding toward him, I circle my arms around his waist. I don't care that we fought, that we both said things we regret, or that my heart can't take all of the conflicting emotions I'm putting it through. All I know is this is where I need to be. It's where I want to be, too.

Not just attraction.

He completes the embrace, wrapping his arms around me so tight, I know I'm the only thing keeping him together. Beau made the call, and now there is no going back, but does he wish he could? What did they talk about after so many years? Was it awkward? I'm sure. But, was it also helpful?

He rests his chin on top of my head. "I'm so sorry, Kit," he whispers and his words sink deep. "I shouldn't have said all that. I was scared and only wanted to protect you. I-I care about you."

My pulse stammers at his admission. I don't come from a world of apologies; they were weaknesses personified. Yet, it doesn't sound that way coming from Beau. His words are honest and humble as he says them through cracked speech, and I believe every single one.

I exhale my earlier tension and sink deeper into his chest. "I'm sorry, too. I said a lot of things that weren't true. I know you want to help, to protect, and you are. But, there are some things in my past I still have to face."

He nods, and when I pull back enough to see his face, to read the pain in his eyes, the tears I've kept at bay begin to fall. He thumbs away his own tears until I move to do it for him.

"I get it," he says, "but I want to be there for you when you face them."

I rest my hands on his shoulders as his find their home on my waist. "I know you do. I've shut you out. Sometimes on purpose, but other times on default."

Our nearness would have freaked me out a week ago, maybe even yesterday, but being here with Beau, the length of our arms the only thing between us feels like the safest place I could be.

"Can we do this together this time?" he asks. "Not as friends?"

I pause and consider the possibilities of a world where we aren't just friends but friends and *more*. Where attraction and a relationship can coexist. Before I came to the Journey Center, "together" implied that I wasn't living up to expectations. I should be doing or carrying more, but now I'm learning that "together" means stronger, not weaker. Beau and I, we work well *together*. It's the kind of connection I've never felt with anyone else before, and I can recognize the rarity of it, despite my attempts to fight it.

It's not just attraction. It's more.

I bite my lip, the very same one that Beau pays special attention to when we kiss. I exhale my qualms and stare up at him, nodding my agreement, or rather, acceptance. "Yeah, I'd like that. Together. Us. You and me." The words pass through my lips and I expect them to feel laden with a weight I felt with Bobby. But the contrasts between them are vast, and that makes all the difference. He holds my heart with reverence instead of revenge and treats me the way I should have been treated all along.

Beau leans in, hovering over my mouth with a question I've already answered. I tug him closer, chasing his lips with a light kiss. We smile though our lips still touch. I'm attracted to him, that fact has been well defined, but it's the *more* behind it that pulls me deeper. I sink into him, all the parts of him that make him attractive. Body, soul, mind. Every piece building on top of the other.

I let myself get lost in his mouth, his touch, and his honesty until the reasons for why he's here come barreling back into my mind. I hurriedly pull away. "Wait, your dad. What happened with your dad?"

His hands fall from my waist and he rubs at his shoulder, releasing the tension that's been building, because it's in my shoulders, too. Retreating, he slumps onto the couch, forearms on his knees, while I fold my arms around myself.

"When I talked to my Dad, I told him I needed help for a friend."

I stand in the middle of the living room as still as one of the sketches in my notebook. Everything is hitting me at once: the contact with Beau's dad, Bobby's threat, finding Jacob, and our friendship migrating to a relationship. I'm hit with all of it at the same moment I want to succumb to the pressure, but I can't. I have to hold it together. *Just a little longer.*

Wringing my hands, I ask, "What did he say?"

"I explained what's going on and that we've been trying to find Jacob. He didn't think he could help, but I was desperate, so I told him. I'm so sorry, Kit, but I told my Dad about Bobby." Beau flips his palms upward in apology, or surrender, likely both.

I'm listening between the lines as he shares, waiting for the moment where I'm hit with information I may or may not want. I start pacing, if only so I won't cave to the worry of what this could mean. "What did you tell your Dad?"

Beau drops his head to look at his feet. "I told him what Bobby told us, that he had information on Jacob. I didn't think he'd know anything, but I had to ask."

My blood pumps faster as my feet move quicker. "And?"

"He knows him."

If it's possible for my heart to stop beating and to still be alive, that's what is happening now. I slam on the breaks. "Jacob?" I ask in a shaky voice.

"Bobby. My Dad knows Bobby," Beau clarifies.

I expel a pent-up breath of disappointment and feel the blood drain from my face. My head is spinning. "Do they work together? Bobby and your dad?"

Beau stands abruptly and steps toward me. "No, no. My Dad said he doesn't work with Bobby, different businesses and all, I guess, but he's heard about him."

I tug at the hem of my t-shirt and face him, the movement oddly calming despite the screaming exasperation. "What the hell do we do now? This is becoming such a mess," I say, rubbing my forehead.

"He wants to meet with you and me."

I peer up at him and see he's studying me for a reaction. I'm overwhelmed; my insides and outsides want to go numb, but I fight against that feeling. I need to fix things. The more people that get involved with Bobby means the more people could fall because of him. And ultimately, I'd only be able to deposit the blame in my own account.

"When?" I ask, like it's already decided that we'll go meet with Beau's dad—the gang member.

"Tonight."

I suck in a breath. "Tonight?"

"He said the sooner the better, and I agree with him. Kit, Bobby is dangerous. The way he looked at you the other night was…vengeful. If he tells you somethin' about Jacob, he'll want something in return. We have to find another way."

Beau's eyes are pleading, and I nod, because everything he said about Bobby is true. All of it. I know what he wants, but I still don't speak up, because I don't want it to be true. I keep quiet in hopes that Bobby isn't capable of harboring a grudge for this long. But, I'm lying again. Revenge is the fuel that keeps Bobby motivated.

He reaches for my hands, holding them delicately between his. "My Dad might be the only chance we have to get ahead of Bobby, to find out what he knows about Jacob and keep our lives."

The way he says *our lives* is sobering. I didn't want to drag him into this, and I don't want to resort to getting help from gang members but here we are. Risking our lives doesn't sound like a good option, either. But somehow, I push past the warning signals blaring in my mind. I focus on the one thing that has kept me going. My brother is the only person I would do anything for, because he's the one I want in my future family pictures. So, I'll do whatever it takes. I'll accept the help however it comes.

I squeeze his hands tightly, pulling from their strength. "What time are we meeting him?"

. . .

I TYPE OUT my message and hit send, hardly believing I am fully invested in my reckless plan. It was always going to come to this. I knew that when Bobby spoke Jacob's name.

Kit: Hey. I want to ask you for something but I know it won't be easy.
Ruby: What is it?

I exhale. Am I really doing this? I'm taking a risk that could result in casualties, likely my own, so I need to be calculated, smart, focused. The time for doing this any other way is up, and I need to have this option in my back pocket, or at least programmed into my phone.

Kit: Could you get me Bobby's number?
Ruby: Probably. Why do you need it?

I re-read Ruby's reply, figuring she would ask this but remind myself again that this isn't her battle. The less she knows the better. I'll have backup, but I won't let it be Ruby.

Kit: It's better if I don't tell you. But know, it could save a lot of people.

A lot of people, meaning the ones who are closest to me. The lives that would destroy me if they were lost. My head falls back against the wall, and I stare at the bathroom ceiling. I escaped in here while Beau called his dad to confirm the time and place.

My phone shakes my hand again, so I look down and see the ten-digit number that stands between me and my biggest fear.

Kit: Thanks, Ruby.
Ruby: Anytime. Be safe.

If only safety was my biggest worry.

CHAPTER THIRTY
July 2014—Age 23

The restaurant's mariachi music is an effective distraction while we wait for Beau's dad, Marcel. That, and the bottomless tortilla chips that I've polished off. I can't say the same for Beau, who's making my chair shake with his knee bouncing. He's been pretending to read the menu, but at the rate he keeps surveying the small entryway, I'm surprised he hasn't gotten whiplash.

"Hey." I must say it too softly, because he doesn't respond. "Beau."

His attention snaps to me, eyes wide like a child caught in the midst of wrongdoing, so I squeeze his arm to ease the worry that's rendered him mute. "Thank you for doing this. I know it can't be easy facing your dad like this, but I want you to know how grateful I am that you reached out to him for me."

He expels a long breath and, abandoning the pretense, sets his menu down. "I didn't think I'd be this nervous. Mama doesn't even know I reached out to him, let alone that I'm meetin' him." He kneads his forehead, and I can tell how much this kills him. He loves his mama and would never want to hurt her.

He sips his water, but then decides to gulp the rest of it. "It's a good sign right, that he's willin' to meet me?" There's a waver in his question, and the rigidity in his body makes me tighten my hold on his arm. "I think whatever happens tonight, you are still Beau no matter what. You're the man who rescues women off the streets, the man who is a hero to foster care youth, you're a helper, an achiever, and my *best friend*." I believe these things about him wholeheartedly, and that won't change by meeting his dad. There are more feelings in me that I choose not to share, even though they are resting on the tip of my tongue.

He gives me an easy smile, and I mirror his expression. "*Best friend*, huh?"

My hand falls away and I cling to my water glass, a smile tugging at my mouth. "Just don't tell Andrea," I say, and then take a long sip as the waitress approaches.

"*¿Hola, cómo estan?* What would you like to order?"

I read our friendly waitress's name tag: Rosa, and smile at her. "*Hola*, yes we'll take—"

Beau's sharp inhale interrupts me, and I follow his unwavering gaze to the door. Marcel is talking to a hostess, and everything from the rich color of his dark skin to the way he holds himself marks him as Beau's dad. Like Beau, he has a strong jawline and the width of his shoulders is staggering, like he could carry the world and then some. He commands the attention of the room in size alone, and I immediately catalog the similarities between Marcel and his son.

I glance at Beau who is sitting straighter in his chair, chest puffed out, and so still that I study him a beat longer to see if he'll blink. His mouth is a tight line that twitches with the grinding of his teeth.

Marcel scans the small restaurant and eventually lands on our table. His brows draw closer at the sight of Beau, studying him as if to determine if he's really his son or an imposter pretending to be him, as if there could be any doubt. The way Marcel's features stay hardened and his posture stands erect don't exactly denote a warm welcome. He's observing us beneath his lowered lids, and I can't help but think he's used to this sort of thing: sizing people up in seconds to see if they're friendly or dangerous.

Realizing she won't be taking our order any time soon, Rosa shoves her pen and notepad back into her apron pocket. "I'll come back."

Rosa leaves as Marcel draws near, his every step revealing more of the hard gangster that's probably made grown men cry. What is Beau thinking right now? I reach under the table for his knee, sliding my hand along his leg in slow motion. Is this what it'll feel like to see Jacob for the first time? Years of each other's lives missed and wary of the other person?

When Marcel finally reaches us, he remains standing behind one of the empty chairs, waiting for us to offer him a seat or deciding if he'll sit. He's pensive, staring at Beau with the same unwavering gaze as Beau had when he'd spotted his father. We all wait for someone to make the first move. Beau is immobile as he stares blankly at his father, and Marcel's fists are balled.

Unable to take the pressure, I scoot my chair back and it scrapes across the tile floor so loudly that it drowns out the five-stringed *vihuela* serenading the customers. Without letting it deter me, I thrust my hand toward Marcel. "Hi, I'm Kit."

Marcel's eyes bounce between Beau and me before hesitantly enveloping my hand in a hearty grip. It dwarfs mine and I gulp, realizing what kinds of acts these hands have committed. Beau stands and pauses, fists dangling at his sides. I watch him decide what to do next, or maybe what he *wants* to happen next. It's not like these men have many warm, fuzzy feelings between them; they're strangers. The intensity of this moment is palpable, and I squirm in the waiting.

"Son," Marcel says the word quietly, but I hear the thickness in his throat as he extends a hand.

Beau regards his dad's offered hand, then he grips it firmly. "Marcel," he says, his voice void of anger, but calling Marcel by his first name isn't a sign that he's warming up to him, either. Every one of Beau's walls are up, and I wonder if maybe we should have met somewhere less public. This first meet-up is entirely too intimate for a restaurant, but here we are, standing in jilted silence for far too long.

When they finally let go, we take our seats and I sigh. The shuffle of menus is ten times louder compared to the silent tension between estranged father and son.

I clear my throat and try to cut through some of it. "It's great to meet you," I say, directing my eyes away from Beau and back to Marcel. I'm not sure if *great* is the appropriate sentiment— awkward might be more accurate, but I have to keep focused on why we're here. Marcel said he'd help.

Marcel nods. "You too, Kit." His deep voice beats like a drum, drowning out all other sound. I wish I could read him. Is he remorseful? Filled with regret? I have no clue since it would be like reading a brick wall.

I swallow my accusations. "Of course."

Nudging Beau gently, he narrows his eyes at me, then his dad. "Yeah, uh, thanks for helping us out."

Marcel lifts his chin. "When you told me it had to do with Bobby, I knew it was time. I've been trying to get that guy pinned for all sorts of shit he's pulled over the years."

Beau crosses his arms. "How do you know him?"

I'm sure I can guess, but I wait with bated breath anyway. Beau told me that his father is a straight up gang member, and Bobby knew his way around the inner workings of gang life, but I never knew the full extent to which he was involved. He seemed so normal on the outside: family, bank job, house, and even a dog. But all of it is a front.

Marcel looks at his menu. "We're rivals."

Beau scoffs. "So, you're in competing gangs and he's crossed you or somethin'?"

"Something like that. He's been a pain in my ass for a while now. He's got his hands in a few different business ventures around the city that I don't agree with. Bobby isn't exactly liked out on the streets." He rolls his eyes.

Bobby isn't liked off the streets, either.

Our waitress swings by with another ice water and sets it in front of Marcel. "Are you ordering food tonight or only water?" Rosa asks with an edge.

I hadn't planned on us being those people who take up a table and only order water, but with everything we are wading through, I don't know if any of us could eat.

I search the menu quickly, trying to find something to order. "How about two orders of churros and more chips and salsa with a side of guac," I say with a look at the giant men overpowering our small table. "Actually, make that three orders of churros, thanks."

She's assessing them herself as she scrawls the order on her notepad.

Beau speaks up after Rosa gathers our menus and leaves. "What kind of businesses are we talkin' here?"

Marcel stares pensively, resting his clasped hands on the table, "Human trafficking." He watches our reactions. "It started with prostitutes from a few different blades, and now it's turned into something else for Bobby. It's more lucrative, I'm sure, but he's crossing lines and recruiting more people to do his dirty work. Conning women into work they didn't sign up for, that's fucked up." Marcel shakes his head and drinks his water, the cup looking like a child's play thing in his large hand.

I don't think I heard Marcel right. *Human trafficking?* I had no idea Bobby had something like that going on.

"For how long?" I spit out.

"My guess is around five years," Marcel says.

Shit. It was happening the entire time I worked for him, and I had no clue. None of us did. I just lived it never giving it a name.

Marcel lowers his lids and studies me. "Like I said, I've been trying to put an end to it. If you have anything that will help us put him away, I'll take it."

Beau leans back in his chair, arms crossed. "Aren't you worried about getting mixed up in things? You know, with your own business."

It's the first time Beau's words contain a hint of accusation. The curtain hiding his bitterness is being pulled back, and Marcel and I are getting a glimpse of it.

Marcel stares at Beau, his son, the son he left, but when he answers, there's defensiveness in his tone. "My business has nothing to do with any of that shit. No prostitutes, kids, none of that. I'm risking my name getting too close to this, but I'm tired of letting it fly by. It needs to end."

Determining whether or not he's telling the truth, Beau pins Marcel with his glare. "So that's all that's in it for you?"

"No, it's not," Marcel says brusquely. "My family is what's in it for me."

Beau swallows hard, tightening his arms around himself. Marcel's admission raises questions for me, like I'm sure they do for Beau. *Why now?*

When he speaks next, Marcel's deep voice isn't quite so hard. "I know you won't believe me, Beau, but after this, after we get Bobby, I'm out. I'm done."

In an effort not to reach out and do something to ease Beau's pain, I rub my hands along my thighs. This is not my battle, it's his. It's his history that he's facing and absorbing.

Marcel lowers his tone. "Did your Ma get the money I've been sendin'?"

Beau nods with a fixed stare at the table.

"Good," Marcel pauses. "You get my letters?"

Beau's head snaps up. "Letters?"

"Dammit," Marcel says with a sigh. "I didn't expect her to give them to you guys. Can't blame her for wanting to protect you from my work, from me."

It's the first time I hear the remorse in his voice, sandwiched between anger and regret.

Beau leans forward, resting his forearms on the table. The two hulking men are closer and with tensions as high as they are, I'm not sure yet if that's a good thing. I'd be no match if Beau decided to reach across the table and punch his dad. Rosa wouldn't be much help, either.

"You wrote us letters?"

It's Marcel's turn to nod. "Birthday cards, letters, gifts, money. It wasn't much, but it's what I had."

Beau shakes his head. "You could've stayed."

"I should've," Marcel says. "And this time, I will. If you want me to?"

I swallow and sit on my sweaty palms, wondering what Beau is going to say to that. Would he accept Marcel's offer to be in his life again? Or push him away? Both responses are warranted.

Beau shrugs and releases a long exhale. "I don't know."

"That's fair. I want to see Bobby put away regardless." Marcel's bent posture straightens at the mention of Bobby again. "He needs to be put in his place."

I clear my throat, hearing the edge in Marcel's tone. "I had no idea Bobby was into all that. I worked for him three years ago, willingly, but nothing ever indicated something else was going on."

"Did he ever mention a private location?" Marcel asks.

I think back to my street days, specifically those spent with Bobby. He had a hotel where I met him and used the same room every time, like he struck a deal with the manager to keep that room available for himself. I strain to remember something, anything, but I'm at a loss. "His family doesn't live in the city and the only spot I know of is a hotel room downtown," I say, defeated. "I don't know anything else, but I know someone who might." My texts with Ruby spring to the forefront of my mind. I've already asked so much of her, but I need a little more.

Marcel nods. "Good, let's start there. I do have one more thing I need to tell you."

I pull my brows together as a pit forms in my stomach. I can feel the magnitude of Marcel's next words before he even says them.

He clears his throat. "Your brother, Jacob?"

"Yeah?"

Marcel blinks slowly before answering. "He's mixed up in Bobby's dealings. I don't know how deep he is, but one of my guys turned up a photo of him as Jacob was getting out of Bobby's car earlier today."

"Today?" My stomach drops.

Marcel pulls his phone out of his pocket and searches for the picture. When he slides it toward me, I cover my mouth and stare at every achingly familiar feature that I've yearned for over the last ten years. Time is standing still. The loud beat of music is silenced. All I can see is the missing piece of my heart getting out of an SUV.

This man is no longer a boy. He has the same curly hair, the same intense stare, but he's taller, lean, and darker then I remember. Darker because of the burdens of life rather than the tone of his skin or shade of his hair.

"He looks like your drawing, Kit," Beau says, his voice muffled by the swirling fog clouding my head.

I don't want to believe that this teen is my brother, because then I would have to believe that he's working for Bobby—the pimp that crushed every piece of me.

The picture blurs as the years knock me out in the middle of this restaurant, being touched by the man I love, and sitting across from a thug I barely know. Jacob is caught up in a life I never wanted for him, a life I had to escape from, and now one I have to save him from. Will he want that?

When I find my voice, there is something I have to ask, something I need to know. The bile in my stomach rises with the possibility. "Is he…" I shake my head, "Is Jacob helping Bobby with the trafficking?"

Marcel looks between Beau and me. "No idea."

The space between his words and mine indicates that it's possible, and it makes me cringe.

I clutch my stomach with one hand and my throat with the other, trying to quell the fear that wants full reign over my body. My regrets are restricting my breathing, causing my breaths to become even more labored. It's trying to consume me, and I don't know how to stop it.

No one else speaks for a few minutes until Rosa arrives with three large plates.

"Churros anyone?"

CHAPTER THIRTY-ONE
July 2014—Age 23

I stare out the passenger window of Beau's car and watch the lights of other vehicles pass by at warp speed. We're both pretty spent after the emotional rollercoaster we've been on today. When will this ride end? I have a nagging pit in my stomach, and I can imagine Beau feels the same. Families are messy.

I know I'll have to face the reality that my brother is working for Bobby by the time I wake up tomorrow, but for tonight, I'm setting that aside. Beau needs me, and I want to catch all of his hurts and be there for him in whatever way I can. He reached out to his dad for me—and for Jacob—someone he's never met, because that's the kind of guy he is, and he makes me want to be that kind of woman.

"Did you want to talk about it?" I ask, breaking the silence.

"Yes and no," Beau replies. "I keep thinking what I'm supposed to tell my mama. You heard Marcel. He wants to see me again. He wants to see all of us."

"Do you think she'll be angry that you met up with him?"

"Who knows. I'm a grown man and can handle Marcel. But I don't think she'll see it that way."

I run my fingers through my hair and glance over at Beau whose hand is tightly wound around the steering wheel, bearing the marks of a tense evening.

"I never thought I'd see him again," Beau admits. "I saw how torn up my Mama was and started hating him, but I was curious, too. I wanted to meet him, exactly like I did tonight."

As we exit the freeway and stop at a light, I zero in on the taillights of the car in front of us. I watched Beau and Marcel interact tonight and became well aware of the chasm separating them. It was as wide as the separation between real life and gang life and as deep as a stack of untold secrets. Beau didn't know that world, because he had a Mama who was willing to distance her family from it at the cost of her own happiness. I get that— making sacrifices for the ones we love.

I reach over and grab Beau's free hand at the same moment we move through the intersection. He accepts my touch and laces his fingers gingerly between mine, giving them a reassuring squeeze. "You doing okay?"

I smile, aware he can't see it in the dark, but I know Beau can hear it. "You always ask me that, did you know that?"

"If you're doing okay?"

"Yeah, you always ask. Why?" I'm suddenly more interested in hearing his response than answering his question.

I watch as Beau talks through a smile. "Because I care about you. I care about how you're doing, and I want to know if you're not doing well. Consider me an interested party."

Nodding, I bite my lip to mask my smile. He might as well have said he loved me too, but then I remember, I still haven't told him how I truly feel, and with everything going on, I don't know if I can. "Alright, well, if I'm honest, I don't know how I'm doing."

I look back out the passenger window, wishing I could say yes to put him at ease, but the truth is that I'm tired. For years, I've been running without ceasing, and now the exhaustion is creeping into the fringes of my life and becoming the main story. I'm tired of running toward my brother and never being able to reach him. I'm tired of running from Bobby, and Lord knows I'm tired of running from myself. Maybe that's why I couldn't decide whether to push Beau away or cling to him like he's the only person that exists in my universe. There's no time to be tired, though, because if I stop for too long, I won't be able to continue.

I turn my head to look at the upcoming stoplight, then catch sight of his blank expression. "Are you scared?"

His brows pull together. "Hell yeah."

I laugh. "I guess it's a silly question considering what we're up against."

He peeks at me as the light turns green. "You mean with Jacob or…us?"

I sigh. "All of it. Jacob, Bobby, Marcel…and us."

Our relationship is new and shaky like a toddler learning to walk. I'm scared we jumped into things, but I'm even more afraid of what this would feel like to experience alone.

His eyes bounce between me and the road, and I realize how starved I am to be wrapped in his embrace. In this instance, I'm not thinking about Bobby, Marcel, or even Mercedes. I'm thinking about Beau and me, and maybe his lips.

We pull up in front of my place, and Beau cuts the engine but doesn't release my hand. He looks at me and I stare back, examining the depths of his familiar chocolate brown eyes.

We don't speak, instead, I let go of his hand and unbuckle my seatbelt. The sound of it retracting and snapping back into place doesn't deter me and his eyes don't leave mine either. The car is dark, made darker by the late night sky clothing us in privacy. My body is moving without me giving it any directions and before I can protest, I'm bending and contorting over the center console until I'm sitting sideways on Beau's lap. Unlike me, he isn't surprised at all as he holds my eyes captive with his. The lingering threats from earlier try to poke holes in this moment, but the forcefield we've designed and created is impenetrable to outside forces. It's just us and no one else.

I curl both hands around the back of his neck, lacing my fingers together and cradling his head like it's the most precious thing about him. I wouldn't be able to choose my favorite part of him if pressed, every part holds a uniqueness like it's a groundbreaking discovery. The smoothness of his skin and the firm hills of his chest leave me wanting, clambering for pieces of him I have yet to become acquainted with.

Our breathing intensifies as the atmosphere becomes heady, but this is what I want, for better or worse, because I know without a doubt that Beau can handle the worse; but, I want to know the *better*.

I bite my bottom lip and his eyes drop to my mouth, so I focus on his. Longing and desire radiate between us.

"I think I like you," I say in a low voice.

He slides one hand up the side of my thigh and my legs tense. Lifting his other hand, he releases my lip from the clutches of my teeth with his thumb. In one sweeping motion, his lips are on mine, pressing firmly and refusing to withdraw. Flirting with the edges of my resolve, we greedily take what we need from the other and somehow, in this moment, it's enough.

It's attraction and more.

It's like and love.

It's him and me.

The steering wheel digs into my back, adding pain to the pleasure as Beau leans into me. His horn doesn't work, which is annoying when you need it, and apparently, great when you don't. Our hushed sounds of delight mingle with the audible tones of our unhindered carnal desires and the lingering scent of spices on his tongue makes my senses run wild.

He pulls away, kissing my face and resting his forehead on mine. "I *know* I like you."

I smile so big, my eyes crinkle, leaving little space for the tears that fill them. I'm overwhelmed with the pleasure I had been avoiding, believing it wasn't for me because I came with a past. But truth overpowers the false beliefs I've taken with me. No more. They're gone along with the stiff arm I used to push Beau away.

Our mouths crash into each other, completely shattering me and sealing the truth of our words. Trailing my wanting hands up his neck, I rub his short, buzzed hair, and then chase the hills and valleys of his chest. Hands caressing my back, he plays with the hem of my shirt, fingers lightly tracing my skin, causing me to arch my body closer to him.

Memories of our first kiss flood my mind, then our second, third, current, and all future kisses that are possible and within reach now that he is *mine*. I smile against his lips as he lifts both of his hands to stroke the sides of my face and my mouth moves rhythmically over his. I open wider, deeper, pushing the boundaries of our closeness as if we aren't already molded to one another.

It's like a roller coaster ride. One moment we're plummeting down the tracks, our lips frantically pushing, pulling, biting. Next, we're climbing slowly, tenderly pecking, and softly dragging our lips across one another, building a slow friction that lights a fire lower in my gut. My pulse hammers loudly and it's unquenchable.

All fear is silenced, the second-guessing gone, and the wall I erected demolished. All that's left is *us*.

Beau deepens our kiss as one of his hands grip my thigh and the other rubs patterned circles around my ear; his lips taste the skin at my neck, and I tilt my head back to give him better access. When his hands become entangled in my hair, all of the pent-up needs in both of us are set free. Our need to touch, grip, and fondle, to be closer than friends. And our need to rely on someone other than ourselves. It overtakes us in a full sweep of unapologetic passion.

It is attraction, but not just *attraction.*

I pull away to see his eyes and reread the future we are writing together. His breathing is ragged and I'm panting just as hard. My next words come out in a whisper shattered by restrained need. "No, I think I love you, Beau."

I clamp my lips together so that nothing else can slip out, not because I regret what I've admitted, but because I don't know how he'll respond. For me, this love has been growing over time with plenty of water, sunshine, and patience. My words came in a stroke of desire lit by the fuse of our own making, but they've been building and can no longer be hidden. Does he feel the same? Are his feelings as strong as mine?

His eyes are hooded and the confidence in his relaxed expression is clear. It's aimed at me like an arrow searching for a target and without all of my doubts crowding the bullseye, it's a clear shot.

"I *know* I love you, too, Kit," he says, cupping my cheek. He settles every nerve that's been standing on end in expectation.

I kiss one of his cheeks and then the other. "I know I love you, too."

His lips find mine with a new level of ferocity we haven't reached yet. It's all-consuming, this love. The previous second-guessing doesn't hold any sway with the honesty of our confession draped around us.

I'm learning to love again, in real time, and it's covering all of the lies that were hiding it.

Beau uncovered the truth.

...

A POUNDING ON the door jolts me awake, and in the aftermath of sleep, I'm confused as my hyper-alert body becomes rigid and my lungs gasp for air.

What happened? Where am I?

The room holds all of my valuables: clothes, shoes, pictures, etc., but this isn't where I was seconds ago. I was in a pitch black basement, water dripping methodically into an ever-expanding puddle while I was tied to a chair.

"It was only a dream," I say through labored breaths before repeating, "It was only a dream."

I hear another knock and a shot of adrenaline runs through me as I touch the cold sweat beads on my forehead. Then, I flip my covers off and set my feet on solid ground. The dream is merging with my reality, and I need to focus on the real and not on the imaginary ropes bound around my wrists and ankles.

After a moment, I swing my head to peek at the clock. 7:08 a.m. *7:08? Oh no, I slept past my alarm.* A different sort of adrenaline surges through me as I scramble around my room, grabbing clothes that may or may not be clean and rush toward the bathroom.

Another knock sounds and I'm pulled in the direction of the relentless thumping.

There's an urgency in my steps, like whoever is behind the door will confirm the world I'm actually living in. Asleep or awake? Alive or dead? Free or trapped?

When I open it and see Beau smiling back at me, holding a bag of pastries and two coffees, I exhale deeply, clutching my chest. "Thank God."

"Good morning to you too," Beau says with a laugh.

I walk straight into his arms, despite them being full, and hug him like I'll never let go. And I might not.

"Kit?"

"Yeah," I say, my face nuzzled against his chest.

"You doing alright?"

His standard question deserves my new standard answer. "I am now." I peel myself off of him and stand to my full height, which barely crests his shoulders. "Bad dream."

Beau gives a slow, understanding nod. "I told you I should have slept over."

I scoff, reaching for one of the coffees. "And what would your roommate say if you were gone *again*? Huh?"

"It wouldn't matter. If you need me, I'll be here."

I smile and melt simultaneously as I take that first, blessed, sip. "Thank you for this. You're speaking my love language."

I wave Beau in, and he heads toward the living room, nudging me in passing. "I hope I've been speaking it for a while."

I purse my lips, trying to hold back a smile as I close the door and follow after him. "So, how long has it been for you?"

Sitting down, he shakes his head. "How long? What do you mean?"

I tuck my hair behind my ears before sitting down to rifle through the bag of decadent pastries. "How long have you…you know, liked me?" I select a fresh chocolate croissant.

He offers me a closed-mouth smile, hiding the bite of a danish behind his lips. "It's been a while." Beau's nonchalance doesn't prevent my heart from skipping a beat.

I take a slow sip of hot, black coffee. "Define *a while*."

He grabs a napkin to wipe his hands with, and then takes a sip from his cup. I know he's making me wait, lengthening the suspense for as long as possible, and I could jump out of my skin in anticipation. "Since I first saw you."

I choke on my coffee. "Wait, what?" I cough a few times to clear my throat. "The first time you saw me was on Figueroa when you handed me the rose and told me to meet you at a random diner if I wanted to leave and never look back."

His gaze is steady. "I remember."

"Beau, I was wearing next to nothing that night. Are you sure you didn't notice me for those reasons?" I ask with a pinched laugh.

"I saw more of you than your body, Kit." Beau's expression is dead serious. "You were scared out of your mind the entire ride back to the Journey Center an–"

I interrupt him. "To be fair, the ride back to the Journey Center was a full-blown car chase, bullets included."

"I'm not saying you didn't have a right to freak out. We all did. But I remember witnessing the exact moment that you finally exhaled and felt safe again. I knew I played a small part in it that night, and I remember thinking that I wanted to witness that every time. I wanted to be the one who made you feel safe every time." His eyes lock on something past my shoulder as if he is reliving old memories in the reel of his mind.

I set down my cup and tuck my hands between my knees. "Mission accomplished."

Beau meets my eyes and smiles, his squared jaw becoming more defined with this action.

Dropping my gaze to the table, I know I need to tell him. He's kept me safe the entire time I've known him. I know he'll do it this time, too, so I clear my throat and start in. "Maybe this would be a good time to tell you about the text I sent last night." Beau's smile disappears. "Try to keep an open mind here, okay?"

Beau's gaze stays with me and he nods.

"I got Bobby's number from my friend, Ruby. I wasn't sure if I would need it, but after talking to Marcel last night, I think we need to schedule a meetup with Bobby." There, I said it. Now there's no going back, and I can only wait for his reaction.

Beau drops his head before raising it again slowly. "What are your plans?"

I swallow hard and squeeze my hands closer together, ready to explain what I've orchestrated. "I told Bobby I wanted to meet. There's a restaurant called Lin's that is small enough yet big enough for a conversation like this one. We'll meet this Friday night at eight."

"What are you gonna say?" Beau asks, bending his concerned expression to his will and trying to be supportive.

I see the effort and love him all the more for it. He knows I have to do this. I need to face my past if I'm ever going to have a future. "I'm going to tell him I want to see Jacob."

"And you think he'll listen?"

"I know he won't, but maybe I can get him to slip up, to reveal something that he doesn't mean to. He might give me a clue without meaning to." I'm trying to be calm, but my mind keeps replaying my nightmare, and I can still feel the rope around my wrists and ankles and the helplessness of knowing it was over.

Beau folds his hands as he leans forward, forearms on knees. His feelings are as clear as fresh spring water; he doesn't like this plan. But his words indicate otherwise. "Okay, tell me what else you have planned. What can I do?"

"I am hoping you, Marcel and a couple of his men could post up around the restaurant and keep a lookout. You know, just in case."

He tries to clarify. "And you'll go inside alone?"

I nod my head slowly. "Alone but with a restaurant full of employees and customers."

Bobby caught me off guard during our last run-in, but I'm not going to let that happen again. This would have been so much easier if Jacob was tucked away in some nice foster family's house, but he isn't, which only gives me more drive to meet with Bobby and get this over with.

"And there's no other option? Monica hasn't turned up any information, has she?" Beau asks, grasping for anything that will turn this ship around.

"No, nothing. I've been texting her, too, but more out of support than anything else."

He drops his head into his hands. "Damn it. I wish we could do this another way. But Bobby is after you and won't stop until you meet with him."

I cross my arms and lean back against the couch. "You're right. He won't stop until he gets what he wants. Bobby is successful, because he doesn't know what boundaries are."

Beau nods slowly. "Friday will be here soon. We should run through a few possibilities if we can to make sure we're prepared."

These aren't ideal circumstances in which to start a relationship but my life came with baggage that's begging to be unpacked, and I can't ignore it, even if the safety of Beau's arms is so comforting that I don't want to leave.

Beau extends his hand in invitation, and unlike what I would've done two days ago, I don't hesitate. Instead, I accept his offering, confirming that we are in this together, that I *want* to be in this together. He pulls me onto his lap and leans back into the cushions. Then, angling my head down, I bring my lips to his. Our mouths meet with a practiced intensity that has me gripping the front of his shirt while he holds my face between his hands.

He pulls back and whispers against my lips. "I love you."

A pounding erupts beneath my rib cage. All of my life I didn't think I could be loved like this. Someone with my past, my present mess, and unknown future is being loved in ways that dig the well of healing that much deeper. I feel like I can do anything, and that's exactly the kind of energy I'll need to see Bobby again.

I reply with the only words that my mind can produce. "I love you, too."

He touches his lips to mine, but then we're startled apart by the sound of Olive's voice.

"Finally," she says, on her way to the kitchen. "Took you long enough."

Beau and I let out a relieved laugh. "I brought you ladies pastries," Beau says to Olive, who is pouring coffee into her mug.

She walks into the living room, grabs a pastry from the bag, and shoves part of it in her mouth. Then, she turns on her heel and yells over her shoulder with a mouth full of croissant, "You know what, Beau? I love you, too."

CHAPTER THIRTY-TWO
2014—Age 23

I set my phone down with an exhale that continues until my lungs are completely empty. I have so many plates spinning and I'm afraid of dropping one, knowing that if one of them slips, they'll all come crashing down—on me.

I asked Ruby if she knew any other places Bobby operates his businesses out of. I'm not expecting her to have an answer right away. Sleuthing takes time, and I wouldn't want to risk her safety, even if I'm about to risk mine.

Tonight is happening. Bobby will meet me at Lin's restaurant at eight, and I'm praying he shows up without any surprises. My nerves are already on edge, and I'm still hours away from staring into his frightening eyes. I can't handle any of his games when there's so much at stake, but I know I'll have to play them regardless. It's like any other game I've learned to play, I'll need a mixture of practice, focus, and a competitive edge, all of which I have in spades.

I've been picturing our meetup, trying to get close to how I will feel without being submerged by the weight of sharing a table with Bobby. It hasn't been easy, yet Beau has been with me through it all. He isn't stoked about our meetup, even if Marcel thinks it's as good a shot as any. But he knows this meeting is more than information on Jacob. I have to do it for myself, too.

I ran as fast as I could when given the chance three years ago, but there is no amount of running that can take me away from the life I lived, the past I endured. I've made peace with the woman I was and the one I became. I need to do the same with Bobby. I'm not looking for peace; I wouldn't expect it from him, but I need to face the fears he invokes.

I need to show him, and myself, that I am learning to love myself again, and there's something about love that drives out fear.

• • •

THE WINDOWS IN Marcel's car are as dark as the black exterior.

We're posted up a block down from Lin's, tucked away in the protection of this car. The flickering street lamps don't shed any light into the vehicle, and I can barely make out the highlights of Beau and Marcel's profiles from their spots in the front seats. It's like we've entered full incognito mode.

"Lin's is a small restaurant, so I can't put too many of my men in there without it being noticeable. I'll have two on the inside and one at the back of the building, just in case," Marcel explains from the driver's seat. He possesses a noticeable calm that Beau and I don't have, and I'm guessing it comes from years of practice in being chill under pressure.

From the passenger seat, Beau asks, "Are they armed?"

Marcel doesn't look over at Beau but he nods once.

Beau's voice reverberates off the silence. "Shit."

Guns are like a second arm to guys like Marcel. But that isn't the case for Beau, and we both know it. Our two worlds are meshing, and I can't help but see the chaos they're creating in the process. We are mixed up in a weird dance with Marcel and his gang, but in order to take Bobby down and somehow save my brother from this mess, we need to blow things up from the inside.

Beau turns away from Marcel and doesn't say another word.

I can't stop fidgeting with my hands in the backseat. I'm nervous, which isn't a good sign since I haven't even seen Bobby yet.

When Beau looks at me, the pressure we're under is clear in his wide eyes. "You ready, Kit?"

"Yeah," I say, a little breathless. I'm not ready. I'm not okay. I'm terror stricken and worried, and seconds away from losing my nerve.

Still, I pull the door handle, because my determination is outweighing my fear. The feelings won't leave me whether I face Bobby or go home. They'll still be there waiting for me to face them head on. I'm robot-stiff as I round the car. Beau grabs my hands, and I'm relieved at the contact, unable to tell which one of us is holding the other up.

He leans in, placing his forehead against mine, and together, we take steadying breaths, wanting to be the strength that the other needs. Beau starts whispering a prayer and his breath tickles my face. "Lord, we need your help. Peace when we're anxious. Patience when we want to act. Compassion when we want to kill." Beau straightens to his full height but not before gently kissing my cheek.

We walk around to the sidewalk and meet Marcel where he's been waiting, and I tug my leather jacket closed, warding off the night's chill, or maybe that's my adrenaline turning on. I peer down and evaluate my outfit: black on black on black. I suppose I'm more of a mood dresser than I thought and this is about as cheerful as I'm feeling.

"We'll be here," Marcel points at his car. "If anything shady goes down, my guys will handle it, alright?" Marcel pins me with his gaze and waits for me to confirm.

I nod but can't manage any actual words. I'm not planning to do anything off-script, but I sure as hell don't want to promise that I won't. There is so much riding on this meeting, and I hope I don't crack under the pressure. It feels like Jacob is within reach, which means I can't promise anything else when the weight of my promise to him is already looming over me. Marcel knows a thing or two about protecting his family at all costs, even if that family is his gang.

Beau envelops me in one last hug, running his hands up and down my back to prove that he's got me covered. He'll be here—waiting, praying, loving—for me. His jaw is clamped down and unmoving while his nostrils flare. He's gearing up to let me go, and I know the feeling exactly, except this time, I'm not pushing him away. I'm coming back. I will come back.

When he lets go, I release a final, angsty breath and start walking the couple blocks to the restaurant. With every step, my pulse beats faster and my hands sweat with the anticipation of being locked in a confined space with Bobby. It doesn't matter that the space is over one-thousand square feet and filled with other people. It will still feel too small. The air is already trapped in my throat, preparing for the moment when Bobby steals the rest.

I could run; I want to hide, but I'm too bolstered by love to be swayed by fear.

Lin's is on the next corner and the only thing that separates Bobby and me is a red hand on the crosswalk sign. My eyes return to the car where I know Beau and Marcel are, and I'm struck by the fact that I've only traveled a few feet. This road felt so much longer as I thought about what was waiting for me. I bend each knee alternately while counting down the seconds until the hand becomes the walking figure, and I can continue on. I feel preprogrammed, as if every movement taking me from point A to point B was decided so I wouldn't have to think about it.

I approach the glass door with the instructions to *push* and do just that. Once inside, I don't search for familiar faces nor do I watch my feet in alarm, and I certainly don't look back the way I came.

I read the sign standing upright and visible in the cramped entryway: *Please seat yourself.* There is a partition that blocks my view of the main dining space, and I suck in a breath, exhaling quickly in case I forget to. My feet keep walking, slowly but with forward progress that leads me to my destination: a single chair saved for me.

My first glimpse is like a time machine, as he is the exact replica of the man I met all those years ago, and it is no more evident than in the smile he gives me, one of many, I'm sure. I shiver. Bobby has always had a yin-and-yang vibe—he smiles while he seethes, he caresses while he cuts, and he loves while he hates.

He locks eyes with me, and I see the dichotomy in them as well. They are the darkest eyes I've ever seen, not because of their color, but because of the evil within them.

Not all monsters live in dreams.

CHAPTER THIRTY-THREE
2009—Age 18

I rubbed the back of my neck, tipping my head from side to side to stretch out the tension as I waited. The chef was taking his sweet time plating the food for table seven, the very same table that had complained twice for the long wait. I had worked six hours so far and had three to go, all at minimum wage and whatever customers determined would constitute a good tip. If I smiled and flirted, I got more, even if I had to grit my teeth to get through it.

I rested my hands on my hips and arched my back. This job was physically taxing, but I was desperate for the money. I'd take anything—either the shitty tips or the ones that actually made a dent in my budget—as long as it would support Jacob and me. The costs only continued to add up when I thought about what we'd need to get by. We would need a place to rent, rather than the pay-as-you-stay motel I'd been living in, and there'd have to be enough money for utilities and food, too. It wasn't cheap living in L.A., so maybe we'd move, but I couldn't do that until I found him.

Slumping forward, my gaze landed on my old sneakers—the ones I had to use glue to keep together—and I questioned yet again what I was doing with my life. I started working at this diner shortly after aging out of foster care when it was apparent my last family had no interest in adopting me. Something about an eighteen-year-old girl with a pension for leaving more than staying wasn't appealing to them. I picked this establishment to work at first, because they hired me, and second, because it was a few blocks away from our old apartment. Call me crazy but I wanted to be close to this place in case Jacob came back here looking for me. It's the only place he'd remember, so even though being back in this neighborhood gave me all kinds of anxiety, I didn't give myself a choice. I stayed and waited.

"Order up," the chef called.

Adding an orange slice and the accompanying dipping sauces to the plates, I loaded them onto the tray like fallen dominoes stacked partially on top of each other. "Thanks, Chef," I hollered, hoisting it onto my shoulder.

I was so focused on not dropping the tray—something that took more practice than I'd anticipated—that I didn't notice the man until after I distributed the plates. He was the sole occupant of one of our corner booths—something I really hated, because it meant fewer tips—but when I couldn't find the host, for a good scolding, I tucked the tray under my arm and marched over toward the man. The first thing I noticed was the way he was dressed. It was far nicer than anyone who ventured into that neighborhood. It's not like we didn't get our fair share of customers, but we didn't get folks that dressed like him. Ever. Everything, from the pristinely pressed suit jacket to the cufflinks to the immaculate hair, it all screamed money.

If his looks were any indication of how he tips, he could sit wherever he wanted.

I sidled up to the booth. "Welcome in, I'm Kit. Can I get you something to drink?"

The man looked up from his menu and a cheshire grin spread across his face. "Whiskey. On the rocks."

Pen hovering over my notepad, I looked up. "Anything else?"

Teeth on full display, the man's mouth twinkled thanks to the overhead lights bouncing off his bleach white teeth. "Not yet."

I subtly eyed his bare ring finger, and then morphed into Flirty Kit. "Alright, *sir*, if you change your mind, I won't be far away." The smile cemented on my mouth coupled with the sway of my hips would do the trick.

The restaurant was busy that night. I served food to regular customers and took orders from hungry strangers, all the while feeling the man's eyes on me. His gaze was unrelenting like his smirk.

After a while, I retreated to the kitchen under the pretense of handing off another ticket to the chef, but really, I wanted to study the man from somewhere safe. He hadn't ordered food yet, which was weird, and no one had joined him, which I also didn't understand. Why come to a diner for a drink that was better enjoyed at a bar? He shouldn't be here, he didn't fit. Was he someone important? I bet he's rich. What kind of car did he drive? Maybe he had a driver.

He was as focused on me as I was on him, which is why I faltered and nearly dropped a tray when he winked at me. However, when I went to his table, he barely spoke, answering my standard questions with two-to-three word replies. Who did that? Rich people, I guessed.

It wasn't until he left, having enjoyed nothing more than his drink, that I scurried over to his table, hoping for more than a twenty-percent tip but expecting far less. Which was why, when I picked up the receipt and flipped it over, my mouth dropped.

No, that wasn't right. It couldn't be. There were too many bills there.

The well-dressed man who had ordered a single drink had left me a five-hundred dollar tip. In cash. And if that weren't enough, the inky scrawl on the receipt didn't lie. He wrote my name at the top and his name and phone number on the bottom.

Bobby, it read. A pretty informal name for someone who appeared to have some say in the world. I tucked the receipt and cash into my apron pocket and hustled back to the kitchen to retrieve another order. What was I going to do with that money? Do I tell my boss? That was more than I made in a week working at that hole-in-the-wall diner. The receipt had my name on it, though. He'd stared at me all night. It had to be for me. And what's with the name and phone number? He had to be at least ten years older than me, and I didn't get the vibe that he wanted to take me on a date, despite his obvious interest.

I worked the rest of my shift with less enthusiasm and more distraction regarding the receipt. The name and number scrawled in black ink were a clear indication that the next move was mine. I didn't know what kind of game that guy was running to be able to tip a lowly waitress five-hundred dollars, but something made him do it. Something made him choose me, and after a string of foster families that didn't choose me, I wanted to know what he thought was so special.

My shift ended, and I snagged my coat and purse, only to march down the street to the corner pay phone. I loaded the coins into the slot and punched in the neatly printed number.

I didn't know that when he answered, I wouldn't be able to take it back. I didn't know that I would be adding years to my search for Jacob, or that I would have to change my name. That I would cringe every time I heard his voice after that first phone call.

I didn't know I had sold my body to the devil himself for five-hundred dollars.

CHAPTER THIRTY-FOUR
2014—Age 23

I'm standing feet from him, repelled by the snarl he has carved into his menacing lips. My hammering heart is sending blood and adrenaline through me at an alarming rate, but I keep my breathing steady and my hands fisted at my sides.

Neither of us speaks; we just size the other up after three years of transformations—mine, not his. His dark hair is slicked back without one strand out of place, no hint of stubble dots his jaw, and as always, he's wearing a perfectly tailored suit. In appearance alone, he is everything he has always been: a monster behind a smooth exterior.

"Mercedes, a pleasure to see you again." Bobby gestures to the chair across from him. My black Converse Sneakers, complete with black soles and black laces, cover the few feet to the chair that will keep me upright for the remainder of this meeting. Hopefully.

"You look…" Bobby's eyes trail along my body, and I have to look away from his intense perusal. "The same."

I bite my tongue, already feeling like this was a mistake. Maybe I'm not strong enough. Or maybe Bobby is too strong.

His comment is meant to be a dig, and I have to remind myself that I'm different. Physical attributes, soul, will-power, everything is different, even if he chooses not to see them. I'm stronger this time around; I can face him.

I take a calming breath, not caring if he notices, and square my shoulders, back ramrod straight against the wooden chair. "It's Kit."

Bobby doesn't like his women to come with too much confidence. If they do, he makes sure to put them in their place —beneath him. The anger that crosses his face happens in a split second, and then it's gone, but I see it and am empowered by the use of my real name and not the one he gave me.

"Would you like a drink? Looks like you could use one." Bobby waves at the waitress, who can't be more than seventeen, younger than I was when I first met him. At the summons, she walks toward our table with a clear lack of enthusiasm.

Clearing her throat, she flips her ponytail over her shoulder. "Hey, thanks for comin' to Lin's. I'm gonna help you tonight. What do you want?" The waitress realizes what came out of her mouth and she corrects herself. "I mean, what can I get you… sir?

Bobby grins up at her. "Your name."

She starts spinning her rubber bracelets around her thin wrists. "Oh. Right. My name's Stacy."

"Stacy. Beautiful. Just splendid. We'll have two Old Fashioneds." Bobby's words are infused with an acrid tasting sweetness. It makes me want to call him out on it, but I don't.

Before Stacy can reply, I cut in. "I'll take water." There's no way I'm going to share Bobby's favorite drink with him. I don't know what his angle is here, but if there's one thing I've learned, it's that he always has one. I see him for the snake he is, slithering around his unsuspecting prey until he coils himself so tightly they surrender. But I won't be that prey.

He raises his eyebrows and tilts his head to the side in question. "What the lady said."

"Okay, um, cool. Be back soon." Stacy walks toward the bar and pulls out her phone.

"What do you think of her? She reminds me a lot of you." Bobby's sinister grin clues me in.

I ball my fists tightly in my lap, piercing the soft flesh of my palm as I grit my teeth. I knew what came next. He'd offer her a gig with the perks she couldn't refuse. But, it was all a glossy veneer on a very matte reality.

I open my mouth with the intention of chewing him out, to tell him that whatever plans he has with that girl he needs to back off. But then I shut it. He's doing this to get a rise out of me, and I can't let him. I need to keep focused on the information he has on Jacob, and then I'll let Marcel at him.

"Are you going to tell me what you know?" I ask through tight lips.

"Mercedes, relax. This dinner is as much pleasure as it is business. We have some catching up to do." Bobby winks and an acid taste fills my mouth.

I'm irritated that he still gives me a physical response. It isn't pleasurable; it's unsettling. "It's only business, and it's only drinks."

He studies my serious expression and exhales. "Right."

The bartender swings by our table and delivers my water and Bobby's Old Fashioned before bustling back to his place behind the bar. I almost feel like I recognize the bartender. I study him beneath my lashes, and then I focus on my water. Is the bartender one of Bobby's goons? The possibility is enough to make me push my cup farther away from me.

Bobby picks up his drink, and pauses, resting the rim against his bottom lip. "So distrusting, are we?"

I cross my arms. "You know me. Always cautious."

"If anyone has a right to be distrusting here, it's me." He sets his glass on the table harder than we both expected, and the amber liquid sloshes over the sides while the large cube of ice clinks against the glass's walls.

There it is, the evil glint in his eyes behind the facade of his smile. I knew he wouldn't be able to suppress it for long, but I'm oddly unaffected by it. I see Bobby for the creature he is. A swell of courage settles over me, like I've developed an immunity against his particular brand of venom.

Empowered by the backup I know I have inside and outside this restaurant, I shake my head slowly. "What do you want, Bobby?"

The first slip-up I've made since walking in this restaurant and sitting down came out of my mouth in the form of five letters. His name sounds like a vile curse rolling off of my tongue.

He's pleased by my slip and pierces me with a fiery look in his black eyes, a smirk tattooed on his mouth. Adjusting his position so that his forearms rest on the table, he leans in as much as his chair will allow and speaks in a low growl.

"You."

CHAPTER THIRTY-FIVE
2014—Age 23

My skin is crawling off of my bones in disgust. I purse my lips and press my crossed arms closer to my chest, needing their protection. One moment I'm riding on boldness, and the next I feel weak, but that doesn't mean I need to look like it. I glance to my left and scan the restaurant, wondering which men are Marcel's and which are Bobby's. Both are here, no doubt.

His sinister voice draws me back. "Look, Mercedes. I'm a man of no attachment. That's how I've built the successful businesses I have, but I haven't easily forgotten you."

My resolve snaps. "Is that supposed to be a compliment?"

"It should be." Bobby leans back, his arm straight as his palm rests on the table.

I stare over his shoulder when his intense gaze becomes too much. "Why?"

"Why?" Bobby repeats.

"Yes. *Why* haven't you been able to forget me? There are plenty of women out there who would actually like to be with you. Why waste your time on someone who doesn't?" I know my jab will bruise, which is the point. I'm taunting him, and we both know it.

"Oh, I'm not talking about the sex," he scoffs. "You were easily and quickly replaced." Bobby pauses for a reaction I refuse to give. I'm made of stone and determined to make sure my expression is, too.

He leans in again, but this time he lowers his voice so I have to strain to hear him. "You were the one who got away. And *nobody* runs out on me. Nobody steals from me."

I knew it was never about me; it has always been about him. His pride was wounded and he ruined lives to rectify it.

I uncross my arms and match his posturing, bringing myself dangerously close to him. I need my words to carry power. "Well, *I* got away."

I left him before he tossed me out, and that power of choice to leave is something I'll always have. He can't take that from me.

My words hit their mark and he leans back in his chair, crossing his arms while I never take my eyes off him. His expression threatens a violence I never want to experience again, and I'm dying to look away, but I continue to face the evil I know well. I won't give in to the fear, even though it hovers so close.

Bobby looks at the table, running his tongue along his top teeth. "You had it good once. I gave you everything you could want, need, or desire. And you repay me by walking out?" He huffs and grabs his drink brusquely.

"The fact you think I, or anyone else who worked for you, had it *good* is your first mistake." I bite my tongue. I can't get distracted by answering questions that won't matter to a sleeze like him. Explaining working conditions is the last thing he cares about and the last thing I should, too. I sigh and press him further for what I really want. "I want to see him."

"You will." He lifts his glass to his mouth, and I notice a perverse grin behind its rim.

I forget my calm persona and slap the table. "Where is he? Where's Jacob?"

Bobby studies me for a beat, and I can tell he's debating what to share and how much. Without any words, he sets his glass on the table and nods his head toward the far wall of the restaurant. Following his cue, my eyes land on a table in the back corner, tucked against the wall. There are two men sitting at it, and I assume they work for Bobby. When one of them looks up at me, I know I'm right. But when I see the familiar features of the other, I want to be wrong.

My heart softens as my emotions rise. *Jacob,* my heart says and my lips follow suit. "Jacob."

I stare at him, absorbing both the old and new features. My eyes unwillingly fill with tears and I choke on a sob. Everyone else in the restaurant fades away, even Bobby, and it's just us: Jacob and me. Fear doesn't exist, time stands still, and hope breaks in. My quivering lips mouth the only words I've held onto for years, *I'm sorry.*

The dim lights make it hard to see every subtle expression on his face, but I still try. He looks back at me and the hard expression relaxes. His eyes jump from the burly man across from him and back to me. I can practically hear his plea in his watery gaze and stooped posture.

I wipe the wayward tear from my cheek. He's been here the whole time? I didn't see him. I never noticed him. But now I do. Now I see that he is alive, safe, and needs my help. He needs his sister.

Bobby interjects my thoughts. "There. You've seen him. Now, are you ready to make a deal?"

"He works for you?" I ask tightly.

"Yes, he's a recent acquisition."

Jacob turns eighteen in nine days, so the file Monica found with the police report of a runaway was his, it has to be.

I close my eyes tightly and drop my head. I'll love my brother, no matter what, but I need to know. "Does he represent you on Figueroa street?" I ask, instead of blurting out, *is my brother a pimp?*

Bobby doesn't answer right away, calculating his approach as a skillful blackjack player on a night at the casino. "No. He helps elsewhere but is valuable to my operation nonetheless."

I immediately think about what Marcel told Beau and me about the women Bobby was trafficking in and out of the city. There really isn't one aspect of Bobby's business ventures that I want Jacob a part of. All of it is tainted with stolen power and manipulated control.

If it wasn't for the warning look in Jacob's eyes, I would rush toward him, but I can't when Bobby's ulterior motives are stealing all of the air in the small restaurant.

My head snaps in his direction. "What do you want?"

He lifts his glass to take a sip. "Mercedes, you're a smart girl. You already know." I watch his Adam's apple bob as he swallows, feeling the burn of the alcohol within my own throat. "It's quite simple. I want my money back."

I grind my teeth. "I never took your money."

He swirls the ice cube around in circles. "I have witnesses."

"They're lying. I never took any money from you!" The emotion simmering under the surface sends my voice up another octave.

Bobby's fist hits the table and catches the attention of everyone. He calms himself, refusing to look at the questioning eyes. "You fucking took *thousands* from me, and I need it."

My mouth drops open and I rest my hands on my thighs. I peek at Jacob, who is watching our conversation, and thankfully, he can't hear it. My protruding eyes try to absolve his false assumptions. "I swear to you. I never took any money."

"I believed you when you told me that the first time. But then you ran. You left like the guilty bitch you are."

I shake my head, muscles vibrating beneath my skin. "No. I didn't plan on leaving, but when I had the chance, you better fucking believe I left. You were…" I search for the worst word, all of them fitting. "Horrible." Crossing my legs, I jut out my chin in defiance.

He makes a *tsking* noise then surveys the restaurant to capture Stacy's attention. "Receipt. Now. Please."

I watch her slowly punch in Bobby's order, pulling two receipts after it prints and walking back to our table.

"Here." Stacy places both receipts in front of Bobby and pulls a pen from her apron before walking away again.

Bobby separates the receipts then reaches inside his suit jacket pocket and pulls out a wad of cash. He starts counting one-hundred dollar bills until he reaches five-hundred and sets it by one receipt. I watch every move he makes as he picks up the pen and scrawls what I know is his number on the bottom of the receipt.

He leers up at me, pushing the cash and one receipt aside before picking up the second. He writes slowly, holding the pen loosely as though he hasn't a care in the world.

He's calculated as he pushes it across the table to me. "With interest."

I stare into his eyes before dropping them to pick up the receipt and read what I don't want to know.

$10,000.

His voice is like an assault on me. "You know, Mercedes. We have more in common than you think."

I set the receipt down and glare at him. "How do you suppose that?"

"We both seize the opportunities in front of us."

My eyes travel back to the demanding number written on the receipt he gave me. It's funny how the five-hundred dollar investment I received at eighteen is now costing me twenty times the amount on interest alone. Never make a deal with a snake.

My shoulders slump. "I need to think."

"I thought you might say that," Bobby says before continuing. "You have forty-eight hours. After that, Jacob will still be under my employ, and I'll have to think of another way to get my money back from you. I'm always looking for new recruits, as you know. Think of it this way..." He looks from me to Stacy and winks at her. "It could be a family business."

Bobby gives a slight wave of his finger, and Jacob stands with the assistance of the guard, a firm hand gripping his elbow as he is led through the swinging kitchen door and out of my sight. I want to yell for them to stop but the words are locked in my throat and bound by the weight of securing ten-thousand dollars. I bite my tongue hard enough to taste blood.

My heart walked out of the room, and now I feel helpless wondering how I'm going to get out of this unscathed. Maybe I won't. Could it be I'm not supposed to? I don't have the money that Bobby wants and without resorting to dirty deals, I'd have no way of getting it within his timeframe. Yet, Jacob's life is on the line, which means our future is, too. I would endure anything if I knew that he was safe minus the deals that promise to pay handsomely and end up costing more in the long run. But did Bobby give me any other choice?

"If you don't want to be with customers, I could use someone with your background to train the girls," he says, standing. "There are more now."

I wince and drop my shoulders. *More women?* Instead of anger wracking my body, it's sadness that overtakes me.

"You know how to reach me," Bobby says, tapping the table. "It wasn't all bad, Mercedes. Remember that when you're thinking things over." He walks toward the swinging kitchen door and disappears through it, leaving me at a table with tainted water and a bill for the mistakes I made when I was eighteen.

This decision weighs as much as the pain in my heart. It feels impossible to go back when I've already gone forward. Yet, the steps I've taken can only take me so far without Jacob by my side. I'd always be looking back if that was where he'd be. I have to find a way to get Bobby his money and keep Jacob safe. There has to be a way even if I can't see it now.

The temperature in my body rises as heat courses up and down my arms, spine, and neck, before settling in my cheeks. I have to find a way for Jacob and for the women that Bobby is exploiting. There isn't a scenario that I'd go back and work for him, but there might be a situation that saves the helpless and spears the oppressor. I just haven't thought of it yet.

I stand abruptly, my chair scraping the floor as a surge of fire lights my fuse and propels me forward. I need to see my brother, even if it's only a glimpse. Pausing mid-step, I turn back around, marching to the table and snatching the receipt meant for Stacy with Bobby's name and number on it but leaving the cash. Rearing back, I jog in the direction Jacob left knowing that it's the same door Bobby left out of too. It's a risk I have to take.

I push open the swinging kitchen doors in hot pursuit as I'm being carried by the fast pace of my feet that won't stop for anything or anyone. Not for Marcel's guards who are on my heels, the kitchen staff that yell for me to leave, or the warning bells clanging in my head.

The kitchen's bright fluorescents are blinding compared to the dim lights in the restaurant, but I keep moving. I need to tell Jacob that I will do anything for us to be a family again. I will pay Bobby whatever sum he wants, fight to see him brought to justice, and protect Jacob regardless of the cost.

An ear splitting sound explodes on the other side of the well-worn back door with rust in certain spots and dents in others. I push hard, launching my body into the dank alleyway behind the restaurant. The putrid smell of garbage and piss hits me without warning and the faint but demanding voices from the kitchen are now grabbing my arms and pulling me against the brick wall, shielding me for reasons I don't understand yet.

I'm not prepared for what I see.

A scream escapes me before I register what's happening. "No!"

My vocal cords vibrate, stretching and straining with the force of the word as it echoes off of the surrounding buildings. The scream is all I hear as restraining bodies prevent my escape. The only color that fills my vision is red. On the pavement, on someone's hands, on the body, and my broken heart.

Maybe I wore black for different reasons tonight.

CHAPTER THIRTY-SIX
2014—Age 23

My screams are shrill and piercing as they cut through the still night air. "What happened?"

I break free from the arms restraining me and rush toward the growing puddle of blood on the cement that will wash away, unlike the scar that will forever be. Kneeling, I hear the sound of tires screeching in the distance as they reverberate off of the walls in the narrow alleyway, but my eyes never leave Beau. "W-What can I do?" I ask Marcel with a stammer.

I saw the blood before I saw Beau. There is so much of it that panic grips my throat, making it hard to speak or breath. Everything happened so fast. One minute, I was barreling outside to see Jacob, and the next, I'm watching Marcel press his hands over Beau's side attempting to stop the flow of red that won't relent. My screams are stuck between the desire to help and the terror telling me to run.

Bile rises with my fear, but I shake my head in defiance and swallow it back. "What can I do?" I ask again.

Marcel doesn't look up at me. "Keep him calm." He's focused on keeping the blood inside of Beau and barking out orders in between. "Jimmy, call an ambulance. Now. Saul, get some towels from the restaurant. Everyone else, get out of here."

I gently run my shaking hand over the top of Beau's head, letting it settle on the smooth, paling skin of his cheek. "Beau," I whisper. "This is all my fault." Sobs wrack my body and I press the back of my hand to my mouth. He was whole and perfect ten minutes ago. How could this happen? Why did it happen?

I feel my way around his body, afraid of what I'll find but needing to inspect him for more wounds. I'm only gathering more blood on my hands in the process, the sticky texture clinging to me with every inch they travel.

Part of my heart drove off in the SUV, but the other part is laying on the ground writhing in pain.

One of the burly men who held me back is on the phone rattling off instructions to the emergency dispatcher. When he flips his cell phone shut, he looks to Marcel for his next orders. "Boss?"

"Get out of here. Hurry, go," Marcel commands in his booming voice. I look up to see them running toward the end of the alley and disappearing around the curve of the building. Marcel grunts. "Dammit. We need that ambulance."

The smell of Beau's blood on my hands, arms, and clothes is causing my head to swim, but I shake it and force calming breaths through my mouth.

We need help.

Beau is quiet, too quiet. His only movements now are sluggish and distant. Worry perches on my shoulders. "No, no, no. Beau, stay with me."

"We're gonna get you help," Marcel adds. Beau is no longer squirming in pain, instead, he's taking shuddering breaths and working for every one of them. A hazy shock fills my vision, the whites of his eyes becoming more visible than the brown I'm used to seeing. Guilt rises up in me as I watch his mouth go slack.

It's all my fault. I did this to him. This is happening because of my demons, not Beau's. I ruined his life by asking him to help with mine, and I can't reverse this. We can't go back and do things differently.

"Beau, come on, look at me," I whisper, tears streaming down my face. I look at my bloody hands hovering over the horror scene that is Beau's body. I reach and grab for one of his limp hands, nestling it in mine while squeezing tighter and willing him to respond, but he doesn't. Every emergency signal I have is blaring and fear is rippling through me and ready to come out of my throat. "He was shot." I close my eyes against the queasy feeling in my stomach. "Someone shot him."

Marcel looks up at me and then to Beau. He nods.

I widen my eyes, my own skin clammy with sweat. "Wh-Who did this? Who shot him?"

Marcel clamps his jaw and doesn't answer.

I look at Beau's ashen face again. His eyes are slits, revealing the barest strips of white. "Don't you dare close your eyes," I demand, slapping his cheeks. "Beau, look at me!"

His eyes fly open, rolling around madly as he follows the sound of my ravaged voice. "Keep looking at me." I cradle his face between my hands as I lean over him. "Don't look away."

He finds my face with his overcast eyes and nods, choking on spurts of air as he grips Marcel's arm. Sweat drips from his forehead, making me dizzy with worry. I shouldn't have let Beau help me. From the very start, I had reservations because this is what it got him, how I sensed things would turn out: a bullet wound.

"I'm so sorry, Beau." My tears charge down my cheeks in a furious storm, highlighting the torment that is swelling inside of me. "I-I d-didn't…I'm sorry."

Marcel perks up. "Hear that? Ambulance is coming."

I strain to hear the sound of hope, and there on the edge of my senses, is the distant wail of sirens coming to our rescue. It's followed shortly by red, rotating lights that bounce off of the dark alleyway and throw us into even more chaos. "They're here, Beau. I'm here. Help is here. Don't close your eyes." I release my hands from his face, leaving two red handprints.

"I-I…" Beau's voice is hoarse and weak, but that doesn't stop him from trying to speak so he mouths the rest. "I lo–" He doesn't finish, but I know what he's trying to say.

"Sh-sh-shhh." I bring my forehead to his as tears blur my vision. "I love you, too."

The sirens stop but the flashing lights continue to flood the area with silent urgency. Doors open and slam, followed by heavy footfalls.

"Ma'am. We're going to need you to move aside."

I peer up through my haze and scoot toward Beau's head while they assess the wounds in practiced synchronicity. My legs are numb, but I don't care, I ignore their screams for relief like I ignore the torn heart inside my chest. A gurney rolls up and another medic is asking Marcel questions that my ears hear but my brain doesn't compute.

"Yeah, gunshot. The shooter's gone," Marcel replies, moving aside.

Blood sputters and spurts with Beau's every breath as the medics apply gauze to the wound in place of kitchen towels. I push myself to stand and trip backward on unsteady legs. They've forgotten how to hold me up and numbness pierces its way through my whole body. Red leaks from my own heart, trickling onto the pavement where it merges with Beau's. I didn't know that learning to love again meant accepting the risk that comes with it.

I glance over at Marcel, and the permanent crease between his brows has deepened and the lines on his forehead have multiplied. I know what it means that he's still here. He didn't book it like he told his guys to; he stayed.

I cover my mouth as I watch the medics work and immediately inhale the scent of Beau's gunshot wound, reflexively gagging at the amount of blood coating this night.

I bite the inside of my cheek and wring my hands together hearing him grunt in pain as they gently slide him onto a stiff board, after which the medics secure his head and lift him onto the gurney. Legs reliable once again, I move in sync with the gurney as he's whisked into the back of the ambulance.

I clamber in and immediately reach for Beau's hand, squeezing it once and holding my breath until he squeezes mine back. I exhale when he does and close my eyes, gasping for each breath between my cries. Life is so fragile. I was hugging the love of my life an hour ago, making promises and hoping for all that love had to offer me. Now, that love is flat on his back with a bullet lodged in his side as a crimson river pours from his body.

I raise Beau's hand to my lips and give his fingers a lingering kiss, wondering, praying, begging that these aren't the last moments we have together.

My future is hanging by a thread, and my prayers just got louder.

CHAPTER THIRTY-SEVEN
2014—Age 23

The ambulance finally pulls into the unloading dock at the emergency room, at which point I'm shunted off to the side. "Ma'am, you'll need to check in at the nurses' station. We need to take him back so the team can assess the wound." The medic steps off the rig and holds his hand out for me to follow. I look at Beau and then the extended hand, begrudgingly agreeing with my swift action to reach for it. I promised him repeatedly on the drive here that I wouldn't leave him and I'm breaking it almost as fast.

Anguish overtakes me as I step down from the rig without a word. They're all gone. Every single one of them. All of my words have been replaced with worry and worry doesn't speak, it feels. Meanwhile, I follow the medics every maneuver, watching silently as they lower the gurney and wheel Beau through the sliding glass doors that separate the still night from the chaotic emergency room. I stay outside, however, allowing the night to wrap itself around me as I wait to wake up from this nightmare. It doesn't comfort, it scolds, and I shiver in response. I want Dina to startle me awake by dropping something or Beau to knock on my front door again. Anything to get me out of my memories.

My body shakes with suppressed sobs that are coming out of hiding. I fight to keep them in, but they push and pull with a strength that overcomes me and soon I'm hunched over, hands on my knees, breathing fast while my tears fall faster.

I try to tell myself that Beau is in the hands of professionals, and there is nothing else I can do. He's safe, for now, and I am, too. But none of my assurances ease the hollow pit in my stomach or erase the images of Beau's limp body from my mind.

I cover my mouth with the next gasp and catch sight of something red on my palm. Slowly, I bring my hands together, studying first the fronts and then the backs. And that's when the panic lets loose. Blood. Beau's blood. All over him and all over me. My chest rises and falls in rapid succession. Panic becomes a second skin as chills and adrenaline blend.

Beau almost died. He still might die. I accepted his help, and that's why he was there tonight. He wouldn't have gotten hurt if I hadn't been meeting with Bobby, if I wasn't searching for Jacob, if I didn't lose my brother in the system, if our mother didn't die, if I could have held my family together. But I didn't. I failed. And now I'm helpless to change the outcome. There are no rewind, erase, pause, or redo buttons. Only the startling realization that this movie is stuck in play.

My hands are shaking but I don't draw them in. They are strangers that need to be kept far away. Strangers that are covered in dried blood and guilt. They were supposed to hold it all together, but now I see nothing but the death of multiple families on my hands.

Tears drop one after another onto my stained hands, loosening the crust and liquifying it once again. I'm in a bind that cannot be undone. Just like in my nightmare when I was bound to the chair of my own making, I can't get out of this by myself.

As I stand alone on the sidewalk, the tears take over. My sobs grow in volume with every heave, every heart pang, and every realization. Streaks become visible on my hands when my tears wash cleansing trails down them. I found love and lost it. Jacob and Beau slipped through my fingers because I didn't have a tight enough hold on them. If only I had hung on tighter.

I don't wipe my eyes. I can't. His blood, the blood I spilled, will taint everything I touch. I sink onto the edge of the curb, sickened by my helplessness.

"Why?" I say quietly, testing my voice. "Why Beau?"

Why Jacob?

Why me?

I wrestle my leather jacket off in a rush, fighting the sleeve that won't release my arm. "Get off me!" I scream, arching my back in a frenzy to escape it. The sleeves are turned inside out when I free myself from its clutches, but I don't care. It can't bring Jacob back or heal Beau. It can't fix the gaping wound in my core.

Frantically, I scrub my hands with it, creating burns from the friction. I'm breathing loudly and the tears in my eyes blur my vision, but I don't stop. I *need* to get the blood off of my hands. I have to before it kills me, too.

In the midst of my hysteria, flakes of dried blood smear across my skin, staining them an abhorrent shade of red that I'll never forget. They are as raw and aching as the heart in my chest.

"I can't do this," I scream, bunching up and tossing my jacket to the ground in front of me. Dropping my head, I fall apart. I lack the power to do anything else, because I'm broken, and that's what broken people do when their efforts don't work—they break.

I'll never forgive myself if Beau dies. I didn't mean to fall in love with him, but I did. And for a few, brief days, it was pure and untouched by my soiled past. It didn't last long before the metaphorical winds rustled the ease, the rain soaked my confidence, and the hail battered my heart. My past was all coming back to consume me in a downpour of bullets and tears. The missing answers, the questions, and all of the broken pieces are on full display.

I still don't have Jacob, and now I don't have Beau.

I'm living my greatest fear, except now I'm losing two people I love for the price of one. The pulse in my hands beats under the scratches and sensitive skin, reminding me that I'm a flawed human. I'm not a hero, like Beau. I don't possess those skills, only the ones to fuck everything up. I've created more enemies in the last twenty-four hours or resurrected the old ones. Either way, I'm in too deep now with bits of blood curving around my nail beds and hiding out between my fingers, but I leave them there. I don't have the energy to deal. All of the fight has fled my body, and I'm glad to be sitting or else I would topple over in exhaustion that I wouldn't be able to come back from.

Another ambulance pulls in as my tears still trickle down my cheeks. Despite the flashing lights and resonant sirens echoing off of the carport, I'm so still, like a statue, or someone who is dead but still breathing. It dawns on me that I'm in the way, so I stand on shaky legs and retreat toward the tall windows near the entrance.

The back doors fly open and another gurney is pulled carefully from the back and wheeled through the automatic glass doors with urgency. I look on, watching the scene unfold like I had done when they took Beau. The turmoil of the last hour flashes across my mind, and I feel like I could be sick.

My jacket is still lying on the road, but I leave it and rush inside to find a bathroom. I press a hand to my mouth, wishing my stomach were as numb as the rest of me, but it isn't and I need a bathroom. Now. I'm going to be sick. I can't stop it.

I search frantically, casting glances up and down foreign hallways, unsure of how long I'll be able to hold off. There is too much saliva in my mouth and my attempts at swallowing it are waning. I don't need a bathroom; I'll take a trash can.

There's a lobby beside the nurses' station, and I spy a trash can against the wall. I rush forward, barely making it before every horror I've been suppressing spews out of me. All of the knots in my stomach are being untied, releasing agony along with it. Bracing the waist-high can's sides, I sink further into it with equal parts embarrassment and reflexive force. My head swims with light and color that fades with every heave. I lack control to do anything else but rely on the trash can to hold me together.

A hand on my back startles me, and wiping my mouth on the sleeve of my shirt, I turn. A woman with eyes so blue I can see my own reflection watches me with concern. "Oh, I'm sorry, I didn't mean to scare you. Are you okay? Do you need anything? Water? A towel?" With her arms extended, she moves to steady me at my elbows. I didn't even realize I was swaying.

"I…uh…I'm…" I jab my thumb behind me but still lack the words to articulate what I need.

"Here, let me help you. Come and sit. I'll fetch you some water." She backs me gingerly into a chair and I sink back, my limbs sighing in relief. I watch the woman in blue scrubs rush to the water fountain, pull out a paper cup and fill it, her light brown ponytail swishing as she moves.

She's back before I can blink. "Thank you," I say, accepting the cup with a jittery hand.

"No problem," she says, sinking down in front of me as I drink deeply from the cup. "I'm Angela."

I lower the cup. "Kit."

"You've been through the ringer tonight." It's a statement, not a question.

"How can you tell?"

Her blue eyes roam my hands, arms, and neck, and then return to my face. I drop my gaze. "Oh."

"Your friend will be alright. The bullet didn't touch any major organs. He'll be sore and tired after losing so much blood, but he'll live," she says with a smile.

I release an audible sigh and nod my head, eyes welling with more tears. Thankfully, this time it's in relief instead of despair. I don't know how she knows this about Beau, but when I see her name badge and the boxy uniform that matches her eyes I realize why.

Angela rubs her hand over my arm, disregarding the fact someone else's blood coats my skin. "I'm here, Kit. And I won't leave you." She stands to sit on the chair beside me.

I lean into her as the tears fall and Angela holds me, both arms gripping my shoulders. "I shouldn't have fallen in love. It almost killed him, and it's killing me," I stutter, admitting more to this stranger than I have to myself.

But she doesn't feel like a stranger anymore; Angela is letting me fall apart again, but this time, in the safety of her arms. "Love is greater than our fears," she says, whispering each word slowly in my ear as she continues to draw me closer.

My body stills in her arms as I ingest her words. I sit straighter in my seat, brows pulled together as I stare at her. "You can't love someone if they're dead. And the guilt of being the one who killed them…" I shake my head and swallow. "What if this never ends? If Beau's life is always threatened because of me? I'd be looking over my shoulder wondering when the love of my life would be taken. I can't do that. I can't do that *again*."

Rubbing my shoulder, Angela doesn't pull back. Instead, she leans closer, catching my gaze.

"Love doesn't bend to fear. It's the other way around."

CHAPTER THIRTY-EIGHT
2014—Age 23

I wake to a rhythmic squeezing tightening around my hand. Dragging my head from the pillow of my arms, I blink rapidly as my eyes adjust to their surroundings. I groggily register that my hand is in Beau's and follow the natural progression up his arm, until my gaze finally lands on his face. He's watching me with a half-smile, alert. Awake. Alive.

"Hi," I say in a hoarse morning voice. "How are you feeling?"

"Never better."

I squeeze his hand back. "Liar"

He shrugs one shoulder. "It's true."

I shake my head, yawning deeply. "Beau, you were shot last night, had emergency surgery to remove the bullet, and now have stitches in your side. I don't believe you."

"I got to wake up to you."

I fight my natural response to smile, because there is no smiling in the pit of destruction I dug for myself. I reach my other hand up to rub the sleep from my eyes.

"What the…" Beau's eyes grow wide.

"Huh? What?"

"Your hand." He turns my hand over to inspect the consequences of my self-destruction. "Your hands…what happened? Did someone hurt you?"

I pull my hand from his and cradle them between my thighs. "No, no. Nothing like that. It was, uh…it was the, um, blood, on my hands. It was hard to get off." My words are quiet as I deal with the embarrassment they bring. The shame of having hurt my best friend, and while I may not have put the bullet there, I taunted the man who did.

"Kit…"

I exhale. Something broke in me last night and somewhere in the middle of finding out Beau would live and Angela holding me together, I found peace. I can still feel it this morning. It isn't the kind that wipes everything away. It's the kind that washes the blood off your hands and fetches your favorite leather jacket from the street, like Angela did.

Beau offers me his hand again, inviting me to take it, to lay my burdens down, even though he's the one sitting in a hospital bed.

So, I do. I take his hand and unload every thought, feeling, and belief I have been navigating since he was pushed through those sliding doors. He listens attentively, nodding and wincing when I relay the gritty truth.

I stand, unable to sit any longer. "All of this escalated so quickly." Swaying, Beau reaches out to help me balance.

"Hey, look at me."

I meet his eyes.

He isn't angry that he's here or hopeless like I feel. He's resolute. "No matter what comes next, I'm not going anywhere."

His confession lights the fuse of my emotion and tears crest like waves in an ocean. I wipe at them and lean forward, kissing him soundly. I'm thanking him for his persistence to be by my side, even when I've been a pain in his…literally.

The hospital room door opens and instead of the nurse, I see Marcel. He's balancing a coffee cup while a woman, who isn't dressed in scrubs, follows behind him. I straighten, giving both Beau and myself a chance to cool off.

I don't need an introduction to know who she is; the physical similarities speak for themselves. The woman looks like Beau, or rather, he looks like her, and I can't help comparing every detail. Dark hair frames her face, stopping below her chin, and while she isn't anywhere close to Beau of Marcel's height, she isn't short either.

Beau's swallow is audible. "Mama."

She pushes past Marcel and rushes to place a kiss on Beau's cheek. "Oh, baby, you're awake. How are you feeling? Do you need another pillow? Need any water? You're probably thirsty, let me call the nurse."

"Mama, hold up, I'm fine, really." Beau looks between me and his Mama before realizing we've never met. "Oh, right. Mama, this is Kit. Kit, this is Ma—" Beau catches himself. "Sherry."

"Kit. I've heard plenty about you, honey," Sherry says with a wink and a smile. She extends her hand. "I hate that I'm meetin' you at a time like this, but I'm still glad to get the chance."

I smile. "It's nice to meet you, too."

"Marcel," Beau says with a nod of greeting.

I don't miss the glare that Sherry shoots over her shoulder at Marcel. Her lips are pursed, body stiff as she determines whether he's worth a glance. Do they know that Marcel saved Beau's life? His hands had more blood on them than mine did.

"Don't mind me. I got breakfast while you two slept. I didn't bring you anything, but I can ask the nurse to order something if you're hungry." Marcel looks to Beau as if he is offering more than breakfast.

Beau's face softens. "Yeah, I could eat."

Marcel looks at Sherry, who immediately darts her eyes toward the opposite wall. He nods and slips out the door without another word or another look in her direction.

There's an audible sigh that passes her lips when the door clicks shut. "Baby, what happened last night? What in heaven's name were you all thinking?" Sherry asks, squeezing Beau's hand between both of hers. "The nurse told me you had been shot, but how'd that happen? Are you and Marcel involved in somethin' together? I can't believe that man, tying you and Kit up in all of his dirty business. What was he thinking?"

Beau settles a hand on her shoulder. "Mama. It's cool. We called him, not the other way around, I promise."

Her brows furrow. "Why would you call him? If you were in trouble, I woulda helped. We could've gone to the police first instead of them lookin' down their noses at all of this now."

Beau looks at me briefly. "I'll explain everything when I can, but know that Marcel was helping us and there was nothin' illegal goin' on, alright?"

The pained expression on her face wanes. "I know you're a man now and can make your own decisions, but I'm still your Mama. And there isn't a chance I'll let you go down the same road as your father. You're too good, sweetheart." Sherry reaches out to cup Beau's cheek.

He nods and leans into her palm. "I should've told you I was going to call him, but Mama you're right about something," he pauses and stares at her without blinking, "I'm a grown man now and I want Marcel back in my life. I understand if you don't want him to be in yours, but I'm ready to try."

Her wrinkled brows relax and she nods. Dropping her hand from his cheek, she points it at his chest. "But you will not be working for him, ya hear?"

Beau's mouth tips into a smile. "I won't. I think Marcel is ready to be done."

Sherry doesn't gasp in surprise, but she does purse her lips. "I believe you, baby, I do." She leans down and presses a kiss to his cheek.

"Thanks, Mama."

"Now, are you going to tell me how you got shot or what?" she says.

Beau rubs a hand along the stubble dotting his jaw. I, too, want to know, and step closer to the edge of the bed. There are so many gaps. He was supposed to stay in the car with Marcel.

Before he can speak, I ask, "Why were you back there? That wasn't the plan."

He exhales. "Marcel's guy texted that they may need more backup in the alley. One of the kitchen staff who was out back smokin' on his break said a guy in a suit entered through the back earlier. We figured it was Bobby and he'd leave that way, too."

I nod and reach for Beau's hand, needing his closeness. "Keep going."

He smiles and continues. "We were posted up outside at the back door, thinking we'd catch Bobby if he planned to make a quick escape. It happened so fast," he cringes, reliving the moment. "An SUV pulled up at the same moment a guy came out with a kid," Beau looks at me, "with Jacob. They came out the back door, gettin' in the vehicle before they even noticed we were there."

Gingerly, Beau massages the back of his neck, rolls his shoulders, and then drops his hand back into his lap. "Marcel and I stood in the shadows, pressed up against the building until

Bobby came out and then…" Beau's voice falls off. "Then, he saw us and I knew from the sneer in his expression that he recognized me. He jumped into the SUV, and we thought we were safe, until someone rolled down a window and stuck a gun out, aiming it between both of us and hitting me."

"Lord, have mercy," Sherry says, clutching a hand to her chest as if to hold the shock in her body. "This is exactly what I didn't want you gettin' mixed up in, baby." Her voice grows louder with every word. She's worried not only because of Beau's wound, but because of what a gunshot in a black man's side means. Especially when a white man put it there.

Beau shakes his head, regarding his hands in defeated regret. I want to wrap him in my arms and tell him that it isn't true. Beau did nothing wrong. He was looking out for me, and it was my fault. I grit my teeth and squeeze his hand harder. He tightens his hold on me, reminding me that at least we have this moment. One step is all we can take.

Sherry grabs his face and kisses his forehead. "Oh, sugar."

I clear my throat when Sherry stands to her full height. "Did you see the shooter?"

Beau frowns. "No. I didn't see. Did Marcel?"

Sherry shakes her head to confirm he didn't. "He told the cops earlier that he didn't see. The restaurant didn't have any security cameras, either."

"Was it Bobby?" I ask, the seething undertones of my question rising to the surface.

He shrugs. "Coulda been."

I sigh heavily. "I'm so sorry, Beau. If it wasn't for me, you wouldn't be in this mess right now. You wouldn't be here," I say, waving a hand over his bandaged body.

"Kit. No, it isn't your fault. We had no idea they'd pull a gun," Beau says. He's trying to be reassuring, but my brain refuses to accept it.

"Yeah, but I dragged you into all of this."

Sherry reaches across the bed to gather my hands. "Honey, please believe this isn't your fault. My Beau wouldn't have let you face whatever you were facing without making sure you were taken care of. I know that in my bones."

I stare at our joined hands. Her touch is soft against my tender hands and it takes everything in me not to break down again like I've made a job of doing.

Sensing this, Sherry scurries around the bed. "Oh, baby, come here." I let my tears fall as I'm wrapped up tightly in her arms. Her motherly touch is undoing me and healing me in every place my heart has cried out for. The only one blaming me for the events of last night is me.

The door to this small, sterile room opens once again and Marcel walks in, reading the temperature of the room before asking, "What'd I miss?"

I give a small laugh and look back at Sherry. "Nothing much."

I had forgotten what it felt like to be surrounded by a family. Despite the tentative glances between Beau's parents built over years of distance, I can feel the love as if it's another person in the room. Maybe it is. Either way, I want everything this is.

I watch Sherry shower her son's face with kisses he only half-enjoys and feel Marcel's hand on my shoulder, encouraging me more through his actions than his words. The torn areas of my heart are being knit back together by the tangible presence of love.

The only thing missing is Jacob.

CHAPTER THIRTY-NINE
2014—Age 23

The smell of blood permeates my clothing. Add the lingering scent of puking in a trash can and sleeping in a hospital bed again, and it's too much for my senses to take. I peel my t-shirt off and shimmy out of my jeans, tossing both into the hamper in my room. I reach for my robe hanging on the back of my desk chair, plunging my arms through the sleeves, and curling up in it.

The cops came by later this morning, questioning Beau and me for what felt like hours. We gave them every detail we knew including the few pieces we had on Bobby despite the lack of evidence. I thought about keeping Jacob out of it, not knowing how deep he was and how much trouble he'd be in, but I couldn't. If there was a chance the cops could find him, I wanted it.

I look between my door and the bed, debating whether I should sleep or shower. In the end, I fall belly first onto my bed, relishing the feel of the plush comforter beneath my body. I'm exhausted after spending another night in the hospital with Beau and his family. Sherry, Marcel, and I have all been taking turns sitting with him, and when I couldn't keep my eyes open any longer, Sherry offered to drop me off at my house to rest.

If only my exhaustion diminished my awareness of the ticking clock counting down at a speed I'm not ready for. Bobby's forty-eight-hour window is closing with every minute I waste, meaning I don't have time to rest my face on this pillow. I need to figure out my next plan more than I need to take my next breath. If only I knew where Jacob is and how I could reach out to him, but I don't. I have no clue.

I relax deeper into the bed, yet my mind races like it doesn't need a break. What *could* happen and what *will* happen if I don't have the money or an answer for Bobby?

My eyes drop shut, but I tell myself they are only resting. I can still open them if I want to. The shower is simultaneously calling my name, but I ignore it. I'll open my eyes soon.

Beau will be in the hospital for a few more days, and there's not much he can do from a hospital bed anyway. I'd like to think Marcel would help, but I'm not sure I can ask him considering how everything turned out the first time. But I do need help coming up with a way to get Bobby out of our lives. For good.

My eyelids are weights sinking to the bottom of the ocean. It's dark and I can no longer see the light from the surface. My mind goes quiet, and this is all I need to let go and let sleep take me.

THE DARKNESS LIFTS slowly, and I try to move my head to the side, but the kink in my neck puts a stop to that. Disoriented and barely able to remember where I am, I press my fingers to the sore muscles in my arms, neck, and stomach.

What time is it?

Did I move at all?

I push myself into a seated position and lean against the adjoining wall. My bedside clock says: 5:08 p.m. Seven hours. I slept for seven hours? I didn't have time to sleep for seven hours. There are problems to solve and people to save, sleeping for this long wasn't part of the plan.

I blink a few times, adjusting to the fading light filtering through my window. When I look down, I wrinkle my nose. I should've showered.

Scooting to the edge of the bed, I let my feet hit the floor and head for the bathroom. Once the water is hot and the room full of steam, I step into the pounding stream to erase the remnants of last night's horror. As soon as the water hits my hands, however, I suck in air and snatch them out of harm's way. I'd forgotten about the burns. Unfortunately, they haven't forgotten about me, yet I have to get clean, so carefully and with gritted teeth, I use them to wash my hair and body.

When I've finished, I wrap a towel around myself and return to my room to dress. As I brush out my hair, I look at my phone and see a text from Beau.

Beau: Miss you. Love you.

I smile instead of cry, a marked improvement since waking up from my much needed sleep. I shoot a quick response back, noting my mirror feelings, and move on to the next notification. Monica's name catches my eye, and I click her message.

Monica: Kit, I have some news. Call me ASAP.

My stomach drops. There's also a missed call, so I look at the time stamp and notice she tried calling three hours ago. My pulse races as fast as my fingers locate her call back number. What does Monica need? Jacob is with Bobby. Does she know this? I haven't updated her, but it's not like there's been much time between meeting Bobby, caring for Beau, and scheming for ways to get ten thousand dollars.

My breaths are shallow and fast as I hear Monica pick up on the other end.

"Hello, Kit?"

"Hi, yeah, it's me."

"Thank God. I was about to try your phone again."

My heart beats wildly. "Sorry for not answering. It's been crazy. What's going on?"

"I have some news on Jacob."

My hands start to sweat. What can she tell me that I don't already know? "What is it?"

"He got picked up early this morning by a patrol car, and they ran his name and found out he was a runaway." Monica's voice falls quiet. "Kit, I have to tell you that he was caught with a lot of drugs in his vehicle."

This new information causes me to sit back on my bed with an ungraceful thud. "Wait, he was caught?" My astonishment is clear, but not because of the drugs. "Where is he?"

Monica sighs loud enough for me to hear through the phone. "He's in jail right now. He, or anyone else, hasn't tried posting bail yet, according to the officer who called the L.A. Family Services to let them know Jacob was picked up. I'm so glad I reached out to other agencies to let me know if they heard anything about him. It's kind of a miracle I know this soon."

My mind is running circles considering what all of this means. Jacob is in jail. He isn't with Bobby. He's *safe*. Mostly.

"Where's he at? What jail did they take him to?" I ask Monica.

She rattles off an address as I write it frantically on a slip of paper. My hands aren't shaking as much as I'd expected, but I'm anxious to go see my brother. I need to get to him before Bobby does.

"I have some time tomorrow. Do you want me to go with you?" Monica asks.

"Yes, please, I could use a ride if you're able to pick me up?"

"I'll come get you around nine. I think visiting hours start then."

Tears prick the back of my eyes when I consider how many times she has done this for other kids over the years and how many times she's been there for me. I shove the slip of paper in my purse in case. "Monica…"

"Yeah?"

"Thank you. I can't tell you how much it means that you're helping me."

She's quiet for a moment, but when she does speak, her voice is thick with emotion. "It never gets easier doing this work, but these small miracles keep me going. I'm proud of you, and I'm so glad you'll have a chance to see Jacob again."

Regardless of the years that sat between us, she is exactly the woman I remember. The one who handed me her business card, but she was actually giving me a piece of her heart.

CHAPTER FORTY
August 2014—Age 23

I'm so nervous I could puke. Sitting at a small table with only a couple of chairs, I wait for the guard to bring my brother in. I don't know how to start this conversation, and I have no clue how it will end, two things that make me wonder what will actually come out of my mouth when it's time.

Monica had dropped me off at the front entrance with instructions to text her when I finished, but even after enduring the process of getting to this room, I still doubt that this is actually happening.

Fidgeting with my hands, I try not to ignore the voice that is whispering my deepest fears. Jacob might take one look at me and say he doesn't want to talk. Maybe he won't even make it as far as coming to our visitation hour. Is he angry at me for not keeping my promise? For letting the system separate us?

I've carried this shame for ten years. Ten years of beating myself up for every mistake. Ten years of searching and never finding. Healing isn't linear, my therapist told me once. And as much as I've worked these feelings out, they have never forgotten my body's address.

What if he does come?

If he comes, I'll have a shot at an apology, and that's all I can hope for.

I look over at the door that's still shut tightly in its frame and close my eyes, focusing on my breathing.

I can do this. I can face another fear.

I can't predict the future or change the past. All I have is the present. My hands rest in my lap, and I start lightly tapping the heel of my hand with my finger to keep me grounded in the present. This tapping technique has saved me the last couple of years, and I do it now despite my sweaty palms and irregular heartbeat.

The grinding of metal on metal snaps me out of my practice. Looking up, I catch my breath. *It's him.* Jacob is being led in by a guard, his cuffed hands and orange jumpsuit clash with his tan skin. His hair is wild with curls, but when his caramel eyes meet mine, I don't see the hardness I expect. I recognize a longing so deep it's familiar.

Standing, I push out my chair and trip over the table leg. I know we can't touch. That rule was made clear before I had been allowed to walk through these doors, but I will get as close as they let me—as he'll let me.

Mere feet are between us, and I fear my heart will explode with so many unsaid words, but there is only one that rolls off of my tongue: "Jacob."

His expression is neutral, but since I was only around him for half of his life, I don't know how to read him. The undertones of every movement he makes are a mystery to me. Folded hands, jaw set, eyes scanning. What is he thinking?

The guard pulls the chair out for Jacob and he slides into the seat. Perching on the edge of mine, I fold my hands in my lap, mirroring Jacob. I'm staring at my greatest disappointment. The one that has caused me sleepless nights, second-guessing, and sacrifices beyond what I should have made. An apology doesn't feel like enough, but it's all I have.

"I–I'm so…" I drop my chin to my chest, guilt riding every curve of my body. "I'm so sorry, Jacob."

My words catch on his name and my throat constricts. These feelings are knots inside of me. This moment was always easier in my head. Apologies usually are. I expect anger, which would feel justified, but his response is the furthest from what I expect.

"Why?"

I snap my head up to look at him. Like mine, his brows are drawn in, legs bouncing rhythmically beneath the table. We both notice at the same time and halt our restless legs. My lips part but I don't have an explanation. He looks genuinely curious and I'm stunned. What am I supposed to say? I can easily lay out all of my failures, but doesn't he already know? Is this a test?

I came prepared to grovel but can't figure out where to begin. "Well, I…you…I mean, when…" I lift my hands, talking more with them than my mouth is.

"You don't have to apologize, you know. It wasn't your fault," Jacob says, the lines between his brows relaxing.

But shock has rendered me silent. "It was my fault we got separated. I told you I'd take care of you, always, and I failed. It's been ten years, Jacob. Didn't you wonder what was taking me so long to find you?" I open my eyes as wide as they'll go, wild with confusion and remembrance.

His smile starts at one corner and soon affects both sides of his mouth. He laughs, and it holds all of the hoarseness of a boy who's gone through puberty and came out the other side as a man.

When Jacob's laughter dies down, he shakes his head. "I don't blame you, Kit. You didn't think I would expect you to fix everything, did you?"

I frown. "Well, you asked me. You relied on me, and I let you down."

"I was also, what, eight? I learned real quick that life doesn't work out how we want it to. It's not like you had any control over it. You were a pawn in this sick game, too."

His expression may be soft but his words feel harsh. I want to cry at the reality that Jacob lost hope somewhere along the way. I never did, and maybe that hurt me more times than I care to count, but it also kept me going. I would've given up a long time ago if I lost hope the way Jacob has.

I deflate and sink back in my chair.

Jacob scans the room then lowers his voice. "Look, I've never forgotten you. Ever. Whenever things got rough, your voice kept me going. I've missed you like hell, Kit, but I never expected to see you again. This is…unexpected."

The hard plastic chair presses into my shoulder blades, so I lean forward. "Yeah. I thought that, too, at times, but I never stopped searching for you. It's taken this long to find you and when Bobby…" I drop my eyes to the table. I don't want to be talking about Bobby right now. I want us to be *us* again.

Jacob leans in closer and one of his curls falls across his forehead. "How do you even know Bobby?"

His eyes bore into me, but I look up and watch more of his curls fall forward. There are many similarities to the boy I said goodbye to. It makes my heart ache to see the years I've missed looking back at me. Jacob still has his mop of curls that makes me want to ruffle them with my hand and remember the familiar relationship we once had. I'm staring at a man who has had his own story with bruises and bloody lips along the way, maybe even a broken nose.

Crossing my arms over my chest, I let out a long breath. "I worked for him, too, once upon a time."

"Running drugs?"

"Not exactly." Drugs were a part of my work, but I stayed away from them. Customers were on them, other working girls, pimps. The two street businesses overlapped in so many ways. *Too* many ways. But I kept my distance, because I wasn't out there to party.

Jacob sits upright. "Not on…"

"On Figueroa." It only takes the name of the blade I worked to explain things. "Yes."

Jacob nods his head slowly, assessing me. I don't see a hard judgment in his eyes, but his lips part slightly. Does he believe me?

"I'm not proud of my past, but it's there. I've been in a recovery program the last couple of years to help me find myself again. Bobby dropped into the picture out of nowhere when he found out you were my brother. How long were you even working for him? What happened? You should be in a foster home, not on the streets." It's my turn to ask the questions that hover over the gaps of time.

He turns his head to stare at the guard positioned near the metal door. The guard stands erect with his hands clenched at his sides, watching the room. Jacob relaxes back into his chair. "I had a string of shitty foster parents. It sucked. I was done, so I ran. I left and got a real job, making real money."

I get it, because I was offered the same money, but a pang builds in intensity behind the walls of my chest. I put on my big sister hat like I had never taken it off. "Jacob, drug money is barely *real* money."

"Don't try to tell me it isn't real money. I supported myself. I took care of everything I needed and then some." There's fire behind his eyes that soon fades, and his next words come out in a whisper. "Now, it's worth shit."

I study his downcast face, hair dangling over his eyes, and see a man marked by loneliness. It's like the ivy crawling up the trunk of a tree. It creeps up and braids its viney strands around every vacant space until all you can see is the ivy, the life beneath it completely hidden. This is what I see in Jacob, a man hidden by the layers that life has created.

I rest my forearms on the small table. He needs to hear me say what I needed to hear years ago. "Jacob, I'm here." My lips begin to quiver, so I pull them between my teeth before continuing. "I'm here, and I'm not going anywhere. We've finally found each other, and if you won't accept my apology, then at least accept my help."

Jacob looks at me with lowered brows and nods.

I give him a small smile. "It'd be great if you could accept my apology, too, though."

He lets out a pinched laugh. "Done. Accepted," he says with a teasing smile. "I know you won't stop until you get it, so consider it a gift."

My tears push against the rims of my eyes. "You have no idea what a gift it is. Thank you."

Moisture fills Jacob's eyes, too, and the hard shell he's worn to stay safe softens, revealing the tender boy underneath, and this time I don't stop myself. Without looking at the guard, I reach across the table and ruffle his hair.

"No touching," the guard snaps immediately.

I mouth a *sorry* to him and give a small wave, turning back to Jacob and whispering so only he can hear. "Worth it."

His lips stretch into a full smile as he shakes his head. "You're gonna get kicked out."

I flick my wrist. "Nah. I'm sure it's like three strikes, and then you're out."

We both laugh through the tears in our eyes. This feels so good. So right.

"Now, what do we do?" Jacob asks as our laughter dwindles, and I'm all too aware of his usage of the word *we*. It brings a wave of relief, dousing the nerves that have been building inside me.

"We face your demons, cut them off, and move forward. Together." This time I don't have to pretend like I have confidence. I just do.

Reaching into my purse, I pull out a deck of cards and set them between us.

"And we play a round of cards."

CHAPTER FORTY-ONE
August 2014—Age 23

When I get home, I text Beau about my plans to visit him later. Then, I email Candace to fill her in on recent events and request a few days off. She immediately responds with concern for miles, but I assure her that he's healing fine, and I'll tell her the whole story another time, which I will. Right now, however, I need to figure out what to do about Bobby. Even though he no longer has Jacob to bargain with, I know it won't lessen his desire to get the money out of me.

My phone vibrates with a new message and I open the text from Ruby. It's been more than a week since I've heard from her, but her reply makes my stomach drop.

Ruby: Hey, I've been trying to find the name of a place that Bobby works out of. I've got nothing. Sorry.

Dammit. I inhale sharply, hovering my thumb over the buttons to respond. A dead end.

Kit: Thanks, Ruby. I'll keep looking into it.

Ruby: Please make sure whatever you're thinking, it doesn't come back to kill any of us. Okay?
Kit: I promise.

I was hoping for more information that I could pin Bobby with, but he slithered away yet again and left me with no tracks to follow.

"HEY YOU," I say to Beau upon entering the room. After a quick scan that reveals it's just the two of us, I sidle over to his bed and lean down to steal a kiss. I don't rush to pull away. "How are you feeling?"

"Hang on." Beau reaches up and curls his hand around my neck to keep me close. He kisses me slowly, savoring every second we still have. When he finally pulls back, he winks. "Better."

"Mhm. You taste good." I find the side of his face with my hands and taste his lips again with mine.

He snakes an arm around my waist, smiling between each peck. "It's—*kiss*—the toothpaste—*kiss*—I finally—*kiss*—got a hold of."

Beau pulls back and traces my face with his finger. "What are you going to do now that you're out of free wager dinners?"

I smile. "I'm gonna make you another wager."

"Oh yeah?" he asks with a smirk. "Please don't tell me I have to lose at Catan."

My smile broadens. "No, I wouldn't do that to you again." I purse my lips and draw out every last piece of curiosity running through his mind. "I bet you don't get out of here this week."

He looks at me sideways. "And what if I do?"

I tap a finger to my chin. "If you get out sooner, I'll take you to dinner. My treat."

He pretends to consider the bet then nods. "Should we shake on it?"

"It only seems right."

I jut out my hand and Beau stares at it but shakes his head. "I have a better idea."

Grabbing a fistful of my shirt at my stomach, he draws me closer until our lips are a brush away. "We should kiss on it. It'll make the deal stronger."

I study him beneath my lashes. "I think you're right."

"I know I'm right."

As our lips connect, we're interrupted by the door opening. "Hey," Beau says, clearing his throat.

Marcel tips his chin in greeting and strides to the end of Beau's bed. "Beau tells me you saw Jacob this morning?"

"I did. It was…surreal. I can't believe I finally got to talk to him." The lightness in my heart is the only proof I have that it actually happened.

Marcel puts his hands in his pockets. "How's he holding up?"

"He's ready to do the time for what happened. I hate it, but it's for the best. At least he's not on the streets and is in the only place Bobby won't mess with him."

"You think he'll be there for a while?" Beau asks, rubbing his thumb across the back of my hand.

"We'll find out Friday when he goes before the judge."

Marcel nods in understanding, and I really think he does.

When my phone vibrates a moment later, I pull it out and see an unknown number. Ignoring it, I return my attention to Beau.

"I'm going to be there for the trial hearing." I shrug, wondering how I can feel the simultaneous lightness of having finally found my brother and the heaviness of his current situation.

My phone vibrates again and I notice the same unknown number. Realizing this could be Jacob calling from jail, I excuse myself from the room. "Hello?" I say, closing the door behind me.

"Mercedes."

My lips press together in a firm line and my lungs stop working. I crush the phone to my ear in a white knuckle grip and get as far away from Beau's room as possible before saying, "What do you want?"

Bobby's next words don't indicate his loss, but I know it's felt. "I'm sure you've already heard about Jacob. Such a shame he decided to turn himself in."

Rounding the nurses' station, I pace in front of the vending machine trying to make sense of what Bobby said. Did Jacob get caught on purpose? I clear the idea from my mind. "I have. Looks like plans have changed." I'm playing a dangerous game, but I need to know if he has anything else up his sleeve.

"They have, but I'm a patient man."

I exhale slowly, not allowing my relief to be heard in the receiver. I suspected Jacob's routine traffic stop, turned jail time, was not what Bobby planned, but I didn't think it was something Jacob had planned either. Maybe I'm wrong.

"Don't think this is over, Mercedes. I'm a man who gets what he wants, as I've explained, and I know our paths will cross again." Bobby's confidence makes mine waver. "I'll get that money out of you one way or another."

This creep thinks he can bully everyone and he has, me included. "You think you can control everyone, but you're wrong. When I left, I left your control, too. I don't answer to you anymore, and I never will." I don't know where the words come from but I'm glad they do. It was about time I put Bobby in his place. He's used to hearing his prey whimper and beg, but I'm not his prey anymore.

Bobby is so silent on the other end of the line that I check my phone to see if we are still connected. We are, so I continue.

"I'm not afraid of you. Jacob isn't either. If you think I'm going to spend my days worrying about you, you're wrong."

"I don't believe you," Bobby spits out.

"Your power means *nothing* to us now." The words feel like a punch leaving my mouth, and I wonder if I've gone too far. I'm not out to make a stronger enemy; I only want this one off my back.

"I'll be in touch," Bobby says quickly, then hangs up. I can't gauge how rattled I've made him based on the tone of his voice, but I'll have to trust he isn't a current threat. I take a few deep, calming breaths, leaning my head against the wall. I can feel my confidence puddling on the floor now that I no longer need the armor. My hands shake with the decrease of adrenaline, and I remind myself that it's over, for now. In the meantime, I need to change my phone number and clear out those texts Ruby has sent. I know Bobby isn't one to make empty threats but neither am I. I'm going to do what I need to do to be safe, but I'm not about to stop living. I won't stop fighting for the women like Ruby—the women like me.

Not until I see Bobby's face through iron bars.

CHAPTER FORTY-TWO
August 2014—Age 23

"Thanks for coming today," Jacob says from across the table, and I immediately note the dark circles under his eyes.

"Yeah, for sure. How are you holdin' up?" I ask, knowing it's a ridiculous question. Jacob was sentenced to a year in prison with the promise of getting into a treatment facility after that.

"Shit. Today sucks. Happy birthday to me." The sarcasm is clear in his voice.

I glance around the room. There is only one other family having a visitation today, but I still keep my voice low. "I'm sorry Jacob. I guess you'll have to enjoy your birthday cake another day. You never told me this wasn't your first offense. You were in jail before for drug running, too."

He swipes a stray curl from his eyes, but the cuffs make it an awkward task. It's hard seeing him in chains, even of his own doing.

Jacob gives me a teasing grin. "You worry too much."

"Someone has to."

Jacob shakes his head. "It was time, I needed out. I was able to fly under the radar for a while, but the sooner I get out of here, the sooner we can start over."

I nod. There's something I have to ask, but I don't know how Jacob will take it. The question has been sitting heavy in my gut since Bobby mentioned it. I have to know. "Jacob, did you…" I run my fingers through my hair, trying to figure out how to word my question.

"What?"

I let out a puff of air. "Did you get stopped on purpose?"

I watch the subtleties of Jacob's reaction to my question. I've been getting better at reading him, and the way his eyes won't meet mine, combined with his non-answer, confirms my suspicions.

"Why'd you do it?" I ask.

Jacob exhales quickly. "Things changed when I knew you were in the picture again. You've always thought you needed to take care of me, but maybe I was trying to take care of you."

I draw my eyebrows closer together. "By getting yourself arrested and charged? You knew you'd be facing harsher punishment this time around."

"Yeah, well, you *knew* what we were up against with Bobby. It's not like he was going to let me walk. I needed to act and fast before he came up with some other fucked up idea to keep me chained to him. I didn't have to think twice. So, I stole the car that I knew contained the drugs intended for our runners. I had one shot and took it. We would never have gotten out from under that bastard's control otherwise."

I rub my temples as I process what Jacob did. "I don't get it. You should have waited. I would've found a way to get us free from Bobby. I told you Beau's dad has connections. We would have figured it out without you needing to sacrifice yourself."

Half of me is glad he is out of Bobby's reach while the other half is shocked at his recklessness.

"I didn't know your boyfriend had family on the inside, but even if I did, it's not like I would've done anything different. No offense to him but Bobby is a different animal. You don't know…" Jacob trails off.

"I don't know what?" I ask. "I've *lived* Bobby's wrath, Jacob. He's the worst kind of man."

"It's not that. There are things you don't know…" His words fade like his voice does. "I needed to get out," Jacob whispers. "I needed to get out while I still had the chance. These chains are more freeing than his were." He shakes his cuffed fists.

"What do you know?" I'm not about to let him off easy. He was about to say something else.

Jacob's expression becomes hard to read. "Nothing. What I do know is that Bobby is shady as hell. I needed out, I told you."

I remember the accusations Marcel shared, and now whatever Jacob knows. There's more that he isn't telling me, but I don't get why. It's not like Bobby can get him in here, and I'm the one he's after. Jacob was only a pawn.

"You can tell me. Whatever's going on, we can figure it out," I say, hoping it will encourage him to share more.

He drops his head. "Kit, I don't expect you to tell me everything you went through on the streets. Some things are… dark. Know I'm safer here, alright?"

I want to ask more questions, but instead, I find myself feeling more sympathetic. He's been through a lot and I shouldn't be pressing him, at least not today, his birthday. He just got booked and doesn't need me pressuring him for information. There've been moments over the past few days that I've looked at him and witnessed the man he's grown into. The stubble on his cheeks and neck tell me I'm looking at a man that I have yet to know fully, but it's in the admissions like this one that I see the boy who was scared, a boy who had to survive without help.

I reach a hand into my purse. "You can't have cake on your birthday, but how about a round of Go Fish?"

He bites the inside of his cheek, stifling a smile as the tension fades. "I could play."

"You sure? Last time the cuffs made it hard for you to pull out a win."

"Ah, hell no. Deal them," he says, pointing his chin toward the deck. "I got to show you I've been practicing."

Our smiles return as I deal seven cards to each of us and fan out the rest of the deck on the table to draw from. Jacob grabs his cards and awkwardly situates them in both hands, moving them around the way he likes them with suits huddled together in solidarity.

I know the memories we're creating are new, but I've held onto the old ones all of these years, and I don't plan on letting them go. Jacob and I are different, too, but different doesn't mean bad.

"I would have done the same thing, you know, getting caught in order to start over and to help you," I admit. "I mean, I did. But I still wish you didn't have to."

Jacob only nods. His jaw is clamped tight and I can tell by the way his eyes fill with tears that my words mean something. "Got a queen?"

"Go fish," I say.

Jacob grabs for a card on the table.

I shrug one shoulder, pretending to sort the perfectly aligned cards in my hand. "I would make you promise me not to do anything stupid like this again, but I would have to promise you the same thing, and I don't think I could do that." My voice breaks as our eyes meet. "You and me, we're it. You're all I have, and I would move heaven and earth to make sure you were safe."

A tear runs down my cheek with another on its heels. "Jacob, can we at least promise not to do anything stupid unless we absolutely have to?"

Jacob smiles through his own emotion. "Deal."

The knowledge that soft spots still exist in him, that his compassion hasn't completely died, fills me with enormous relief.

"Do you have any fours?" I ask.

Jacob lifts a card from the ones in his hand and slides it over, the sound of metal clinking as he does it. "So, you gonna tell me more about this Beau guy?" Jacob says with a grin, and I'm thankful for a change in conversation.

"What do you want to know?"

"What's he like? I mean, besides having a gangster Daddy."

I laugh. "Ex-gangster, alright? And Beau is the most optimistic person I've ever met," I explain with a smile. "He sees the beauty in people, even when they can't see it in themselves." I peer down at my lap, still smiling. "Do you have any twos?"

He shakes his head in disbelief and hands me another one of his cards. "I can't wait to meet him." Jacob says. "As long as you like him, I'm cool."

"I love him," I hear myself saying. Each time I say this out loud, it sinks in a little more.

"Well, good. Hopefully, he won't be too disappointed by your troubled brother."

I ignore his comment. My actions will speak louder than words in this instance. Like with Ruby, it doesn't matter how many times I say it, the proof is in what I do or don't do. "Any eights?"

"Ha. Go fish." His voice raises an octave as he pushes his chest out further.

"Cool it, hot shot. I'll get more cards from you next time," I say in a whisper.

"So, did you ever hear from Dad?" Jacob asks with an edge, his jaw working beneath his cheek.

I consider my father, the man whose only redeeming quality was absolutely nothing. I can't say I'm not disappointed that he never came after us. It would have made for a great story if he had, but I let go of that idea long ago and focused on what was more attainable.

I shake my head. "I never heard from him and honestly, I haven't searched for him. He's gotta be, like, in his fifties now, right? Probably still working just as hard," I say. "Maybe one day we'll see him again."

Jacob looks bored. "Maybe. You have any aces over there?" His gaze drops to my cards.

I roll my eyes and pluck the ace out of my hand.

It's his turn, but instead of asking me for a card, he looks around the room as if something were on his mind. "Kit?"

"Yeah?"

"Can you make me another promise?"

I relax my facial muscles and lower the hand holding the cards, my heart galloping at a steady pace. I've been here before, making promises I almost couldn't keep. I nearly lost two people I love because of them. Yet, as I look at Jacob, grown, rough around the edges, but with our shared blood running through his veins, I know I would make any promise he asked of me. I would do it all again, because I know how to love again, and that love has unlocked doors in my heart that were bolted shut.

My eyes never leave him. "Anything."

"Promise we'll share a couple of real burgers when I get out of here." A wide grin stretches across his face.

I break out in a matching grin and laugh with him. "You punk." I kick him in the shin.

"Ouch! You better give me your nine for doing that."

"Wait, how'd you know I had a nine?" I'm smiling ear to ear.

Wrists held close together, he snatches the nine from me. "I told you I've been practicing. And paying attention."

I bite my cheek and shrug. "And, of course we'll get burgers. I *swear* it."

"Good," he nods once. "And one more promise."

I purse my lips before asking, "Are you going to ask for a milkshake, too? Maybe some fries?"

"No. None of that. Though, we aren't skimping on the meal. I want those things too, okay?" He points at me as if to emphasize the serious nature of this promised meal.

I laugh. "You got it."

"I want you to promise that whatever comes next, we do it together. Not you more than me or me more than you. Together."

My playful smile warms, and I know this isn't a promise I'll have a problem making. It's already been made.

"I promise."

EPILOGUE
One-year-later
July 2015—Age 24

"He told me to be here at noon, but it could take a while," I tell Beau for the thousandth time. "Hopefully, not too long, though." I look down at the take-out bags at my feet.

"I have nowhere else to be," Beau confirms, also for the thousandth time. "You nervous?"

"Do I look nervous?"

Beau turns in the driver's seat to study me then scrunches up his face and makes me laugh.

"Stop," I say, swatting his shoulder. "You know I can't take you seriously when you make that face."

"You don't look nervous at all…now." Beau winks and grabs my hand.

We're waiting in the visitors parking lot to pick up Jacob. Today's the day he gets out of jail, and it happens to be a week before his nineteenth birthday, so I get to throw him a giant surprise party this year to make up for the bust of a birthday last year. Emphasis on the *surprise* since there's no way he would actually be cool with a party.

Beau looks out the windshield with a serious expression. "What do you think he'll look like?"

His question makes me laugh. "Considering I saw him yesterday, probably the exact same, minus the jumpsuit." When I look over at him, I can see his question was only meant to poke fun at my apparent jitters. "Alright, Big Guy, you win. Thanks for the help settling my nerves."

"Anytime, Squirt." He leans over, expecting to plant a kiss on my cheek. I don't give him the chance. I turn my head lightning fast and catch his lips with mine. I hold him there, savoring every flavor that makes up Beau, the man I love.

He pulls back, but only slightly, and whispers against my mouth. "What do you think Jacob will say when he sees us making out in the car?"

I pause and look out all the windows in case he's nearby. "He'll probably cheer us on. You know how much he loves you."

One of the sweetest things I've witnessed has been the development of Jacob and Beau's relationship. Turns out they have a lot of similar interests in common and, well, me. Beau tags along often when I go to see Jacob. He's been in this position before, visiting kids in jail who need a friend. Beau has some serious magic about him, because he's befriended Jacob *and* a few other inmates. They've even started a support group of sorts to talk and pray together. I think the kids in jail will always hold a piece of Beau's heart, and today, I finally get to hug the one who holds a part of mine.

"I got you something." Beau sits up and uses one of his long arms to retrieve a bag in the back seat. He produces the gift and places it in my lap.

"What? Why? It's not our anniversary."

"Oh yeah, and when is our anniversary?" Beau questions.

I stare out the windshield. "Well, it was...when we were...or maybe..."

Beau throws his head back and gives a hearty laugh. "I thought so. Let's say August is our anniversary month, alright?"

"Deal." I extend my hand to shake on it.

Beau takes my hand in his without looking away. "Now open your gift before I tell you what it is."

I lean forward and plant a kiss on his rough bearded cheek, then I pull out the tissue paper in an excited rush. Inside are two glazed mugs. The first one I pull out reads:

I Like His Beard.

I clutch my chest. "Thank God. I was worried these were going to be more Olive-level crudeness."

"Pull out the other one."

I exchange one mug for the other and stare at the second inscription, except this time there's a juicy peach beneath the lettering.

I Like Her…

I start laughing, and Beau is soon to follow. He kisses me through my smile, and we get lost in our own world again. The same one we've lived in since the moment our eyes locked, the place we avoided for the sake of friendship, and now the world we protect with the ferocity of our love that has only gotten stronger and achingly sweeter. Like a peach.

It isn't until I set the bag aside and catch sight of a figure moving toward us that I jump into action. "There he is," I practically scream.

I leap from the passenger seat to see Jacob in his street clothes sans cuffs. "Jacob," I yell, rushing toward him with my arms open wide. When he sees me coming, he stops to brace himself. I leap into his arms and he spins around once before setting my feet down on the pavement. I don't release the vice-like grip I have around his neck.

"Hey, sis. It's been a while," he says, but I can barely hear him over my tears. I'm so happy at this moment, I could burst.

"Hey, Jacob. Good to see you man," Beau says from behind us, at which point I decide I can let go of Jacob.

Beau wraps him in a bear hug, and there are a few reciprocal slaps to the back.

I immediately loop my arm through Jacob's when Beau releases him and we head for the car, slowly, I might add, because I'm not in a rush. I want to savor this first *real* hello. One that has even more depth, because I know the man I'm hugging that much more. Jacob has been through the ringer. It was tough getting him to share much, there's still plenty I don't know, but I'm learning to be patient.

"Are you excited to start the program at the Journey Center?" I ask, filled with so much joy, I'm surprised my feet are still on the ground.

"Yeah, I think I'm ready," he says hesitantly. "I'm not looking forward to the fact we won't get a chance to talk for another year, but I get it. It gives me a chance to be focused on recovery. It'll be weird to know you're there working, and I won't be able to stop in and say hi."

This is the hardest part about the next phase in this court-ordered journey for Jacob. "I'm not too excited about it either, but at least we have a couple of weeks before you have to start."

"You'll be surprised how fast the year goes," Beau says.

Jacob nods and squeezes my arm in the crook of his elbow. I know what the Journey Center meant to me, and I can only hope Jacob has an experience that changes his life, too. I believe in this place with my whole heart.

I elbow Jacob's side. "What's the first thing you want to do now that you're out of that cement fortress?"

He doesn't have to think about it long. "Eat a big, juicy burger with fries and a milkshake."

"You sound like your sister," Beau says, rolling his eyes in jest.

I peek around Jacob and point at Beau. "Well, we are siblings, and I hope you're hungry, because we have a few burgers in the car."

Beau releases a strong laugh. "A few? We stopped at six different places on our way here."

"Wait, for real?" Jacob asks.

"Yeah. I didn't know what kind of burgers you liked, so I got a few for you to try out. You don't want your first burger outside of jail to be gross, do you?"

Jacob bumps my shoulder with his as he laughs. His gaze drops and his smile broadens as he lifts my left hand. "Nice rock, sis. How are you going to wait a year to marry this one?" he asks, jabbing his thumb toward Beau.

I look over at Beau. "Do you want to tell him or should I?"

Beau laughs. "You know you're going to be the one to tell him so go right ahead."

My face breaks into the biggest smile. "We're getting married this weekend."

"Really?" Jacob looks between Beau and me in disbelief. "Don't play with me now."

"Yup. We've already been engaged for six months. It's time." Beau says.

"Congrats! I'm glad I'll at least get to be there."

"Duh. That's the whole point. It's not going to be anything huge. I don't want the show, only the people." I've waited long enough to marry Beau, but I would've waited however long I needed to so Jacob could be there. He's going to play an important role in the ceremony.

"I have something to ask you." I stop and turn to face Jacob when we reach the car. The sun is brilliantly bright today and bouncing off of the caramel undertones of Jacob's curls, making him look like a man-boy again.

"What is it? You know I'll say yes," Jacob says with a laugh.

I look down at my feet and then back up, my eyes misting over the longer I wait. "I want you to walk me down the aisle."

I didn't have to think twice about asking Jacob to do this. It's the only option I would ever have chosen, and I can tell by his expression how honored he is. This means something greater for us.

Jacob clears his throat. "I'd love to."

"Good. I got you new clothes to wear for the wedding, I hope you don't mind, and I brought them to Beau's house since you'll be staying there until the program starts."

Jacob turns to Beau. "I see she hasn't wasted any time getting things planned."

"Oh, come on," I say, tugging Jacob's arm and taking the last few steps to Beau's car. "You know it's going to be the second best day of my life."

Jacob climbs in the backseat and starts buckling his seatbelt. "Wait, what's the best day of your life?"

I look at Beau and then Jacob, both of my guys in one place. They are my family that I had to wait for and then fight for. My smile widens, if that's even possible since I haven't been able to stop.

"This one."

· · ·

ALL OF OUR friends are here.

Andrea, Jordan, Candace, and Monica, are among the few guests. Marcel sits in the front row, towering above everyone else as Sherry sits beside him and, dare I say, enjoys it. It's taken time to get here, where Beau's parents can sit next to each other without the weight of past mistakes clouding their visions. Marcel kept his word and left the game and has been getting to know his family again. I'd even venture to say Sherry is warming up to having Marcel around more. In fact, I'm positive that's the case since her fingers are currently laced with his.

The rest of Beau's family is here, too—my family. The ones that pulled up an extra chair at the table for me, and Jacob, too. Their anxious smiles beam with the expectancy of what today means for all of us.

Janet, my floor supervisor when I arrived at the Journey Center, is performing the wedding ceremony and is standing on the narrow stage at the front of the chapel behind Beau. I've been stealing looks through the small window in the door, watching the humans I love filter into the room waiting for me.

"Are you ready yet?" Jacob asks from behind me.

We've been standing out here for an extra five minutes, waiting to walk down the aisle, but my nerves are starting to get the better of me. "Yeah, hang on a minute," I tell him on an exhale, pulling my red lipstick out of my bouquet and adding a few more swipes.

"You've said that every minute for the last five minutes."

Mister Punctual likes to remind me of this, but he is still learning that I always show up fashionably late. "Here, come stand next to me so we can get a picture together."

He laughs. "Another one? We've taken at least fifty since we've been waiting out here."

I raise a finger. "I need one more for my cubicle wall at work."

He walks over to stand beside me, pulling his cell phone from his pocket. "Do you even have any more available space to hang a picture?"

I peer up at him and lift one brow. "No, but that's what Beau's walls are for."

Shaking his head through rolling laughter, Jacob lifts his phone and snaps a selfie that I know will be the winner. I might even pin it next to the first picture we took together after being reunited. He was still wearing orange—not his best color—and we both sat in the visitation room at *our* table. A guard took it for us, and our eyes shone with fresh tears and hopeful tomorrows.

Stepping closer to the door, I mentally count all of the seated bodies and start nervously fluffing my veil. "What if I trip?"

Jacob shoves his phone back into his pocket. "Isn't that why you wore sneakers?"

He has a point. I prefer my Converse Sneakers to heels, even if I will be substantially shorter than Beau. That's what steps are for and why Beau is standing below the first step of the stage, waiting for me and looking every bit the heart-stopping gentleman in his tuxedo.

Clutching my wildflower bouquet, I smooth my free hand over the slim-fitting silk dress that drapes effortlessly over my figure. "What if *you* trip?"

Jacob stands beside me, a few feet from the door we'll pass through. Together.

"If I trip, I know you'll catch me."

Tears fill my eyes as I look at Jacob. What once was lost has now been found, and I'm not just referring to my brother. I dug up more layers of love I didn't think existed. I love him more today than I did before, and I never thought that would be possible. But our love has grown. It's hung on for dear life and has transformed through every trial we've put it through.

I smile through my tears and peer down at my dress. "How do I look?"

He's silent, and when I finally look up at him, I see him wiping a tear off of his cheek. "More beautiful than I've ever seen you," he says, offering me the crook of his elbow.

I feed my hand through and grip his arm. "Hang on tight so we don't fall," I say with a wink. "Even if I am wearing sneakers, you never know what will happen."

Jacob smiles and leans forward to give two knocks on the large oak door. When it opens, every person stands and the piano changes its tune. I don't register the decorations we worked late into the night to finish, nor my nerves for that matter, because my eyes meet Beau's and I'm hooked; I can't look anywhere else. He raises his hand to cup his mouth in awe, and I know instantly he is crying, like I am.

I hear Jacob whisper in my ear before we start walking. "Is this still the second best moment of your life?"

Without tearing my eyes away from Beau, I shake my head, because my love has grown twice the size I thought it was capable of. "Hurry, grab your phone," I say through my smile.

He leans in. "What?"

"You heard me. Grab your phone and take a picture of my face."

Jacob does as I ask, because he's the best little brother a girl could ask for. He snaps a quick photo of what I know for certain is the best day of my life. It's clear in the tears slipping down my cheeks and passing over the biggest smile I've ever worn.

"I take it back. I really don't think anything can beat this."

I squeeze Jacob's arm again as we begin our short journey down the aisle. I'm heading toward the arms of the man who helped me face my past, stood with me in the present, and made me believe that a future was possible.

He also took a bullet for me, so there's that.

The End.

Author Notes

What an absolute joy ride I had writing this book! Each one I write holds a piece of my heart in both story and truths, and I am honored for another chance to share it with you.

My goal for this book was to shed light on an aspect of foster care that is often overlooked. When sibling groups enter the system, the hope is that they would stay together, but as you've read through Kit and Jacob's story, that isn't always the case. In fact, it is rather common that siblings would separate based on the availability of foster families, temperament of the other children in the home, ages, etc. With more children in the system than there are foster families to house them, siblings may not even be in the same city and can easily lose touch.

As I wrote this book, I had the absolute pleasure of interviewing my friend, Charisa, who has worked with and for foster care agencies for decades. She taught me so much about the relationships built between social workers and foster children, the backend database structure, and story after story of teens who have run away or aged out. Her wisdom and insight were instrumental in creating this story and bringing full color to the realities of the system, and they were sobering.

There are many kids who end up aging out when they turn eighteen without a family or a clue of what comes next. Therefore, life and work on the streets becomes a viable option. Enter the Journey Center, which is based on a real outreach center in downtown L.A. They are the living hope of this book series, and I am so honored to share a glimpse into what they do to help eighteen to twenty-five-year-olds who are aging out. They provide housing, job search assistance, financial support, and a community to lean on. It's a remarkable place with a powerful mission.

In my research, I was astounded to learn that L.A. county holds half of the entire state of California's foster children. Social workers have historically had too many caseloads and are overworked because of it, but their reasons for doing what they do every single day are remarkable. It is common practice that social workers would give their business cards directly to teens who would often reach out for a host of different reasons. Some of them with news of college degrees, families of their own, and gratitude for the role of their social worker. And still others who would call when they were in a bind, having run away from their foster home or were living on the streets and needed help. I applaud social workers for the roles they play in helping these young people find support in the midst of a life they didn't ask for.

The stories of adoption and foster care are close to my heart, and while our family has never been foster parents, we did have the joy of adopting our fourth child via private adoption. He came to us with a story—a family—when we brought him home, as every child being adopted does. I am so passionate about standing in the gap for children who are navigating a world without their biological parents. For those of us who have experienced the power of love, let's give it out freely like it costs us nothing and means absolutely everything.

Lastly, this series is marked by the stories of women who have experienced the dark sides of street work. Prostitution is an ever-growing business because of the high demand, let's deal with that. I write their stories to call attention to the hidden realities happening on our streets, usually closer to home than we would think. They are humans, like you and me, and deserve love in its most honest and healing form. Love really does conquer all.

If you are interested in seeing my inspiration for some of the characters, scenes, outfits, etc. discussed in this book, you can find me on Pinterest @authorchristinahill.

I also love connecting with readers on Instagram and TikTok: @authorchristinahill. If you loved the book, please consider writing a review on Amazon and GoodReads. This is such a tangible way to help authors and for the message of this book to reach more beating hearts.

With all of my love,
Christina

Acknowledgments

I am incredibly thankful to every individual who has supported me throughout this process of writing another book. Shoutout to all of the phenomenal writers within the indie author community. Seeing you pursue your writing endeavors has only spurred me on to continue in mine. Special thanks to Katie, Erica, Marie, Lindsey, Tracey, and Beth. Your input in this story helped in ways I could gush about and others I wouldn't have words for. You each have become more than readers and critique partners, you've become dear friends that I hold in such high esteem.

My husband, Samuel—We did it, again! Publishing two books in one year is no joke, but we did, together. You are always the first to hear about my story ideas, the first one I go to when I'm stuck, and the person who knows every single piece of myself I've put in this book. You know it all because you know all of me. Thank you for taking this journey with me and loving me through those late nights and early mornings. You're a champion in my book.

Mom and Dad—You'll always get a notable mention in my books, because you were the first ones whispering in my ear to *go for it*. And now here I am, going for it. Thank you for seeing me through another story, another therapy session, and still another endeavor that felt bigger than me at times. You are always there to pour out your love and support through it all.

My sister-in-love, Erica—You are the best sister-in-law a girl could ask for! You agreed to read through and edit my book while teaching, being a mom, and pregnant. I can't tell you how much this has meant to me to have your detailed eye look through everything. You're amazing.

My kids, the Fab Four—Though none of you are old enough to read my books yet, you are somehow still my biggest supporters. When you tell your friends, "My mom wrote a book," it truly makes my heart swell. You are all the best!

My friend, Katie—To say I could have written books without your input is crazy talk. Your thoughts and perspectives on this storyline were invaluable to me. You were the first to finish reading the entire manuscript of a very early draft and you didn't run and hide. That deserves a few rounds of thanks! I am honored to call you my best friend and now an MVP critique partner. I'm going to make you a plaque that I better see on your wall the next time I come over.

My friend, Brenda—You've walked through the launch of two books with me, and I'm so pumped for the partnership we've found. Did you think this would be the case when we first met on a mission trip? A full decade later and we're still kickin' it. Thank you for creating another phenomenal book cover for Kit's story and sharing your craft.

Charisa—Thank you so much for allowing me to interview you for the drafting of this book and allowing me to call and text you throughout the writing process. You helped in countless ways to find the heartbeat behind this story and the message within. Thank you for also being the voice on the other end of the line when kids were calling and needed a comforter.

Lei—Thank you for your time chatting on the phone and sharing about your experience working with the foster care youth in downtown L.A. I asked you to sum up what you did on a daily basis and you replied, "Everything." From setting up rooms for youth to move in, helping them find jobs or get into school, and making dinner for family game night. You really do it all and your role as "mother" to every kid who passes through is nothing short of miraculous.

My editor, Krys—I am very appreciative of your sharp eyes as you've read and re-read this book. Your support for indie authors is both seen and personally felt, and I'm thrilled to have had the opportunity to work with you.

Foster Families—To all of the current foster families I reached out to in order to glean from your experiences and hear the situations you've witnessed, thank you a million times over. I am inspired by your daily commitment to step in where there is a gap and to love beyond reason.

About the Author

Christina is a lover of love who has been writing stories in her head since middle school. She also holds the titles of 'mom' and 'babe' and lives in Montana with her four children, husband, and cat.

When Christina isn't reading or writing, she is wrangling her kiddos, homeschooling, taking baths, baking, or watching PBS.

For more information or to sign up for my newsletter, visit www.authorchristinahill.com.

Love Finds a Way
Book Three

Coming 2023

Fresh out of rehab, Jacob Lopez is trying to rebuild his life from the ground up. When his sister, Kit finally found him, he was a mess. Running away from foster homes, selling drugs, and working for a notorious gang leader on the streets of L.A. before that man put him in jail. He's ready to let his past go and move forward, but it isn't ready to let go of him. Instead, it comes back to haunt him in the form of a red-headed woman he never expected to see after their one night together.

Ruby Red took over the family business when her mother died from an overdose. She's working the streets as a prostitute to support her addiction, hoping one day she'll have enough to get her daughter out of the same foster care system that raised her. It isn't until she recognizes Jacob, the only man who made her feel anything, that she doubts her decision to leave the city.

Now, for once, she wants to stay.

Time isn't on their side when the biggest threat to keep them apart enters the picture again, and he wants revenge. Fueled by rekindled love and familiar hate, they have to decide if love is worth the risk and if it can find a way through the darkness.

Love Finds a Way

PROLOGUE
October 2015—Age 19

Jacob

Dear Kit,

It's weird writing you a letter you'll never read.

My roommate is gone and it's just me, sitting in our dorm room at the Journey Center. It's quiet. So quiet that I can hear my own thoughts, and they're screaming at me. I'm so damn sick of it.

Even though it's only been one year, two months, and ~~three~~ four days since I got arrested, I still remember everything. The things I admitted to and those I didn't. I've got a past, like you, and one that includes the gang leader, Bobby, also like you. I never expected to find *us* again. To love a sister I said goodbye to a long time ago, but I did. You may not understand why I've kept everything from you, but in a lot of ways, I think you do. Deep down, I think you know you'd do anything for the ones you love. You did everything you could for me, and that's what I'm doing for you.

I've been working through all my shit in therapy, and my therapist says writing is a good way to get stuff out—especially for someone like me who has kept too much locked inside for only me to know and nobody else to find out. So, that's what I'm trying to do…get it out. Except I'm not planning to show you this letter, because I love you. Remember that, okay?

It's been eating me alive these past couple of years, and now that I have family in the picture, now that you and Beau are in my life, it keeps me up at night. The information I have, the past I've been witness to, it all makes me feel ~~guilty~~ evil. But, I'm not. I just know what will happen if I open my mouth and tell somebody. It'll hurt people. It'll hurt us and now that there is an us—a family—I'd rather let it die with the old me. The one who went to prison, did drugs, and sold them. But I have to get the words out before they kill me.

So, I'm writing you a letter. I'm going to tell you everything I know, not just because I have to get it out, but because I feel I owe it to you and the past you survived. The women you've told me about and the prostitutes you worked with, I owe it to you and I owe it to them.

It's easier to think of people as a *them*. You don't know *them*, so it's easy not to care. Yet, when you give *them* a name, it changes everything. When they become a sister, a friend, or a neighbor, *them* isn't a collection of random people anymore. They're an individual, and it's personal. So, even if I could keep it all inside, I couldn't. Not when *them* is named Kit.

We've lived a ~~good~~ great life this last year. Aside from the part where I was in prison, you visited me in jail often, and I know if you could, you'd visit me here in rehab, too. Your letters keep me going while I'm in this blackout period where contact with the outside world is limited and all I have are my thoughts.

But maybe not seeing you face to face is why everything's coming up now. You're not here to ruffle my curls and for me to complain about it, even though I really don't care. I like that you do that. It reminds me of the times we had when things weren't so heavy. But they are now, and you're not here. It's just me, my memories, and this pen. A dangerous combination for someone like me who knows too much.

I hope one day I'll have the courage to admit to you what I'm going to write. That I can tell you to your face, preferably years later, and confess what I know. Maybe things will change by then. People will be caught, jailed, and killed by the time I tell you. Maybe Bobby will pay for what he's ~~done~~ doing. I hope so.

Remember, I'm doing this because I love you.

Don't forget that in the facts I'm about to tell you, okay?

Don't forget me.